LIGHT &
SHADE
FOR CHARACTERS

3dtotal Publishing

Correspondence: **publishing@3dtotal.com**
Website: **store.3dtotal.com**

Every effort has been made to ensure the credits and contact
information listed are present and correct. In the case of any
errors that have occurred, the publisher respectfully directs
readers to **store.3dtotal.com/pages/information** for any
updated information and corrections.

First published in the United Kingdom, 2025, by 3dtotal Publishing.

Address: 3dtotal.com Ltd,
29 Foregate Street, Worcester,
WR1 1DS, United Kingdom.

Soft cover ISBN: 978-1-915992-19-2

Printed and Bound in Shanghai, China, by KS Printing.

Visit **store.3dtotal.com** for a complete list of available book titles.

Editor: Philippa Barker
Designer: Fiona Tarbet
Lead Editor: Samantha Rigby
Lead Designer: Joseph Cartwright
Studio Manager: Simon Morse
Managing Director: Tom Greenway

Front cover artwork by individual artists as credited
throughout the book.

Back cover artwork © Andrés Moncayo and Isabella Agosti.

50%

of net profits donated

TO CHARITY

In 2022, 3dtotal Publishing became successful enough to make a pledge to donate **50% of its net profits to charity**. This continues to be possible due to the incredible support from all our customers, employees, and partners. At the time of printing, we have donated over $1.62million (USD) to charity.

We focus our giving on three charitable areas: **environmental**, **humanitarian**, and **animal welfare**. We use organizations such as Effective Altruism and Founders Pledge to guide who we help within these causes. Some ways of doing good are over 100 times more effective than others, so donating this way hugely increases the impact of our contributions.

See **3dtotal.com/charity** for full details.

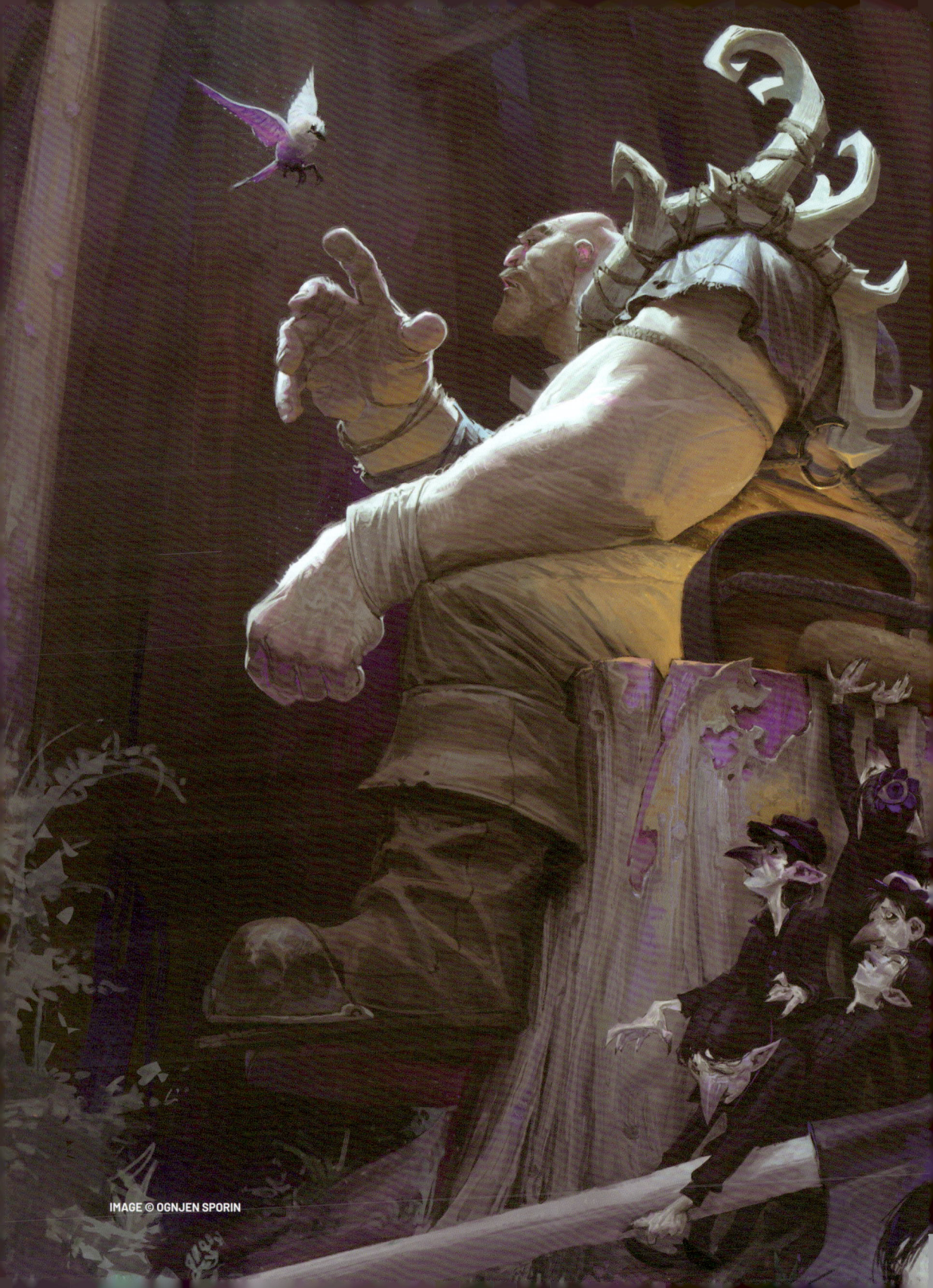

CONTENTS

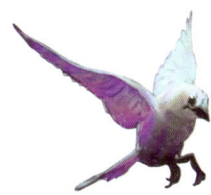

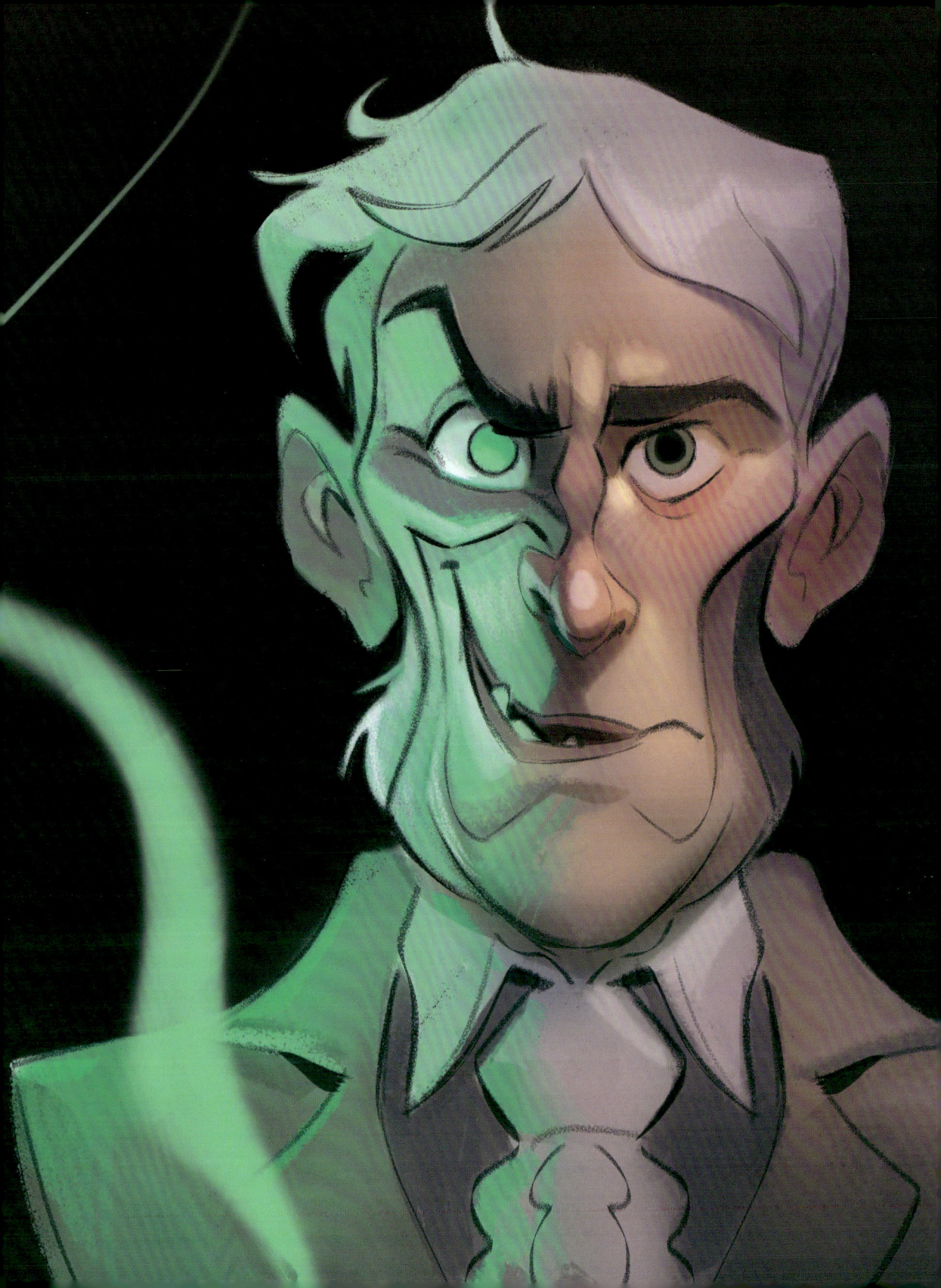

GETTING STARTED

BY KENNETH ANDERSON

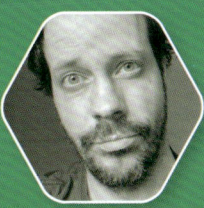

Kenneth Anderson
Character designer & illustrator *charactercube.com*

Based in Glasgow, Scotland, Kenneth is an artist who specializes in designing characters for animation and illustrating for books and magazines.

INTRODUCTION

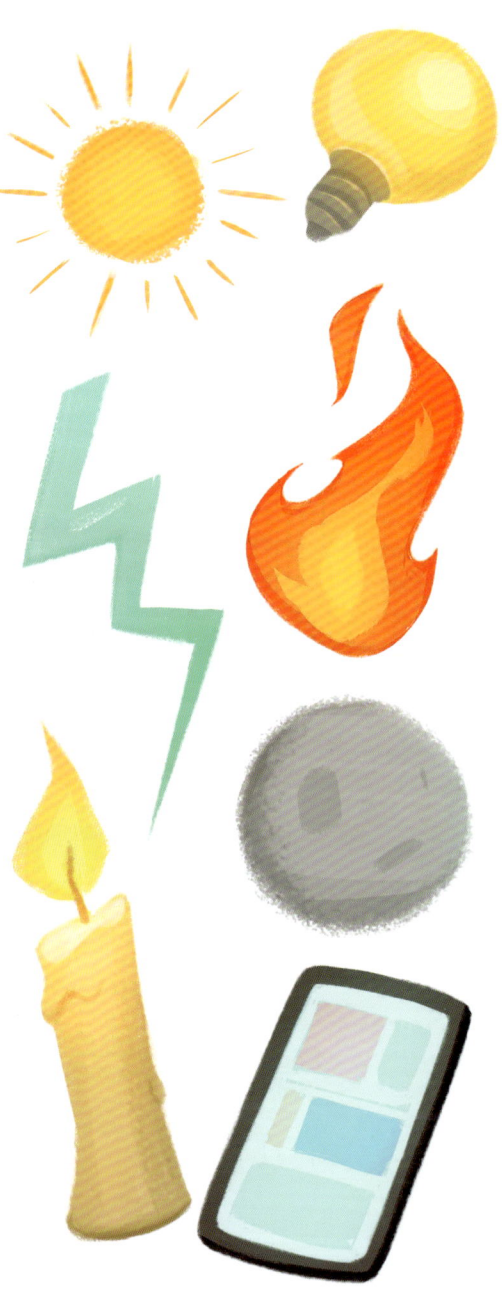

What comes to mind when you think about designing characters? Maybe it's the idea of playing with shapes and manipulating them into interesting combinations? Or perhaps pushing character proportions in weird and wonderful ways? Or experimenting with contrast to make a character visually compelling?

All of these factors are fundamental to the process, but have you ever considered how light and shade can be used effectively in your character designs?

WHY IS LIGHT & SHADE IMPORTANT IN CHARACTER DESIGN?

Whether you realize it or not, you have likely been using light and shade in your character designs quite instinctively for some time. Light and shade are a core part of what it means to see – something most people have experienced to some degree since birth – and are therefore an essential part of everyday life. Without light hitting the world around you – creating lights and darks, and showing the forms of objects in your environment – you wouldn't see anything at all.

Because of this, it's not particularly groundbreaking to add a shadow on the ground beneath a character, or to add shadows to a character to show their form. Nor is it unusual to immerse the character in a cool lighting set-up to convey something about their personality or mood. All are pretty standard in character design.

To take your character designs to the next level, you will need to delve a little deeper. This book will teach you how to treat light and shade as more than something that just happens to a character, and instead think of them as vital tools in a character designer's toolkit.

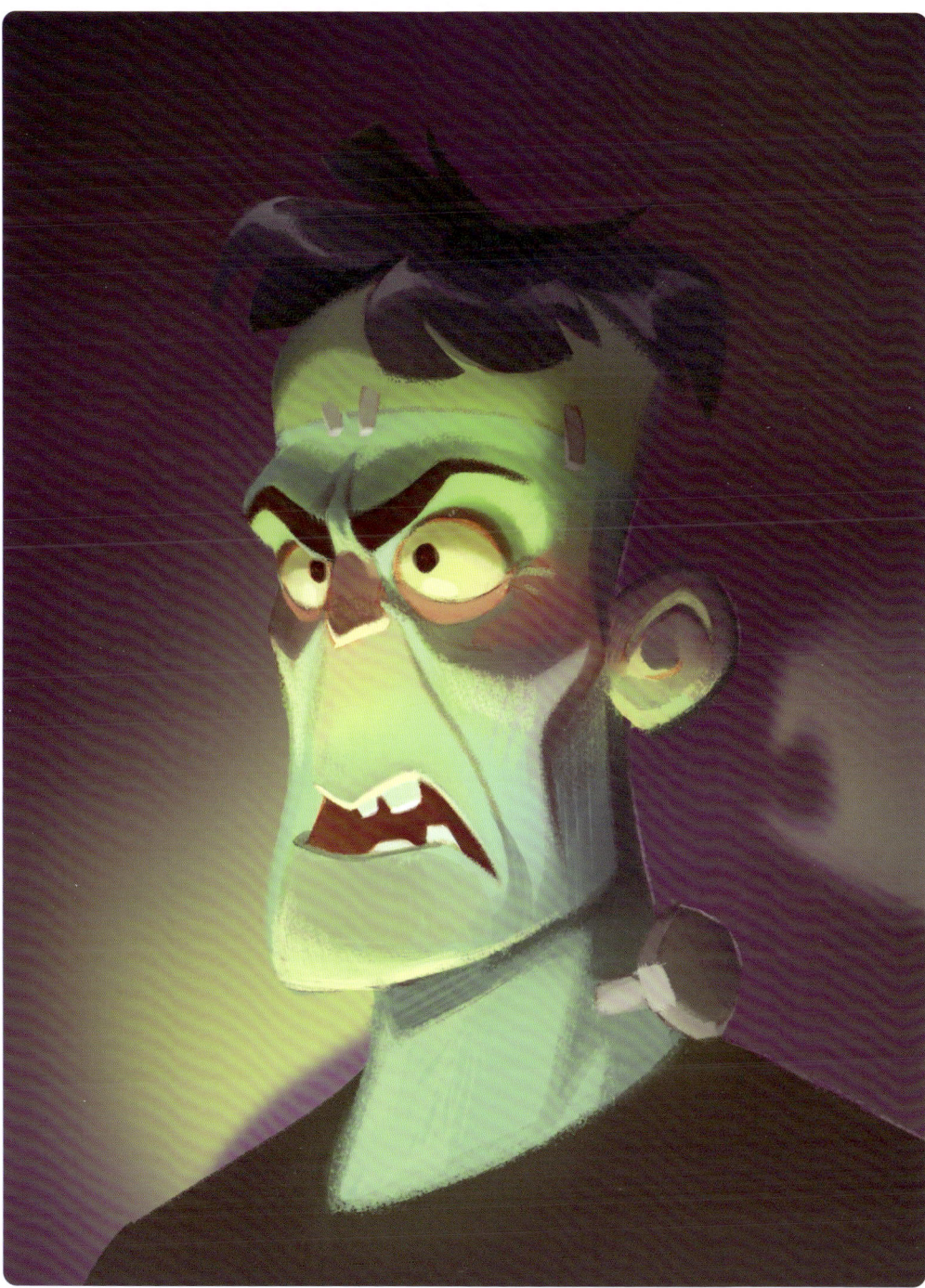

▲ Effective use of light and shade can give a character design visual interest and intrigue

THREE WAYS OF USING LIGHTING

For the purposes of simplification, it can be helpful to think about three distinct ways of using lighting when designing characters...

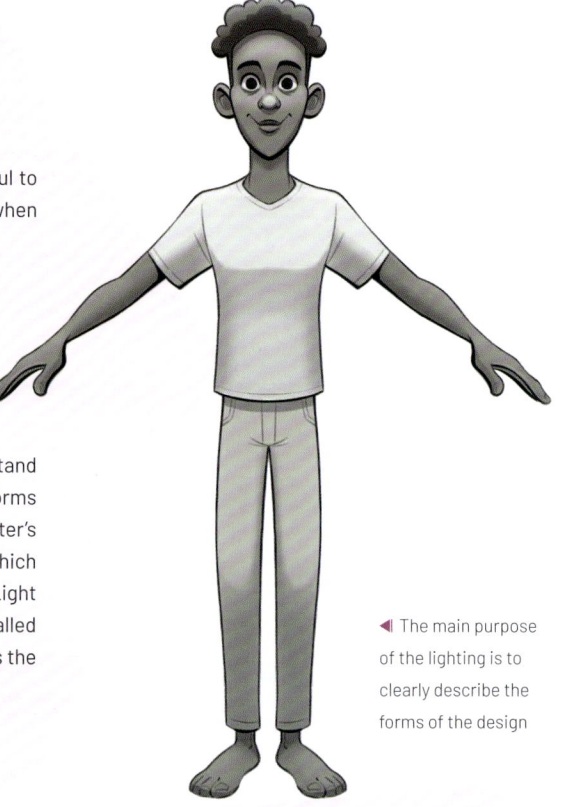

01 DESCRIBING FORM

Just as light and shade allow you to see and understand forms in the real world, they can be used to depict forms in your character designs. How round is a character's head? How angular are a character's hands? Which parts of a character's design overlap one another? Light and shade will help to illustrate all of this. This is called descriptive lighting – lighting that simply describes the forms of a character.

◀ The main purpose of the lighting is to clearly describe the forms of the design

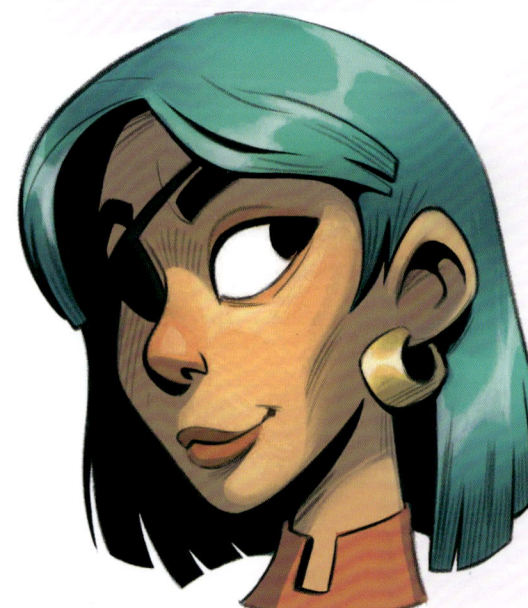

02 STYLIZING

As a character designer, you can take descriptive lighting one step further by making stylistic decisions with your use of light and shade. Remember how light hitting objects and creating shadows can communicate the form of an object? You can push the stylization of a character by making conscious design choices in how you manipulate light and shadows to describe the character's forms. You can also use light as a key feature in your character designs, or get creative and experiment in the ways you represent light and shade.

◀ Specific style choices have been made when lighting this character – the heavy blacks represent shadow areas and the hatching lines represent half shadows

03 STORYTELLING

You can also use light and shade to enhance storytelling in a character illustration by conveying an emotion, mood, or atmosphere. Doing this is the difference between a stand-alone character design and a character existing in a world, environment, or setting, with all the storytelling that entails.

▶ The lighting in this piece serves to enhance the emotion and aggressive energy of the character

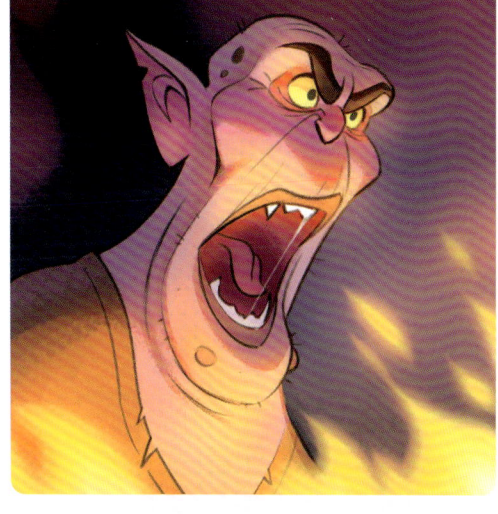

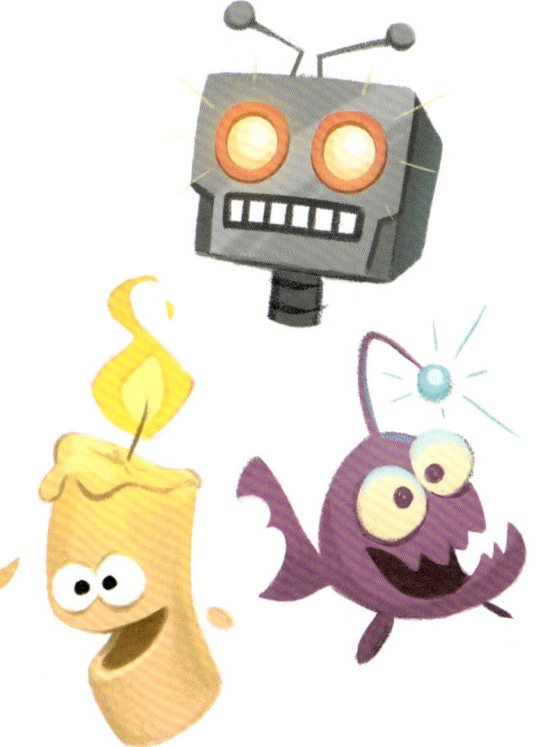

MAKING INTENTIONAL DESIGN CHOICES

These three ways of using lighting in character design are all interconnected. Describing the form of a character is stylizing a character, whether intentional or not. And stylizing a character is storytelling, as every design choice means something and communicates a little of the character's story. Your goal is to make these choices intentionally. Thinking about them in isolation first will aid your understanding of the concepts and allow you to bring everything together coherently.

This book will help you to understand the fundamentals of light and shade, then explore how you can apply these to your character designs in interesting and useful ways. While the chapters in GETTING STARTED won't go into too much detail on how to draw, the eight tutorials that come later will cover the practical drawing process, demonstrating how these light and shade techniques can be applied to a wide range of characters in varying styles.

THE FUNDAMENTALS

Without light, you wouldn't be able to see or understand the forms of objects in the world around you, let alone interact with them. Light is what allows you to see. Without it you are quite literally in the dark!

There are numerous sources of natural light, including the sun on a sunny day, or moonlight on a clear night. There is also fire, lava, lightning, and bioluminescence. Human-made light sources also come in many forms, such as light bulbs, candles, TV screens, computer monitors, and phone screens.

Shade, or shadows, are areas where light doesn't reach: your shadow on the ground on a sunny day, the dark space under your bed, or in an attic without lights.

It is this interplay of light hitting various surfaces, and its resulting shadows, that allows you to see the dimension, forms, and shapes of objects in the world.

While this may seem like a very technical chapter, you need to first understand these fundamentals before you can approach using light and shade in your character artwork.

HOW LIGHT WORKS

Light is a form of electromagnetic radiation that acts both like a wave and like a particle. It consists of various wavelengths and travels incredibly fast – the speed of light!

Only some wavelengths of electromagnetic radiation are visible to the human eye. These wavelengths are known as visible light and form a continuous spectrum of colours, traditionally described as red, orange, yellow, green, blue, indigo, and violet – just like in a rainbow.

◀ Visible light forms a constant spectrum of colours

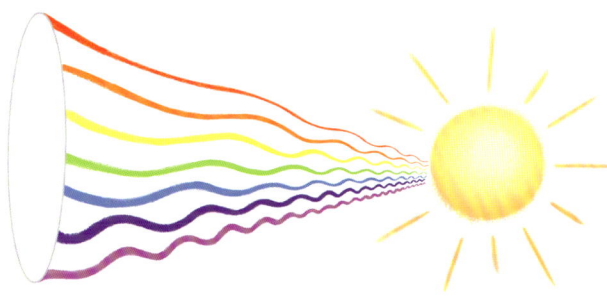

▲ When all visible wavelengths are present at the same time, as with sunlight, they combine to produce white light

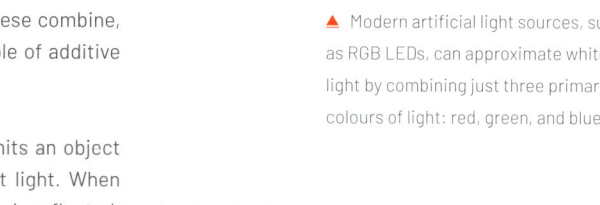

Every light source emits different combinations of visible-light wavelengths. An incandescent light bulb, for example, will appear yellow/orange, as it emits predominantly those wavelengths. In contrast, a cool-white LED emits more blue wavelengths, giving it a more blueish appearance. Sunlight, however, contains all the visible wavelengths of light, and when these combine, it produces white light. This is an example of additive colour mixing.

When light emitted from a light source hits an object without obstruction, this is called direct light. When light hits a surface it is either absorbed, reflected, scattered, or transmitted, depending on the nature of the surface.

▲ Modern artificial light sources, such as RGB LEDs, can approximate white light by combining just three primary colours of light: red, green, and blue

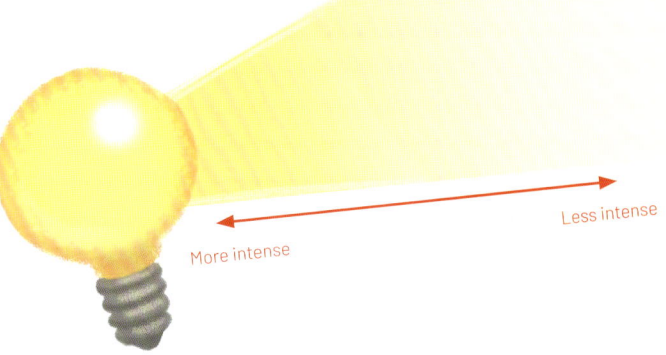

▶ As light travels over distance, it also loses intensity and power

More intense

Less intense

ABSORBED LIGHT

Sometimes light is absorbed by the object it hits. This depends on the object's material, texture, and colour – such as a matt surface – plus the nature of the light.

▶ Light can be absorbed by an object

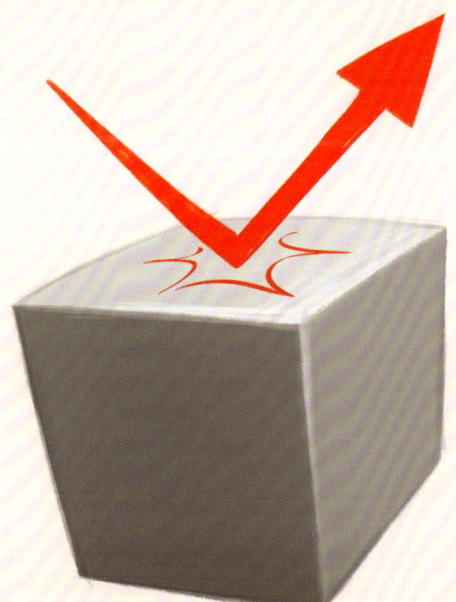
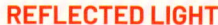

REFLECTED LIGHT

Light that bounces off an object is called reflected light. When visible light reflects off an object, the human eye is able to detect it, allowing you to see the world around you. When you look around, you are actually just interpreting light reflecting off objects in your environment.

◀ Without reflected light, you wouldn't be able to see anything

BOUNCED LIGHT

Light doesn't just reflect once, but will continue to reflect off surfaces in an environment, losing intensity as it goes. When light reflects off a surface, it can become a weaker secondary light source and illuminate objects nearby. This is known as bounced light.

▼ Bounced light can illuminate surrounding forms

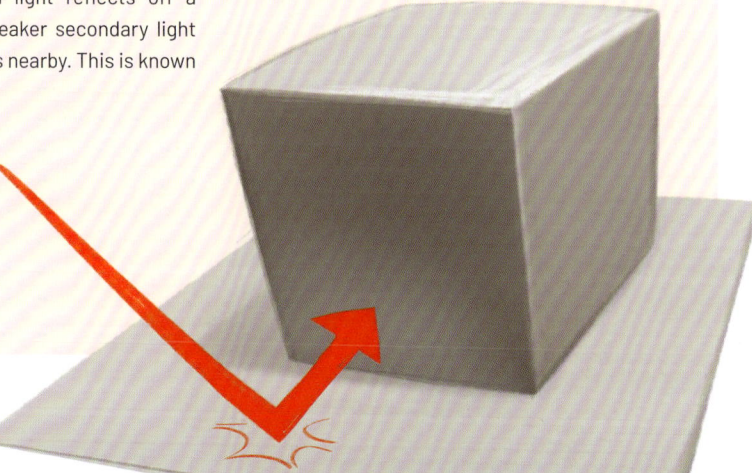

SCATTERED LIGHT

When light hits a surface, the way it reflects will depend on the material and texture of the surface. Imagine shining a light on a woolly jumper and then on a mirror. Each surface will respond differently to the light. While the mirror will reflect the light near perfectly, the woolly jumper won't. This is because of a fundamental difference in their surface textures: the woolly jumper scatters light, whereas a mirror reflects it.

Mirrors are usually made from a very thin sheet of metal underneath a thin layer of glass. Some metals in particular are good at reflecting light and, when combined with glass, create a very smooth surface with little or no texture. As the mirror's surface is so smooth and doesn't easily absorb light, this results in a near perfect reflection.

Of course, there is a range of reflectivity in between the extremes of a woolly jumper and a mirror. A polished apple will reflect better than a carpet, and a piece of polished stone will reflect better than a loaf of bread.

▼ When you look in the mirror, you're looking at light bouncing off its surface and straight back into your eyes – the light rays bounce back at an equal angle to how they hit the surface

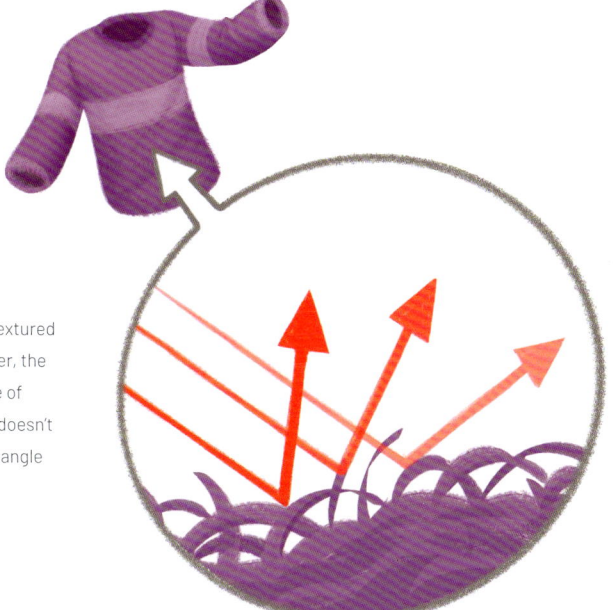

▶ When light hits an uneven textured surface, such as a woolly jumper, the light rays scatter in a multitude of different directions – the light doesn't reflect back at the exact same angle

DIFFUSED LIGHT

A similar effect occurs with diffused light as it does with scattered light. As light passes through a material or atmosphere, the light diffuses in different directions as it bounces around and off the particles in the material. Again, the light bounces in multiple directions, rather than in the same direction, resulting in a weaker, unfocused light.

▶ On a cloudy day, sunlight travels through the clouds, bounces off and around the cloud particles, before some of it eventually passes through into the world below

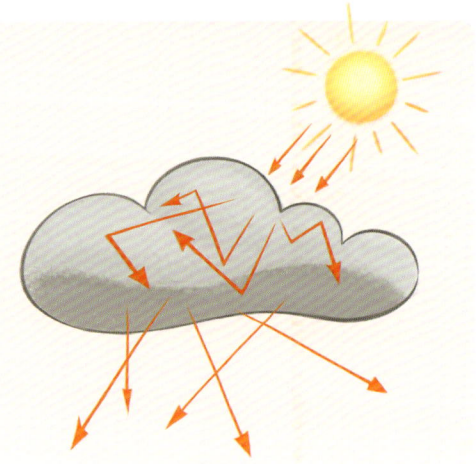

AMBIENT LIGHT

When light bounces, scatters, and diffuses around an environment, it creates what is called ambient light. Ambient light is a secondary light source that is usually weaker and more diffused than a direct light source. Ambient light can help to illuminate areas of an environment that are in shadow.

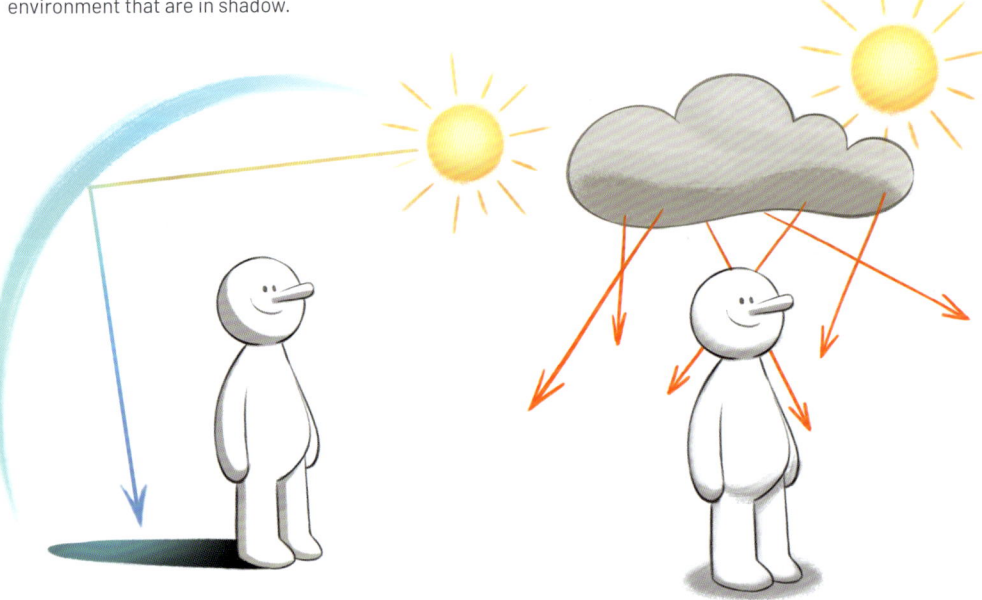

▲ Blue light from the sky can be seen clearly in upward-facing shadows on a sunny day

▲ Diffused light can come from an overcast sky

TRANSMITTED LIGHT

When light hits an object and some of that light passes through it, this is known as transmitted light. Imagine a piece of glass with light passing straight through it. (Sometimes this happens at a right angle due to its smooth reflective surface.)

▶ Transmitted light is where light passes through a material

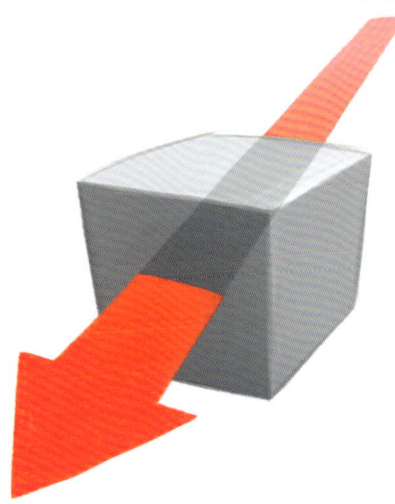

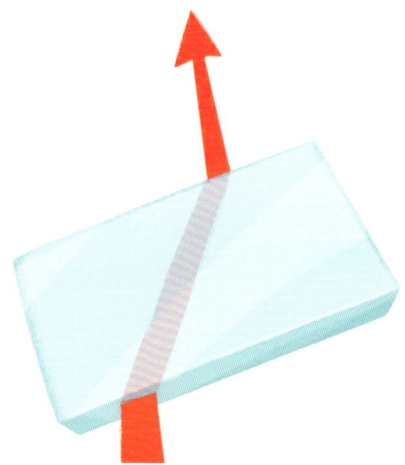

REFRACTED LIGHT

Some materials will refract light, changing the direction of the light rays. Shine a light on a piece of crystal, for example, and the light will change direction.

◀ Refraction happens when light changes speed as it passes through a material, resulting in it changing direction

SUBSURFACE SCATTERING

A semi-transparent material blocks some, but not all, light. In this instance you may see subsurface scattering, which is what happens when light bounces around under the surface of the material, hitting the particles inside, and creating a kind of glow.

▶ Observe the subsurface scattering as light passes through and bounces around beneath the skin

If you hold your hand up to a strong light source, such as the sun, you will notice a slight glow in your fingers. The sunlight passes through the edges of your fingers, scattering (bouncing!) around beneath the skin and reflecting off the red blood inside. This is most noticeable on fleshy parts of the body, such as the nose and ears, when exposed to strong light from behind. It's also more noticeable on people with lighter skin tones, as lighter skin allows more light to pass through.

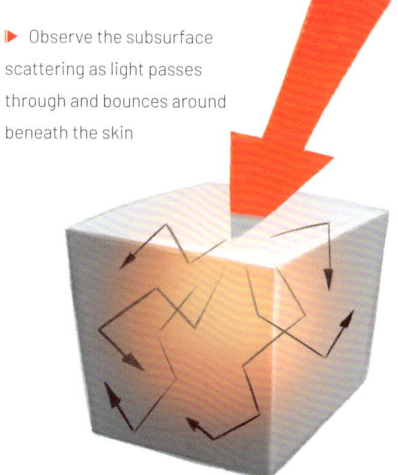

UNDERSTANDING SHADOWS

When direct light hits an object, any areas the light can't reach will be in shadow. Light and shadow go together – you can't have one without the other! Direct light is generally strong and directional, creating well-defined form and cast shadows.

FORM SHADOWS

The interplay of light and shade reveals the form of an object and creates what is known as a form shadow. Any surface of a form facing direct light will light up, while any surface facing away from the light will be in shadow. There may also be areas or planes of an object that catch some of the light, but not all of it, due to the direction in which the planes are facing. (This can be seen on the cube.)

Form shadows can have hard or soft edges. Smooth curved surfaces, such as a sphere, will have soft gradual transitions from light to shadow, while forms with sharp edges and corners, such as a cube, will create shadows with hard distinct edges.

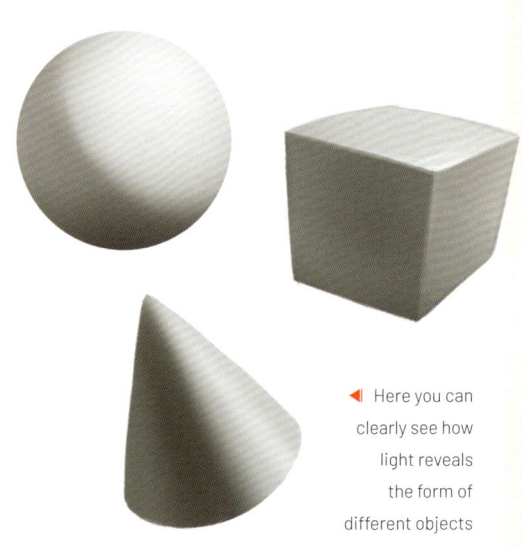

◀ Here you can clearly see how light reveals the form of different objects

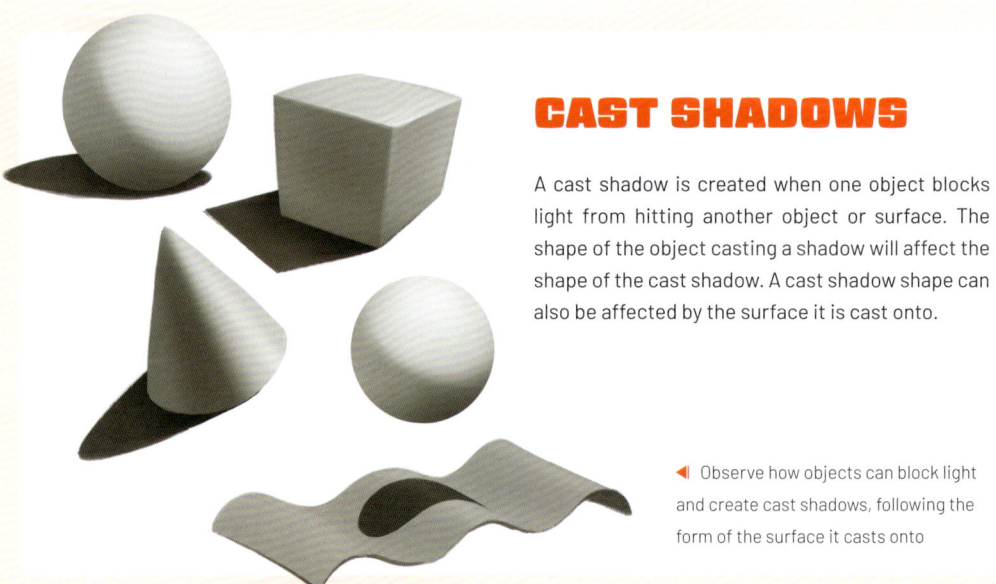

CAST SHADOWS

A cast shadow is created when one object blocks light from hitting another object or surface. The shape of the object casting a shadow will affect the shape of the cast shadow. A cast shadow shape can also be affected by the surface it is cast onto.

◀ Observe how objects can block light and create cast shadows, following the form of the surface it casts onto

LIGHT SOURCES & SHADOWS

TYPE OF LIGHT SOURCE

The type of light source that's in action will affect the form shadows and cast shadows. A strong direct light source, such as the sun, will create strong, clear form and cast shadows.

A diffused light source, however, lights a scene more evenly and creates less defined shadows; as the light is scattered in all directions, some of it bounces into the shadow area and blurs its edges.

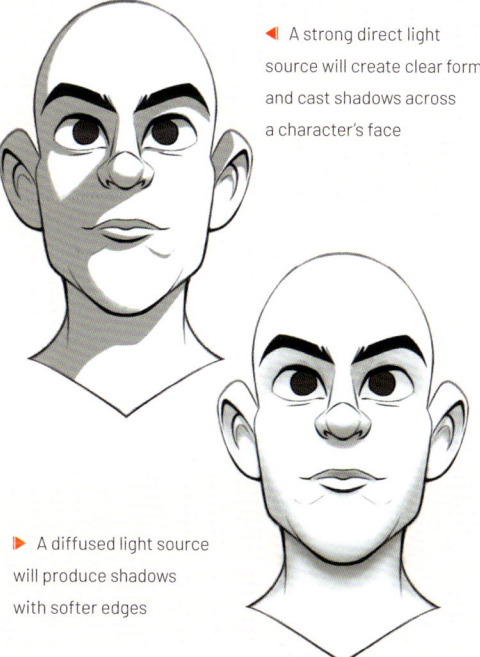

◀ A strong direct light source will create clear form and cast shadows across a character's face

▶ A diffused light source will produce shadows with softer edges

ANGLE OF LIGHT SOURCE

The angle of a light source will also affect the form and cast shadows created. A good example is when your ground shadow changes depending on the time of day. This is due to the position of the sun in relation to your body.

When the sun is high in the sky, it casts a shadow directly below you. Shadows are longer earlier in the morning, or later in the day, when the sun is at a lower angle in the sky relative to your body.

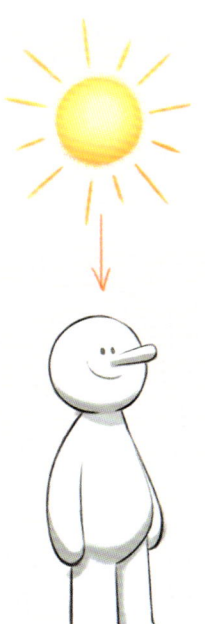

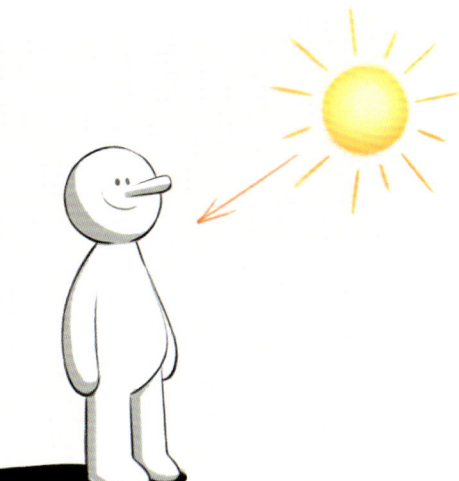

▶ The position of the sun will determine the length of the shadows it casts

DISTANCE FROM LIGHT SOURCE

The distance between a light source and an object can also affect the appearance of shadows. Light is most intense at its source, losing intensity as it travels. The further an object is from the light source, the greater the surface area the light can reach, changing the size and shape of the form shadow.

The distance between a light source, an object, and the surface it casts onto can affect cast shadows, as shown below. An object close to the surface will cast a smaller shadow with crisper, sharper edges, while an object that is far away will create larger, softer shadows.

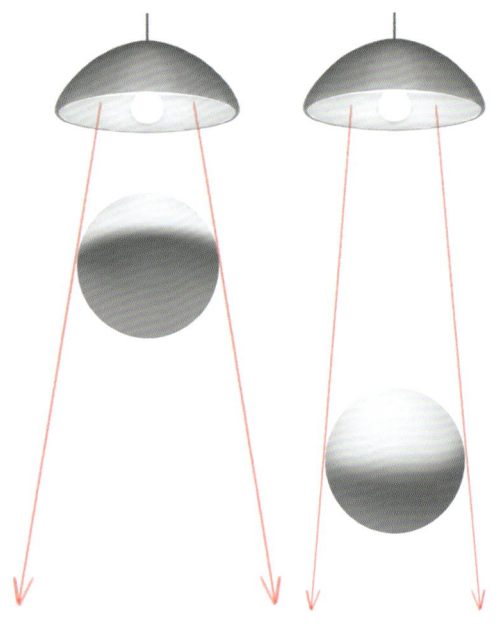

▶ The object closest to the light source receives more intense light, but the object further away receives light on a greater surface area

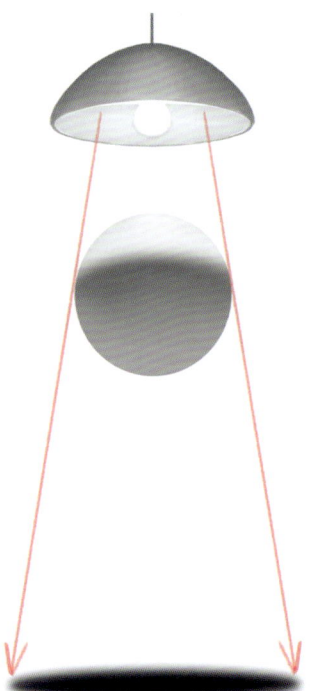

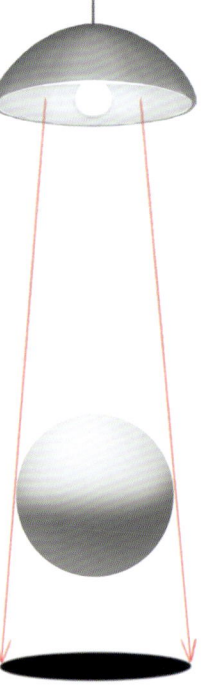

◀ The more distance between an object and a surface, the more light has a chance to scatter and bounce around the environment and into the shadows, softening the cast shadow

COMBINING SHADOWS

While it's possible for form shadows and cast shadows to be present at the same time, the overall shadows don't combine in intensity. A cast shadow overlapping a form shadow won't make the overlaps darker, though it may appear to in some scenarios.

In the example below, it may look like two shadows are combining to form a darker overlapping shadow, but this is actually caused by the presence of two light sources. There are two unseen direct lights, each creating its own cast shadow. Where these cast shadows overlap, you see what appears to be a darker shadow. In reality, the two lighter 'shadows' are just areas of less intense light, not actually shadows.

Another interesting way that shadows can interact is when soft-edged shadows meet hard-edged shadows. In the bottom-right example, there are two cast shadows: one comes from an object close to the light source but far from the surface it casts onto, while the other comes from an object closer to the surface it casts onto. This results in a combined shadow that has both hard and soft edges.

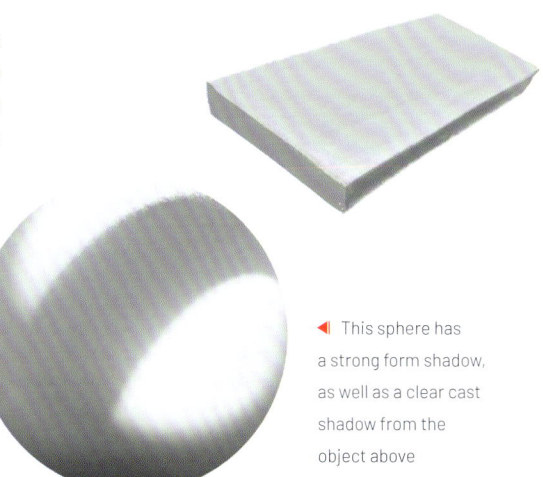

◀ This sphere has a strong form shadow, as well as a clear cast shadow from the object above

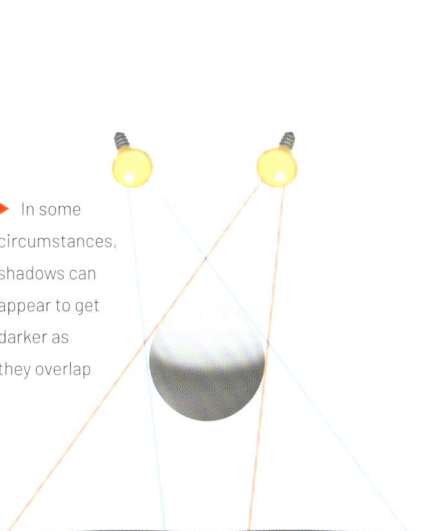

▶ In some circumstances, shadows can appear to get darker as they overlap

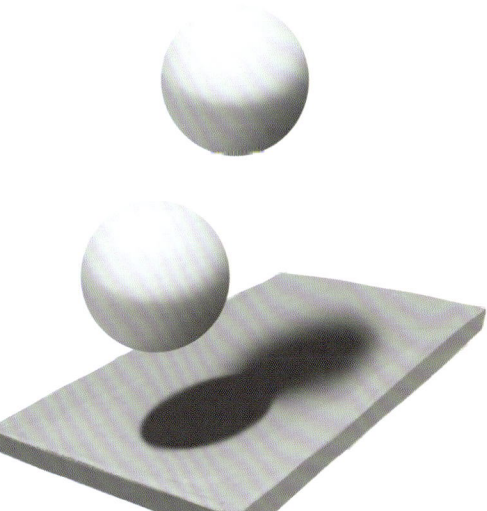

▲ An example of a soft and hard shadow merging into one single shadow shape

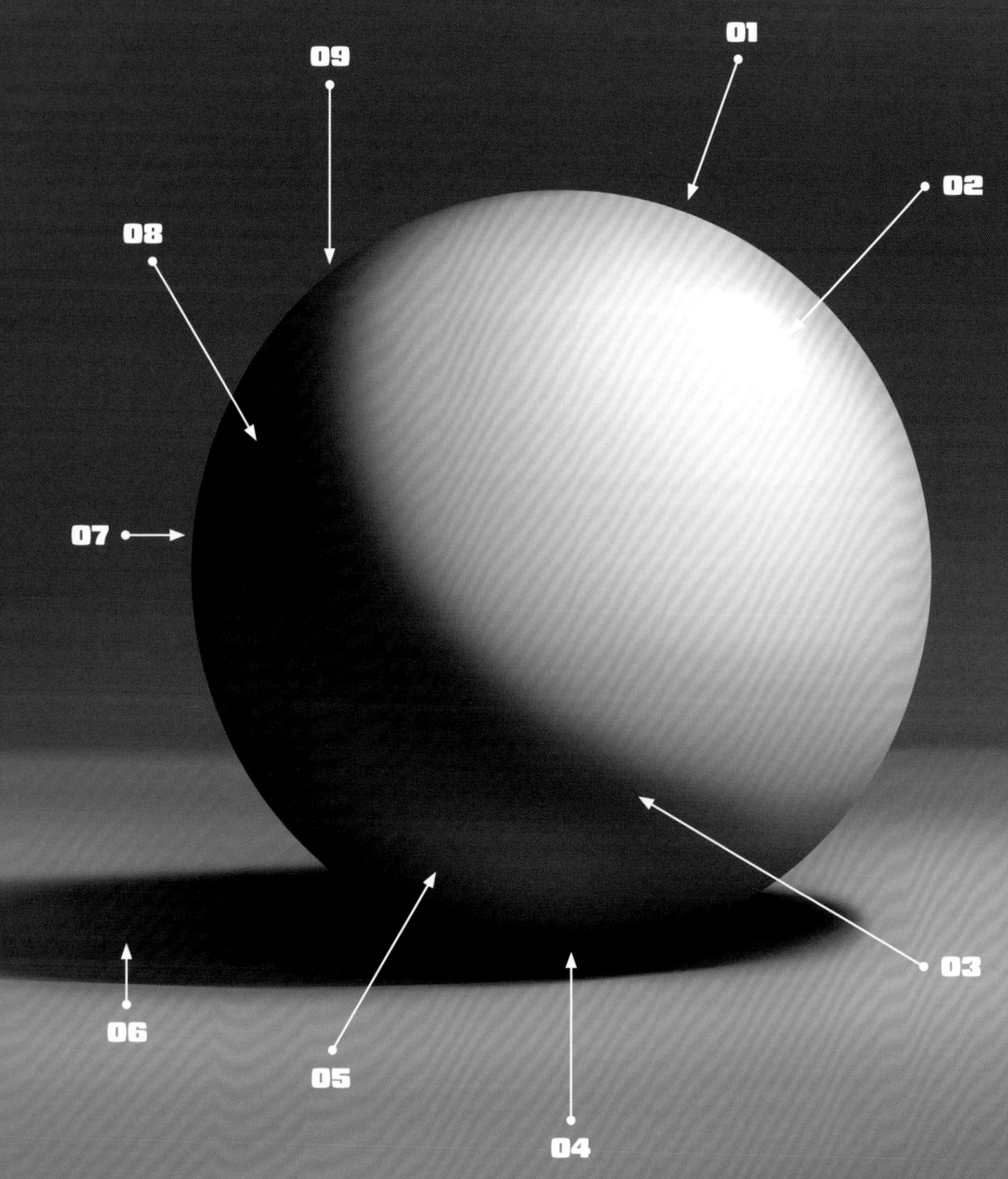

SHADOW ANATOMY

Now you have a basic understanding of form and cast shadows, let's explore them in more detail. The angle of light in relation to an object significantly affects the shadows created. Always start by looking where the direct light is coming from. In this image, the light shines from the top right.

01 LIGHT SHAPE

Where the light hits the object.

02 HIGHLIGHT

Most noticeable on shinier surfaces, this is where the light source reflects off the surface of an object and into the viewer's eye. Its position will change depending on where the viewer is in relation to the light source.

03 SHADOW EDGE (OR TERMINATOR)

The boundary between the illuminated and shadow areas of the object's form – the point where the form transitions from facing the direct light to facing away from it. It appears darker because it is the dividing line between where light hits and where any bounce light is reflected into the shadow area.

04 AMBIENT OCCLUSION

The area where little to no light can reach, usually in crevices or corners, or in this case, at the base of the sphere. It is usually the darkest areas of a shadow.

05 REFLECTED LIGHT FROM BELOW

This light bounces off the surface below the sphere and lights up the lower part of the form shadow. Bounced light is much weaker than direct light, so areas of bounced light will never be as bright as areas hit by direct light. Reflected light generally won't affect areas already in direct light.

06 CAST SHADOW

The shadow cast by the sphere onto the surface below it, blocking the direct light. The shape of the cast shadow matches the shape of the sphere, but due to the angle you're observing it from here, it appears more like an oval.

07 FORM SHADOW

The overall area not illuminated by the direct light (as opposed to the light shape). As the object is spherical, the shape of the resulting form shadow is curved.

08 CORE SHADOW

The dark area of the form shadow that isn't as affected by reflected light. The size of this area depends on the amount and direction of reflected light hitting the object.

09 REFLECTED LIGHT FROM ABOVE

Bounced light from the environment (ambient light) illuminates the top portion of the shadow area.

The sphere is perfect for depicting the basic anatomy of shadow because it simplifies the concept with a very simple form. However, things can get trickier as shapes become more complex. Notice how these different forms affect the light and shade areas, cast shadows, shadow edges, and bounced light. Taking the time to understand how light works on simple forms will help you to figure out complex forms more easily when you move on to lighting and shading characters.

▶ The cylinder's rounded form shows the shadow anatomy quite clearly, but the circular top is a flat surface that is lit according to its relative position to the light source

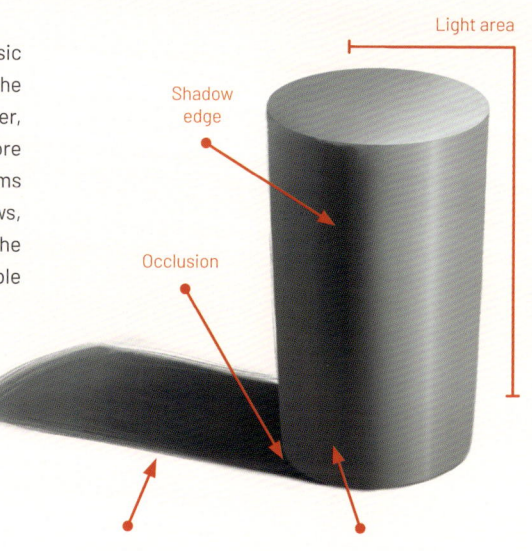

Light area

Shadow edge

Occlusion

Cast shadow

Form shadow

▼ The cone is similar to a cylinder, but note how the shadow details are affected by the circular forms coming to a point

Form shadow

Light shape

Bounced light

Cast shadow

Shadow edge

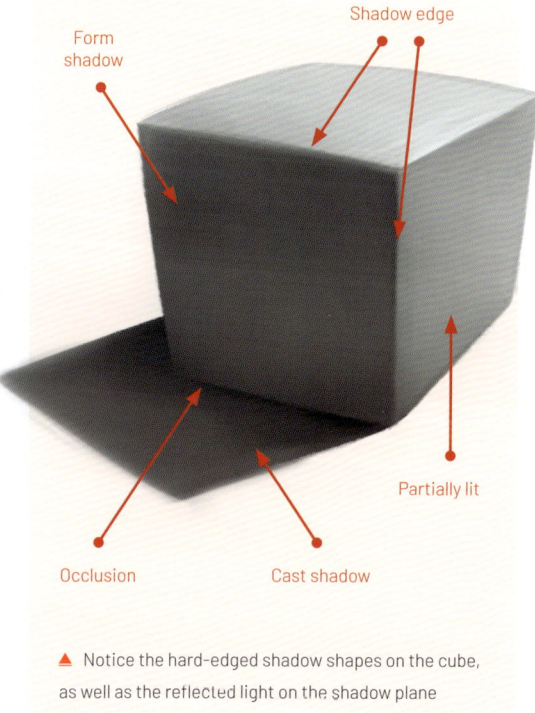

Shadow edge

Form shadow

Occlusion

Cast shadow

Partially lit

▲ Notice the hard-edged shadow shapes on the cube, as well as the reflected light on the shadow plane

Now you have a better understanding of these basic forms and their shadows, you can start to imagine how more complex forms might look.

◀ A character's head can be broken down into simple shapes to help you figure out how the various shadows will appear on each form

◀ Any anatomical feature of a character can be broken down into these basic forms

LIGHT, SHADE & COLOUR

It can be difficult to understand how to apply coloured light to your character designs without first studying light and colour.

WHITE LIGHT

White light is important to your understanding of how light and shade works from a colour point of view. Different light sources contain different amounts of the various visible light wavelengths. This is why some light sources appear yellow-orange, while others may appear bluer.

As mentioned on page 12, the sun is an example of a white light source, made up of all the wavelengths of light visible to the human eye: red, orange, yellow, green, blue, indigo, and violet – the colours of the rainbow.

You can recreate white light by combining just three primary light colours: red, green, and blue. This is known as RGB lighting and is used in televisions, computer monitors, phone screens, and even stage lighting. You will also find it in the colour wheel picker in digital painting softwares.

As shown in the diagram on the left, red and blue light combine to make purple, green and red make yellow, and green and blue make cyan. Combining colours of light is known as additive colour mixing: adding individual colours together to create new colours and combining them all to create white light. Although RGB lighting only uses three colours, by varying their ratios, saturation, and brightness, you can recreate all the remaining colours of the visible spectrum.

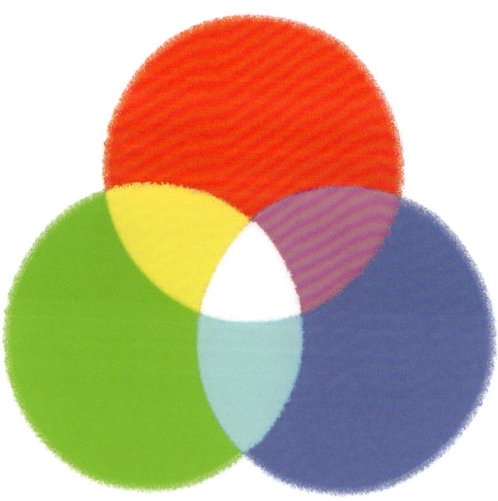

▲ This RGB Venn diagram shows how red, green, and blue light combine in different ways to create other colours

LOCAL COLOUR

The inherent colour of an object is known as its local colour. For example, the local colour of a red ball is red and the local colour of a green ball is green. This is due to light wavelengths. As covered on page 12, different colours of light have their own specific wavelengths. Red has a particular wavelength, green has a particular wavelength, and so on. White light is all of the visible wavelengths of colour combined.

The local colour of an object is determined by which wavelengths of light it absorbs and which it reflects when white light is shone on it. When you see a red object, the surface is reflecting the red wavelengths of white light back into your eyes. When you see a green object, its surface is reflecting the green wavelengths, and so on. When you see a black object, however, that surface is reflecting almost no wavelengths of white light. In contrast, a white surface is reflecting most of the wavelengths of white light.

If you paint a wall blue, it would be more accurate to say you're painting the wall with paint that reflects blue wavelengths of light while absorbing the rest. The human eye then perceives this reflected wavelength as the paint being blue.

Why is it important to specify white light here? Because otherwise it isn't clear what the local colour of an object is. If you shine a pure red light on a blue object, it won't reflect much light and the local colour won't be clear. It is only by shining white light on an object that you can get an accurate idea of what colour it really is.

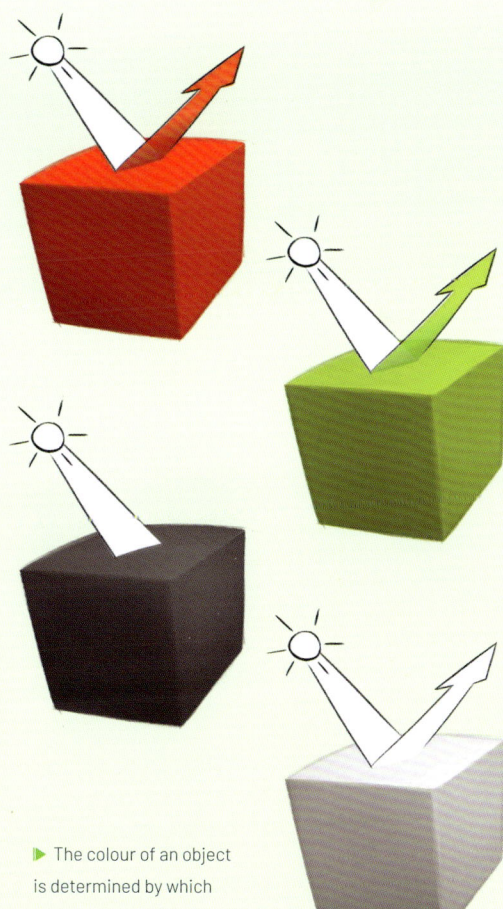

▶ The colour of an object is determined by which wavelengths of light it absorbs or reflects

ARTIST TIP **PRIMARY COLOURS**

The three primary light colours (red, green, and blue) don't match the primary colours used when talking about mixing paint: red, yellow, and blue. Colour-mixing with real paint works very differently to colour-mixing with light.

COLOURED LIGHT

What happens if you use coloured lights instead of white light? If you shine a red light on a matt white object, you can expect the object to look red. If you shine a blue light on a matt white object, you can expect it to look blue, and so on.

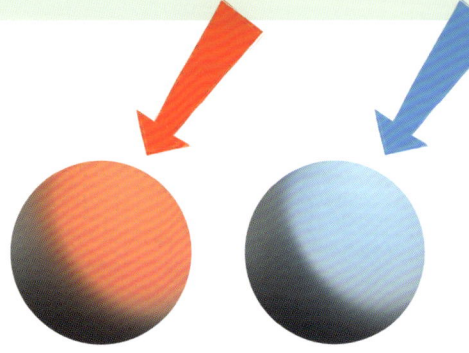

▲ White objects will appear the colour of light shone on them

This is because white reflects all visible colours. If you shine a coloured light on a matt black object, however, it won't reflect any light at all, as black objects absorb all the visible wavelengths of light.

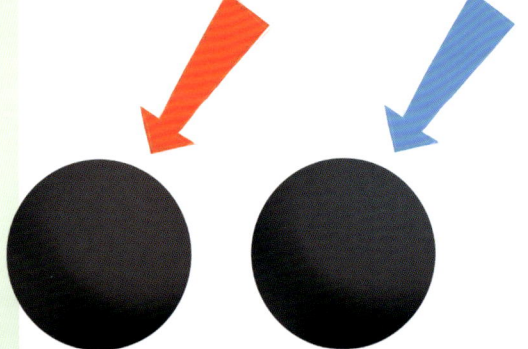

◀ Black objects absorb any coloured light shone on them

What about a coloured light hitting a coloured object? A red light hitting a blue object will result in the blue object appearing black. This is because a blue object will only reflect blue light. In this scenario, the red light would be fully absorbed, reflecting nothing. The same is true if a red object were lit with a blue or green light.

What if you light a red object with a red light? Or a blue object with a blue light? In these examples the colour will intensify slightly, as the object reflects the colour of the light back on itself, increasing saturation.

▶ Shining a red light on a red object intensifies the colour

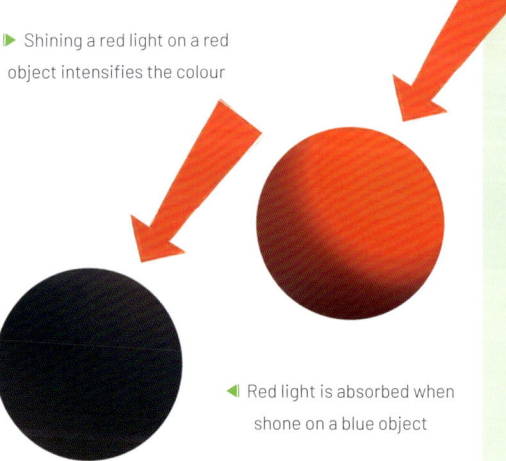

◀ Red light is absorbed when shone on a blue object

You may have noticed that the black objects in these images do reflect some light, and the blue object does in fact reflect some red light, and so on. This is where theory meets reality. There are various reasons why things might not turn out exactly as expected:

- **Colour purity** If the local colour of an object isn't 100% red, blue, green, or black, it may also reflect some other colour wavelengths of light.

- **Light purity** If a light source itself isn't 100% one colour, you may see some light reflection from the additional colour wavelengths.

- **Surface reflectivity** A more reflective surface will reflect some light despite the local colour. This is why the previous examples specify a matt surface.

- **Colour saturation** If the local colour of an object is less saturated, it likely has more white or grey mixed into its pigmentation. Because of this, it will reflect a wider range of colour wavelengths. The value of the local colour here is important, too; a desaturated, dark-valued colour will reflect fewer colours than a desaturated, high-valued colour. This is because it is reflecting less light overall due to it being darker. Remember, black absorbs light, and white reflects it!

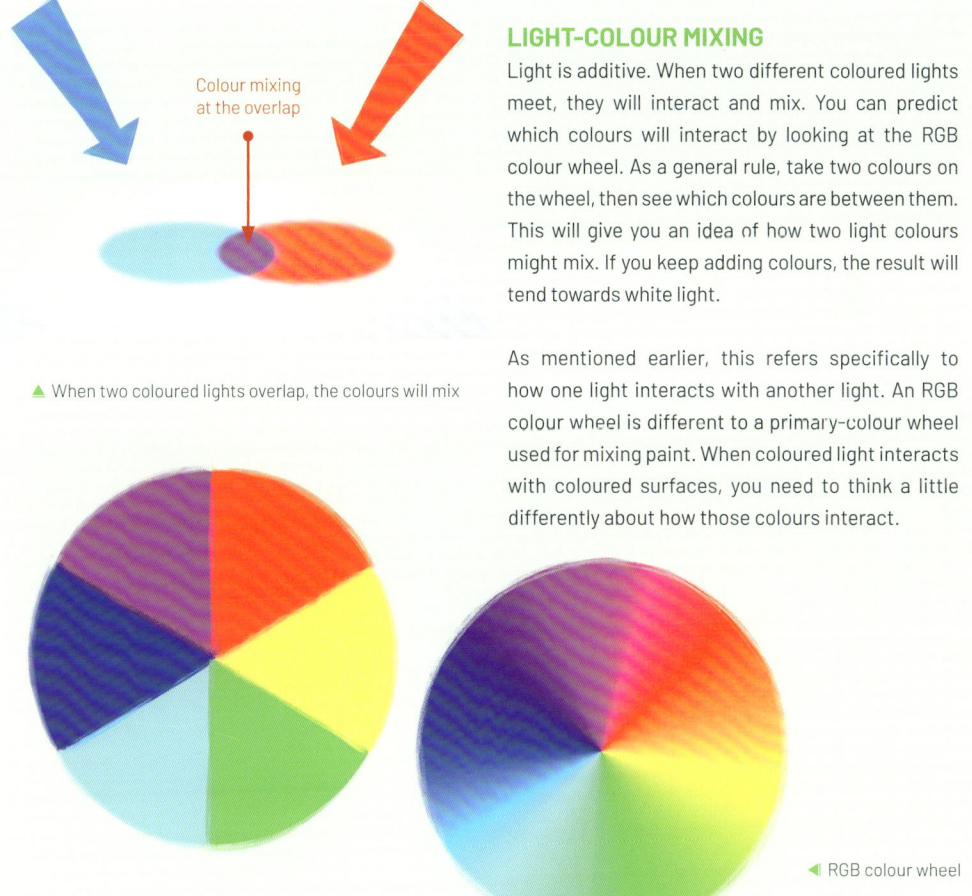

Colour mixing at the overlap

▲ When two coloured lights overlap, the colours will mix

LIGHT-COLOUR MIXING

Light is additive. When two different coloured lights meet, they will interact and mix. You can predict which colours will interact by looking at the RGB colour wheel. As a general rule, take two colours on the wheel, then see which colours are between them. This will give you an idea of how two light colours might mix. If you keep adding colours, the result will tend towards white light.

As mentioned earlier, this refers specifically to how one light interacts with another light. An RGB colour wheel is different to a primary-colour wheel used for mixing paint. When coloured light interacts with coloured surfaces, you need to think a little differently about how those colours interact.

◄ RGB colour wheel

LIGHT & SURFACE-COLOUR MIXING

When a coloured light hits a coloured surface, the colours don't interact in an additive fashion. Instead, some light colours are absorbed and some are reflected by the surface. For example, when a red light hits a blue surface, the colours won't combine to appear purple. The red light wavelengths will be absorbed by the blue surface, making it appear almost black.

Remember that no surface or light source is ever perfectly pure. Always expect some amount of colour reflection and absorption, even if the surface is mostly one colour. When you use paint, you are mixing paint colours in what is known as subtractive colour-mixing. The more paint colours you mix together, the more light colours are absorbed by the paint, making the paint darker. Theoretically, you could make black paint if you were to mix all of your paint colours together. In reality, you would end up with a muddy dark brown because the pigment colours are not perfectly pure.

To summarize, when coloured light meets coloured light, additive colour-mixing rules apply: lights combine to make new colours and all combine to make white light. When coloured light meets a coloured object, subtractive colour-mixing rules apply: wavelengths are absorbed or reflected by the object, depending on its colour. Light and pigments don't mix in the same way as two lights.

While this may seem complicated, you need an understanding of both of these processes to know how to recreate light and shade in your artwork, particularly for more realistic character designs.

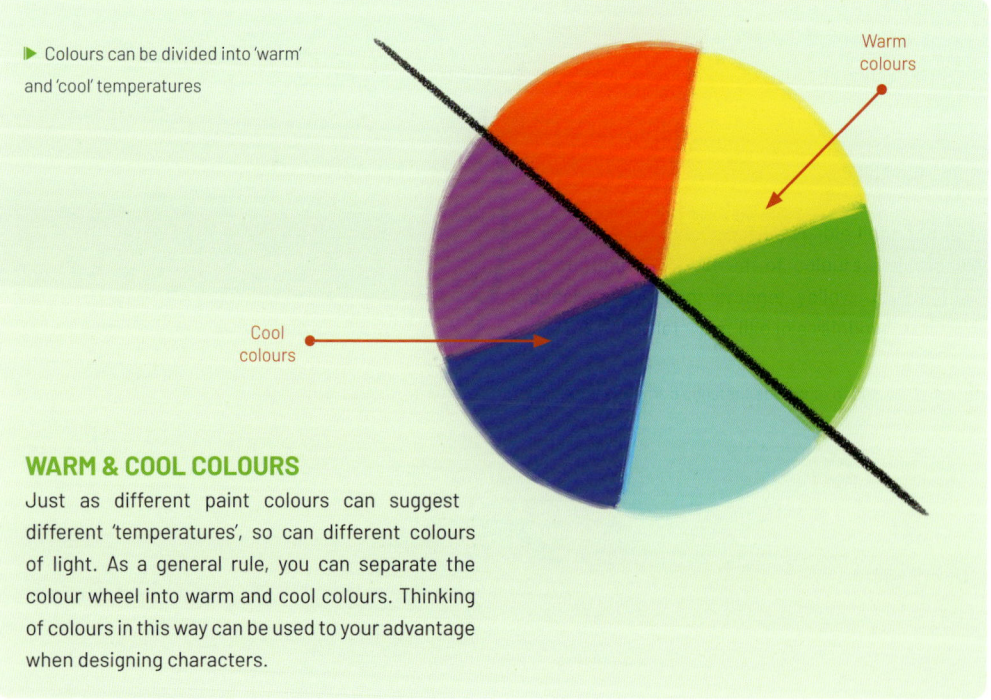

▶ Colours can be divided into 'warm' and 'cool' temperatures

Warm colours

Cool colours

WARM & COOL COLOURS

Just as different paint colours can suggest different 'temperatures', so can different colours of light. As a general rule, you can separate the colour wheel into warm and cool colours. Thinking of colours in this way can be used to your advantage when designing characters.

BOUNCED LIGHT & COLOUR

When white light reflects off a coloured object, that colour is reflected too. This generally only happens in the shadows, where the stronger direct light can't reach. Additionally, if a bounced light is the same colour as an object, you will see an increase in colour saturation where the light hits.

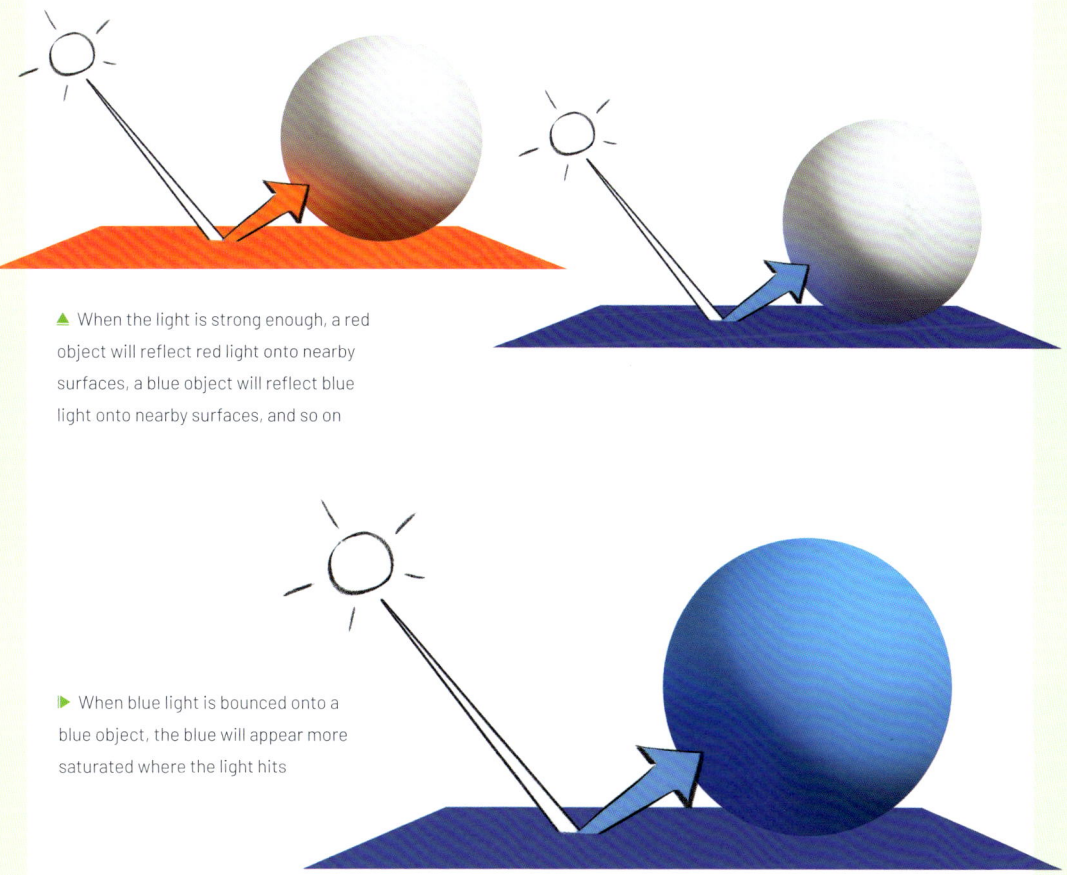

▲ When the light is strong enough, a red object will reflect red light onto nearby surfaces, a blue object will reflect blue light onto nearby surfaces, and so on

▶ When blue light is bounced onto a blue object, the blue will appear more saturated where the light hits

LOCAL COLOUR VS ACTUAL COLOUR

When it comes to coloured-light interaction, local colour doesn't always look as it should. There are numerous variables that can affect the perceived colour of an object. In reality, there is a big difference between the local colour of an object and the actual perceived colour of an object due to the surrounding environment and various ambient light sources that hit it. This is true of almost every object you see in the world around you. Understanding this will prove useful, especially when creating more realistic characters and concept art.

COLOURED LIGHT & SHADOWS

WARM LIGHT, COOL SHADOWS

It's also important to consider how coloured light affects shadows. Have you ever been told that warm light produces cool shadows, and cool light results in warm shadows? This is somewhat of a myth and isn't universally true.

One scenario where this does occur is outside on a sunny day. Imagine a white ball outdoors in the sunlight. The sunlight will hit one side of the ball, making it appear warm. In contrast, the shadows will appear slightly cooler. This is because the sky is a blue ambient light source; this cooler blue light

reflects into any areas of shadow that point towards the sky.

If you move the white ball inside a room with yellow walls and a warm light source, the results will differ. The bounced ambient light from the yellow walls will warm the shadows and there is no sky to influence the shadow colours. Ambient light is what really determines the colour, and therefore the warmth or coolness, of the shadows. The local colour underneath a shadow also plays a role, as you can see below.

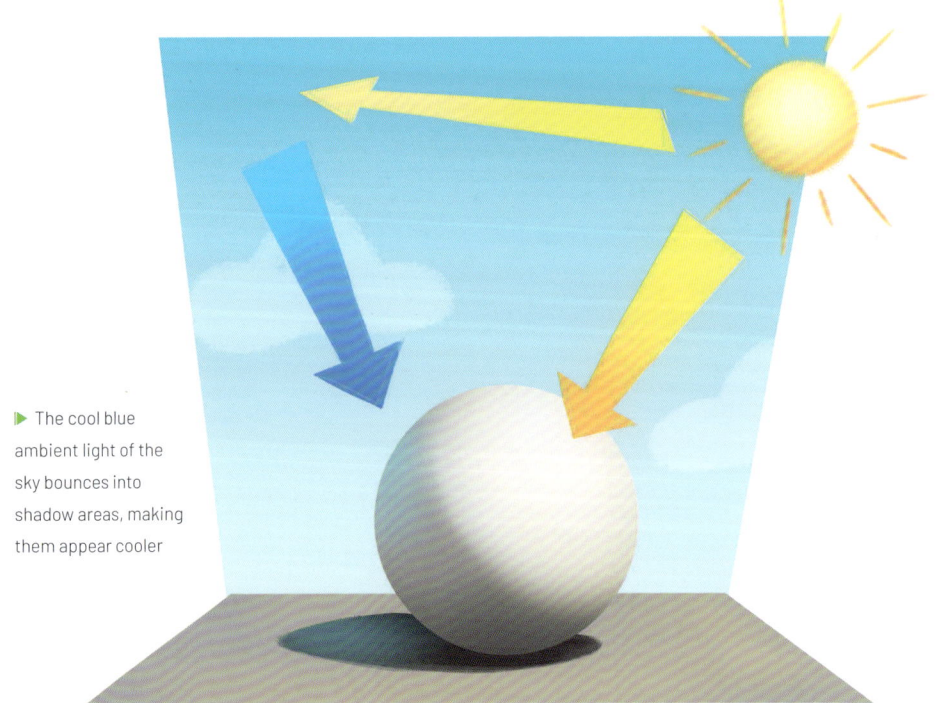

▶ The cool blue ambient light of the sky bounces into shadow areas, making them appear cooler

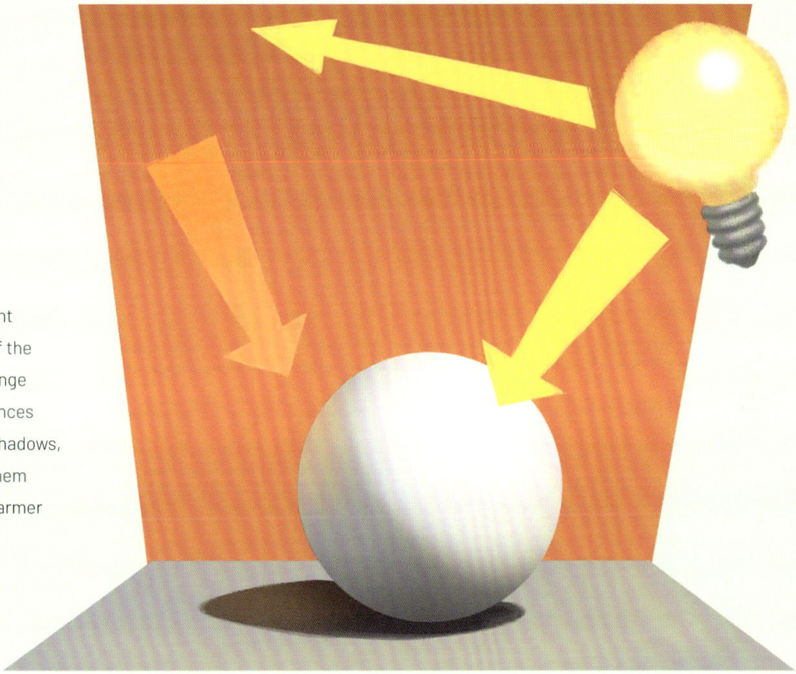

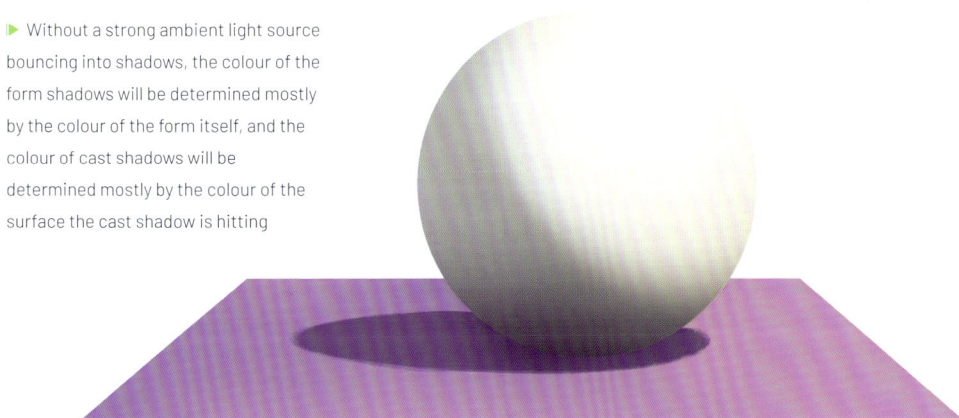

► The light hitting off the warm orange walls bounces into the shadows, making them appear warmer

► Without a strong ambient light source bouncing into shadows, the colour of the form shadows will be determined mostly by the colour of the form itself, and the colour of cast shadows will be determined mostly by the colour of the surface the cast shadow is hitting

Understanding these fundamentals is essential for representing light and shade in a believable way. It can be the difference between a character design with a nice colour scheme and a character design that looks like it really exists in a world of light and shade.

Now comes the fun part... How do you apply all these ideas when designing characters? The following chapters will show you.

DESCRIBING FORM

The most fundamental way of using light and shade in character design is to describe a character's form. The goal is to use lighting to clearly describe the structure of a character, their mass and shape, and whether they are simple or more complex.

How you describe form can, in part, be a stylistic decision. For example, the style of an animated TV show may call for characters with basic shadows.

Or you could be required to provide information about a character's form as part of a 3D production pipeline, giving 3D modellers a clear reference from which to model a design. It's not uncommon to create turnarounds and model sheets to aid in this process, ensuring a character's forms are clearly communicated. As a character designer, you must not only be able to visualize forms in your head, but also draw them effectively.

▲ Every colour has an underlying greyscale value, which you can see by removing the colour information

TOOLS & TECHNIQUES

When recreating light and shade in your character drawings, you can use traditional materials, such as paints or pencils, or digital tools, such as digital-painting software. Whichever you prefer, you must use value and colour. While you are already familiar with colour, value refers to the relative brightness of a colour (or grey tone). In other words, how light or dark it is.

You can use lighter or darker colours, or greyscale tones, to represent light and shade in your artwork. It is the relative contrast between the darks and lights that recreates light and shade. A good way to practise this is through observational drawing – for example, create a physical still life of white spheres and cubes, then draw what you see. This will train your eye to discern the values that make up light and shade.

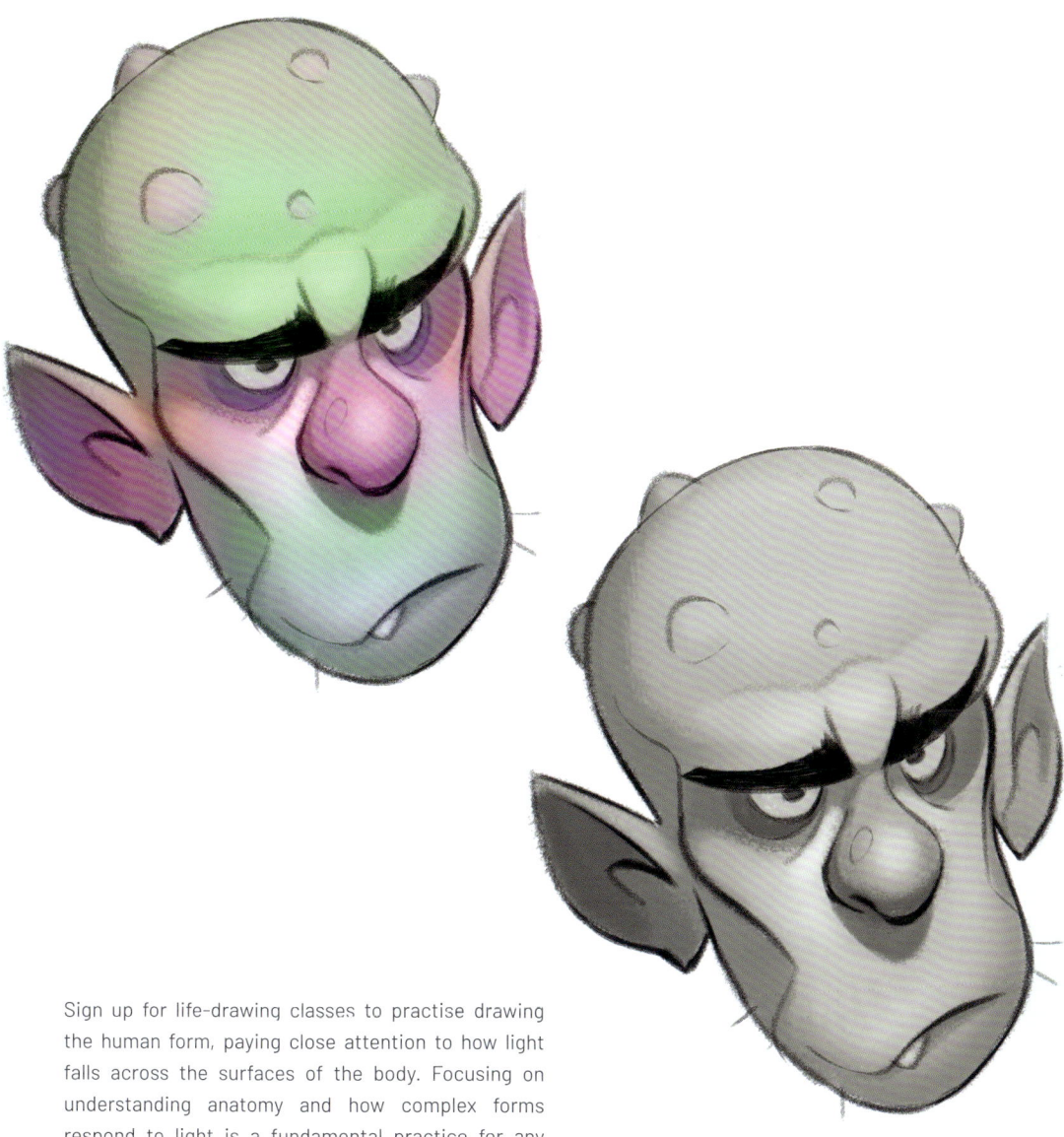

Sign up for life-drawing classes to practise drawing the human form, paying close attention to how light falls across the surfaces of the body. Focusing on understanding anatomy and how complex forms respond to light is a fundamental practice for any character designer.

If attending a life-drawing class isn't possible, study from photographs or life-drawing websites. Anatomy books are also a great resource. The more you can learn about drawing the human form, and translating what you see into values, the easier it will be to incorporate light and shade into your character designs.

▲ Here you can see the values underlying a coloured character; value is what describes form

VISUALIZING FORMS

To draw shadows on an object or character, you must first visualize its form. Try to view it as a volume, rather than just a flat shape. 'Volume', used interchangeably with 'form' in this chapter, is the idea that a two-dimensional drawing can represent something volumetric, and appear three-dimensional, on the page.

▶ If you add volume lines to flat two-dimensional shapes, they start to appear more three-dimensional

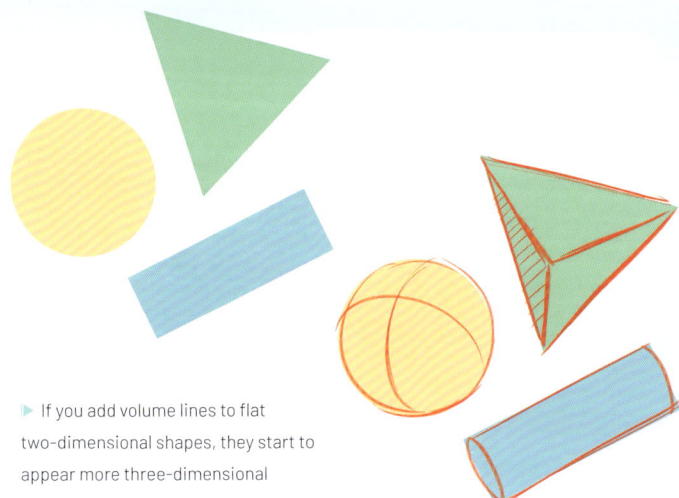

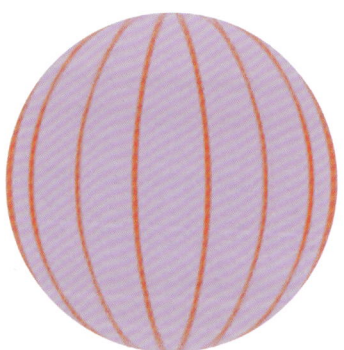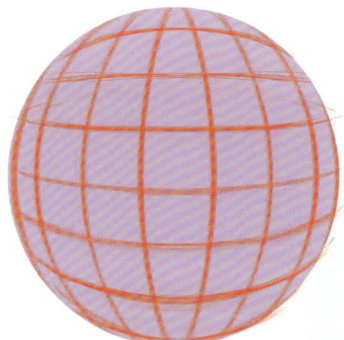

▲ The resulting grid represents different planes of the form

Visualizing form in this way takes a lot of practice. It combines knowledge of perspective, foreshortening, and the ability to visualize things in 3D. Using a form or volume grid can help with this. A simple circle can become a representation of a sphere just by drawing volumetric lines over it, top to bottom and left to right, resembling a kind of wire mesh or grid.

If you struggle with this, try this practical exercise: use a black marker pen to draw lines around an orange, following its form. Next, try it with a banana, drawing

lines along the plane changes on its surface. This can help you to think volumetrically and understand how forms translate into three dimensions.

Next, look at the objects around you and imagine drawing on them with a black marker. How would those lines look? Once you can visualize the grid, it becomes easier to understand how light would hit the object. If every grid square represents a plane of the object, you can see how some of these planes would face a light source, while others wouldn't.

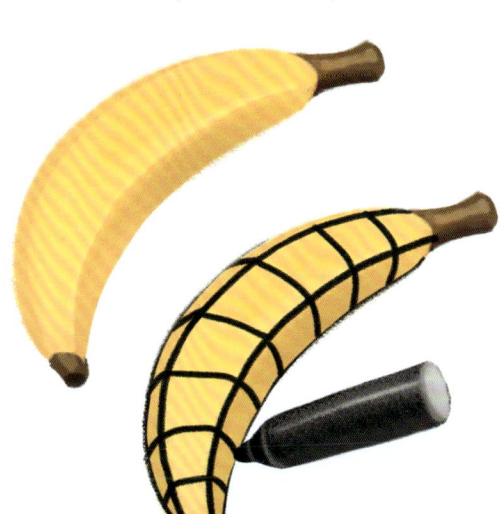

▼ Draw along a banana's various planes

▲ Draw lines around the form of an orange

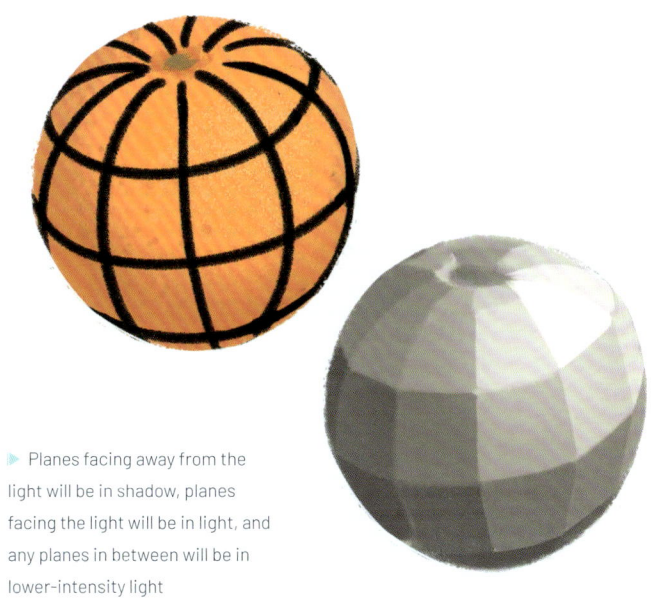

▶ Planes facing away from the light will be in shadow, planes facing the light will be in light, and any planes in between will be in lower-intensity light

To add a simple shadow layer to a character, you must first visualize their form in your head. Adding a grid can help you to see them volumetrically. Using the grid as a guide, you can then add a shadow layer that follows the subject's form. The grid lines will help make clear which planes face towards and away from the light source.

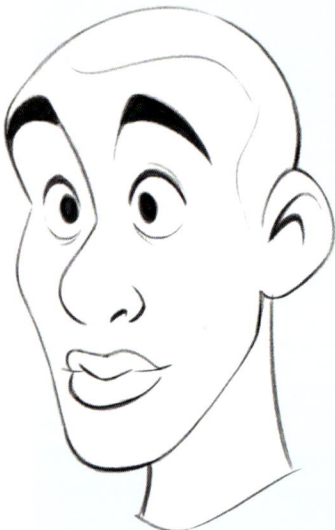

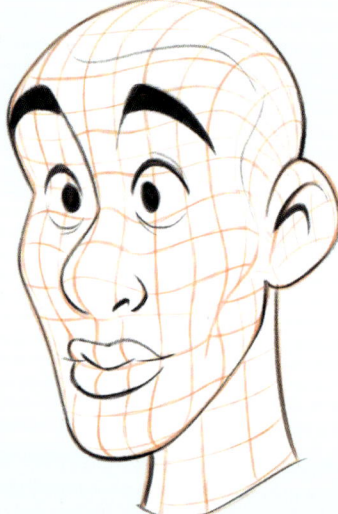

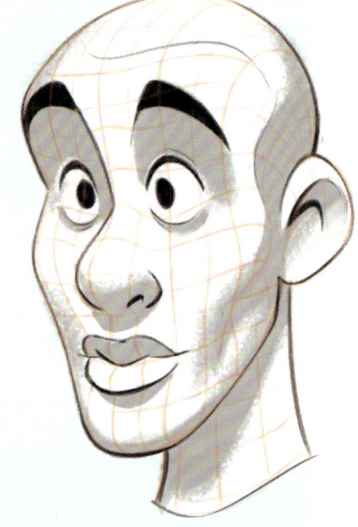

▲ A simple character, without any shadow

▲ Drawing a grid over a character will help you to view them in three dimensions

▲ The grid will provide a guide when adding the shadow layer

You could also visualize other very different forms for the same basic character shape. As before, the first step is always to visualize the character's forms. If you get stuck, simply draw a form grid over the top. The more you practise thinking in volumes, the easier it will become.

▶ Two different ways of visualizing forms on the same character

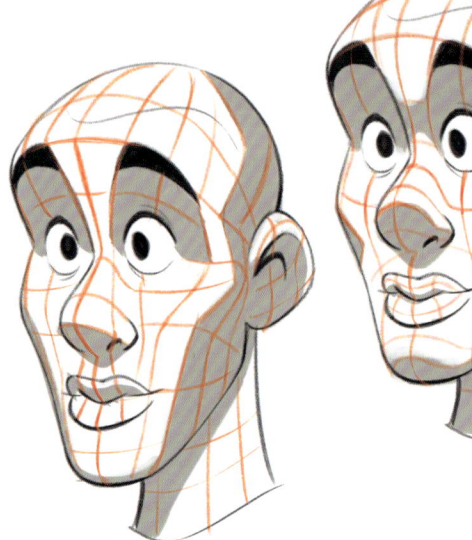

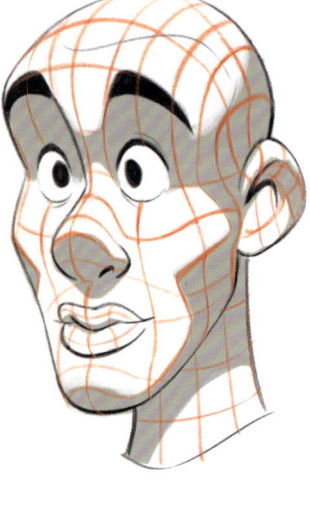

Neutral lighting

Dramatic lighting

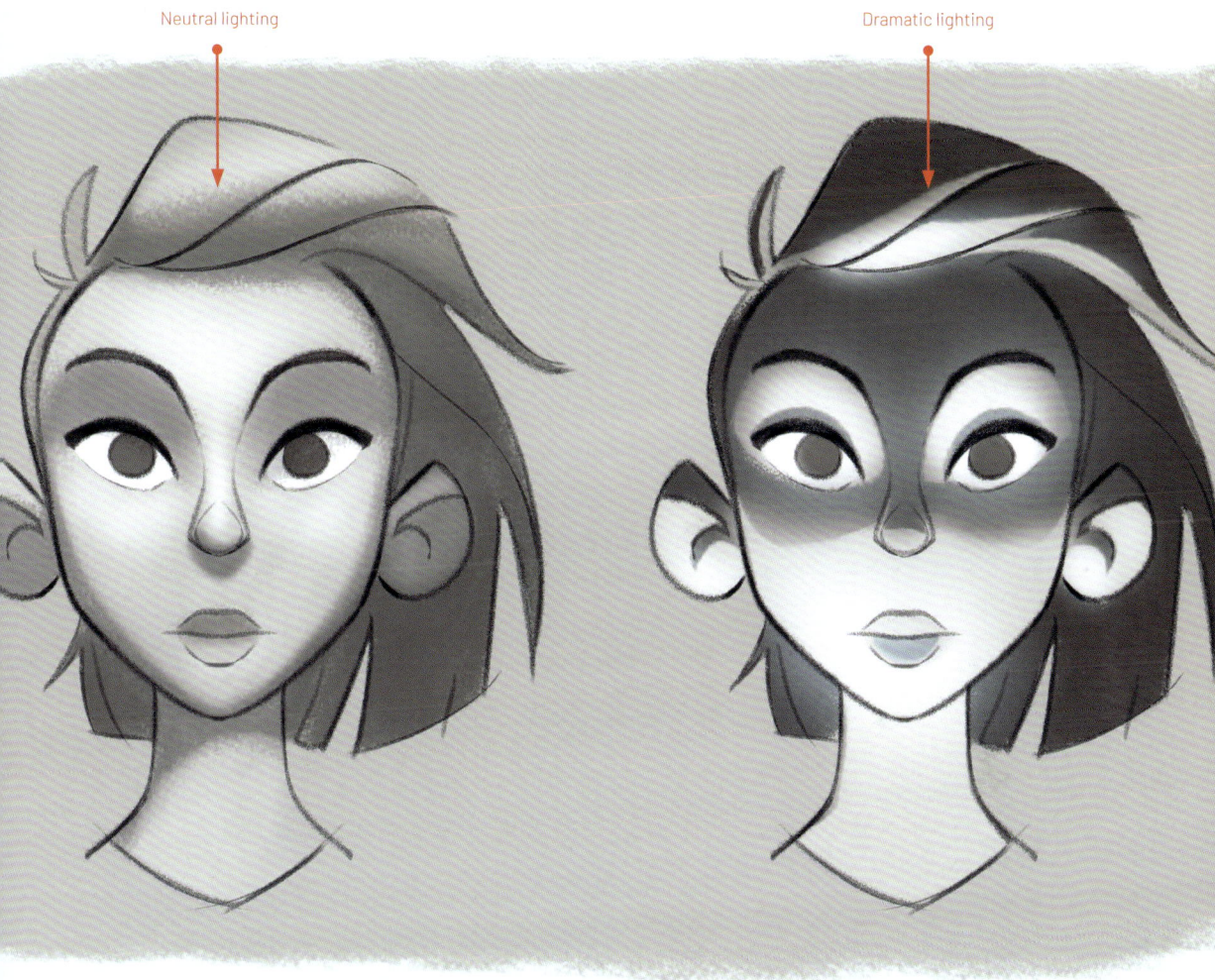

NEUTRAL LIGHTING

When using light and shade to describe a character's form, it is often best to use fairly neutral lighting, since the focus is on communicating form rather than being creative with lighting. More extreme lighting can certainly look impressive, but it could also be a distraction to understanding the true form of a character. You want to show the volumes of the character without any distraction or ambiguity of form.

A simple overhead light source is clear and easy to understand. It also feels most natural, as people are very familiar with overhead lighting, such as ceiling lights or the sun. While extreme lighting set-ups do convey form, they tend to show very specific parts of form and aren't necessarily best for communicating the clear overall design of a character. It can also help to use a slightly diffused light source, particularly for more realistic character designs. This helps to eliminate any ambiguity caused by harsh form and cast shadows.

SIMPLE LIGHT & SHADE DESIGN

Now let's look at a couple of examples of using light and shade to describe different types of characters.

Let's start with simple shadow design, similar to what you might find in an animated TV show, such as *The Simpsons* or *Gravity Falls*, or a simple comic, or certain types of book illustration. The simplest form of shadows you can use in character design, this style only uses two values: light and dark. The only way to make these shadows simpler would be to remove them altogether.

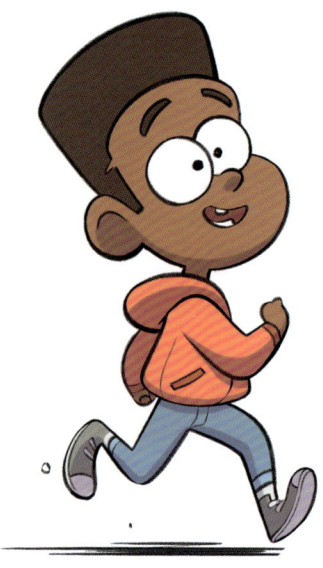

▲ A simple character lit from above, with a simple two-value shadow design

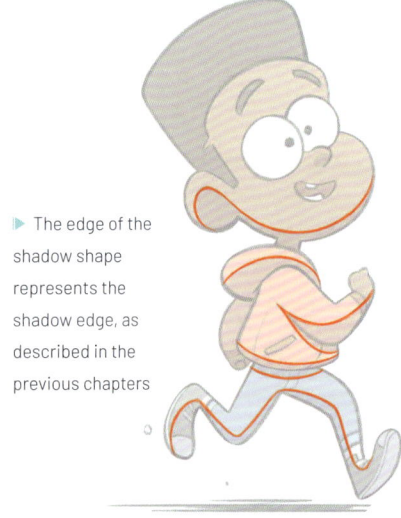

▶ The edge of the shadow shape represents the shadow edge, as described in the previous chapters

ARTIST TIP EXPERIMENT

How you approach shadows will depend on style. This book is just a guide and there will be times where you will want to experiment with these ideas. Not being mindful of volumes is a reasonable style decision if done consciously.

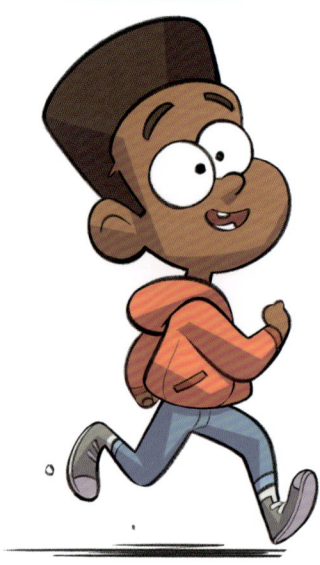

▲ Even with a simple character design, be mindful of the volumes of the shapes, otherwise the shadows can end up looking odd

Shadow design on very simple characters is often used to aid clarity and make a character's forms more readable. The simpler the character-design style, the simpler the shadows should be. The light areas, rather than being drawn separately, are implied by the shapes of the shadows. Since the goal is to describe form, it's important to ask where the shadow edges are. In other words, where does the form transition from facing the light to facing away from it? On a simple two-value shadow design, this is the key variable at play, as it's the only element that conveys the forms. Using a form grid can still help here, even with a very simple character design.

With more complex character designs, it's still possible to convey complexity with only a single shadow layer. This complexity comes from the use of more nuanced and detailed shapes in this layer.

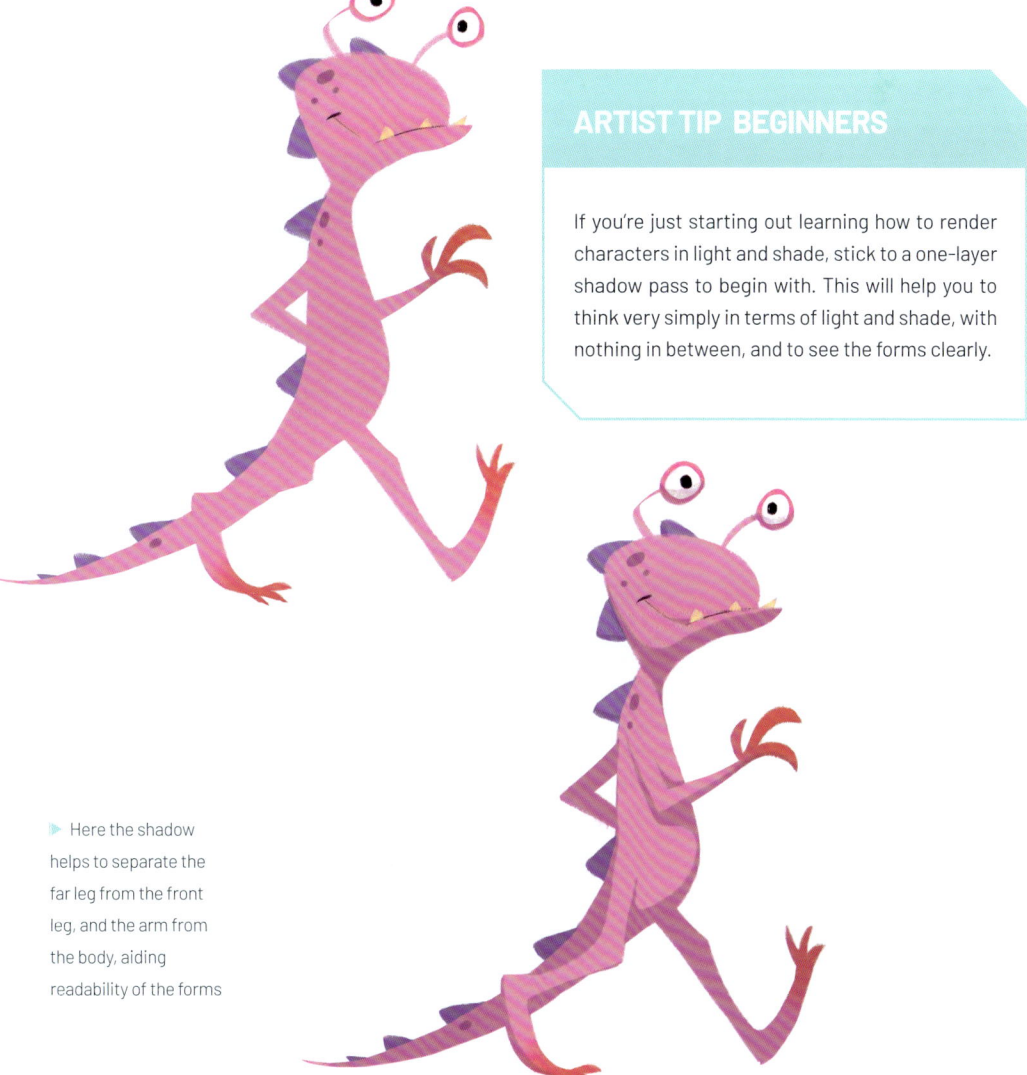

ARTIST TIP BEGINNERS

If you're just starting out learning how to render characters in light and shade, stick to a one-layer shadow pass to begin with. This will help you to think very simply in terms of light and shade, with nothing in between, and to see the forms clearly.

▶ Here the shadow helps to separate the far leg from the front leg, and the arm from the body, aiding readability of the forms

Being able to show a complex shadow using only two values is the perfect place to start for any character design or style. If you can abstract your lighting down to this simple two-value structure, and keep the design clear and readable, you have successfully described a character's form. This provides a great foundation on top of which you can build more complex shadows.

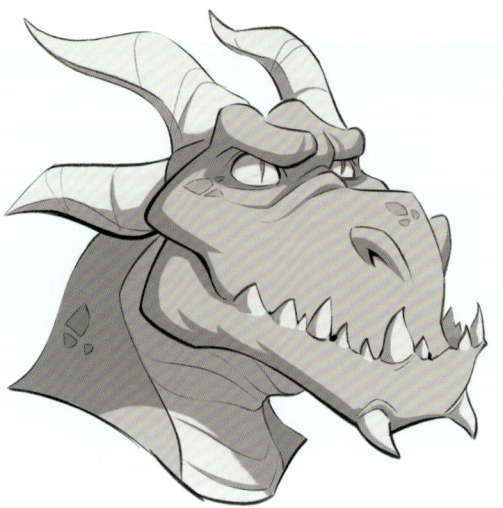

▶ This design has more complex forms, resulting in a more complex shadow shape

HARD & SOFT EDGES

The simple hard-edged two-value shadows are more of an abstraction of reality. While they are perfectly valid, depending on the style of a character, they can risk giving the impression that a form has distinct hard planes, even if it doesn't.

The world is full of both hard-edged and soft-edged forms, as are characters. You can use both to describe more complex forms, still only using one shadow layer.

Hard-edged shadows

Soft-edged shadows

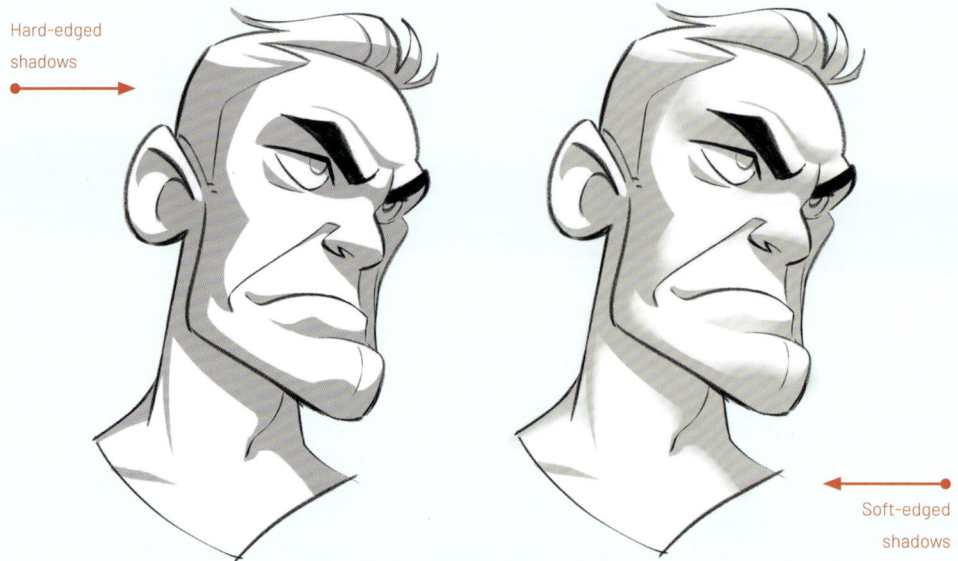

▲ Introducing soft edges increases the complexity of a shadow design and the suggested forms

42

REALISTIC SHADOW DESIGN

Now to explore the opposite extreme: realistic light and shade. Commonly used in video games, feature films, and detailed illustrations, this approach emphasizes realism over abstraction. The goal is to approximate the look of a character as though they were a three-dimensional object in the real world, reacting to light in a natural way. The forms should be described with much more attention to detail and focus on the way light and shade work in reality.

When drawing this type of character, the same ideas generally apply. As the goal is to communicate forms, it still makes sense to use a top-down soft light source to minimize harsh contrasts in shadows. If the lighting is too extreme, the clarity of the forms will be lost.

If working with a 3D modeller who will take your concept art and turn it into a 3D model, the clearer the forms are in the concept, the better. Ideally this would be supported with a character turnaround or concepts from various angles, as a character modeller needs to see the design's front, side, and back to fully understand its volumes. Adding a simple shadow pass on each drawing in the turnaround will also aid understanding of the character's forms from all angles.

Realistic illustration styles are another context that demands well-executed light and shade, and the ability to describe form well.

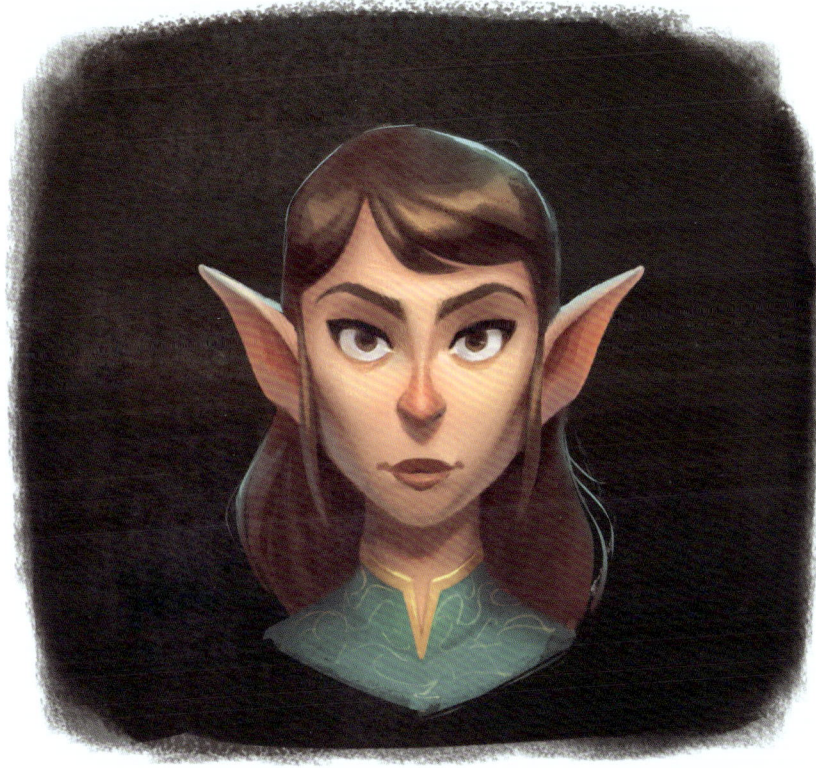

◀ With this more realistic character style, greater attention is paid to realistic light and its relationship to form

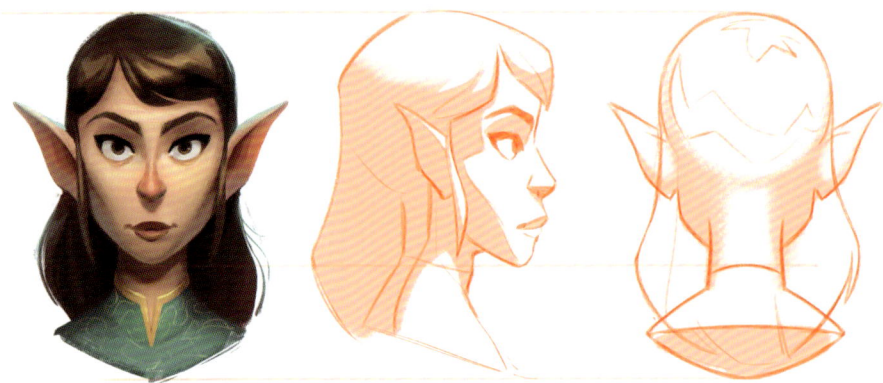

▲ A character turnaround will help to fully convey the character's form

BUILDING FORM

To construct a complex form, start simple with a two-value pass of shadow and light, then build up the complexity. Even the most complex forms can be simplified into basic shapes and planes. Starting with a form grid will help immensely when trying to visualize the volumes of more complex characters.

Just remember, a good descriptive shadow is built on a strong basic shadow. First, establish the shadow edge (the point where the light ends and the shadow begins, as shown on page 23) and the major shadow shapes. Next, add more nuanced shadow shapes to break large forms into smaller ones, before introducing hard and soft edges. At this point you can introduce the intricacies of shading discussed earlier, such as bounced light and ambient occlusion.

The main risk when using realistic descriptive lighting is that there's little room for error and it's therefore easy to get wrong. You are so used to seeing realistic lighting in your everyday life that when a design doesn't look right, it's easy to spot. That said, it's not always necessary, or desirable, to create a character with light and shade that looks one hundred per cent realistic. Believability is a much better target. Additionally, there is no reason why you couldn't create a very simple, stylized character, but render it realistically.

▲ Breaking up complex forms into simple shapes and creating form grids can help when approaching more complex lighting

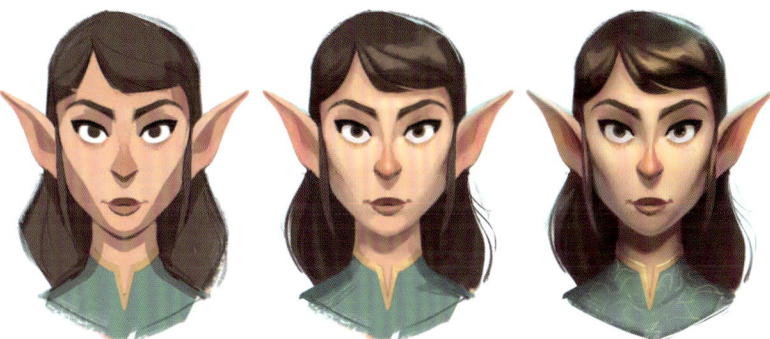

▶ Start simple
and build up the
complexity from
a strong foundation

EVERYTHING IN BETWEEN

This chapter has looked at two extremes of descriptive light and shade for characters – simple lighting and complex lighting – but there are countless possible variations in between.

The common thread to these three approaches (see below) is that the character forms are clear in each. The choice of lighting ensures the volumes read well, which should be the primary goal of any descriptive lighting. On one hand, more realistic designs require a deep understanding of light and shade in the real world, and how to translate them into drawings. On the other hand, simpler character styles can often use a more abstract treatment of light and shadow while still conveying forms effectively.

The lighting style for a character can fall anywhere along this spectrum. It's up to you to decide where your character's light and shade should fall and why. This process of choosing and refining the way you represent light and shade is called stylization, which is explored in the next chapter.

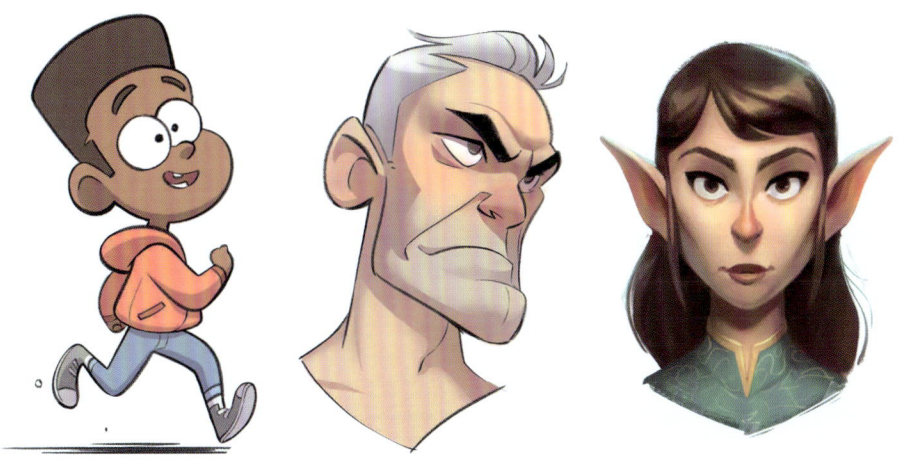

▲ Three different ways of using descriptive light and shade in character design

STYLIZING

WHAT IS STYLIZATION?

Imagine a line from left to right. At one end is a simple character design, similar to *The Powerpuff Girls* or a *Minecraft* character. At the other end is a more complex, almost realistic, character design, like one from *Red Dead Redemption* or *Horizon Zero Dawn*. In between these two extremes you can create all manner of styles depending on how you push and pull your design choices.

Design choices are typically determined by the story being told. Imagine you are telling a story for young children, versus telling a story for adults. Instinctively it makes sense to approach each with different visual stylization more suited for the audience. Stylization is simply a process of abstracting reality – making design choices about how to represent reality and the final look this creates.

The medium the character will exist in should also be considered. Is the character intended for games, TV animation, or picture books? While there is a lot of crossover between these, the final style is often influenced by the limitations of a particular medium.

Every element of a character's design is on the table when it comes to stylization: the proportions, shapes, colours, and so on. The focus for this book, however, is specifically on decisions regarding light and shade in character design and how these choices help inform the final style of the character.

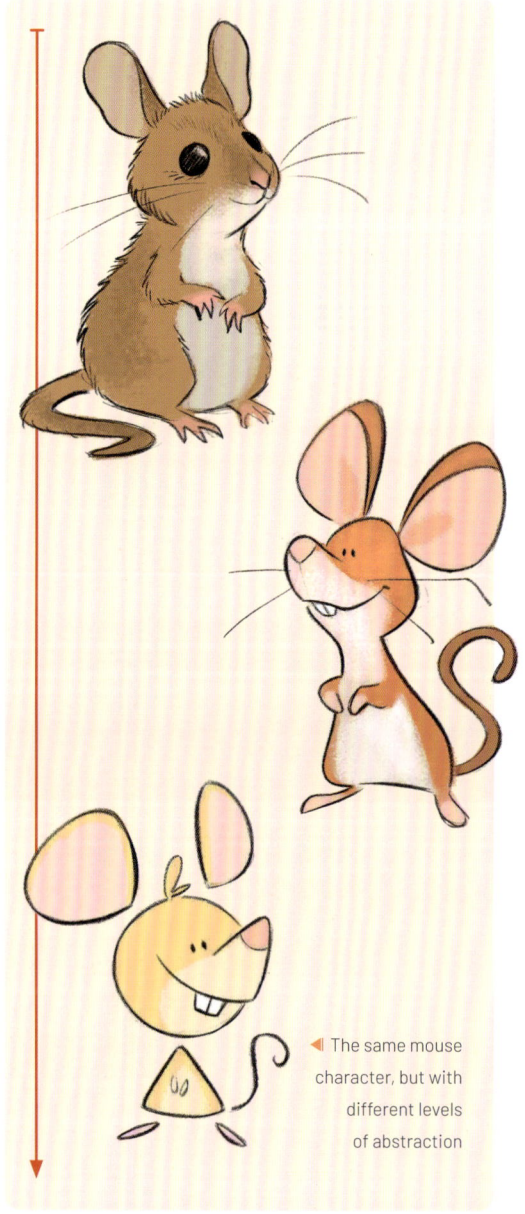

◀ The same mouse character, but with different levels of abstraction

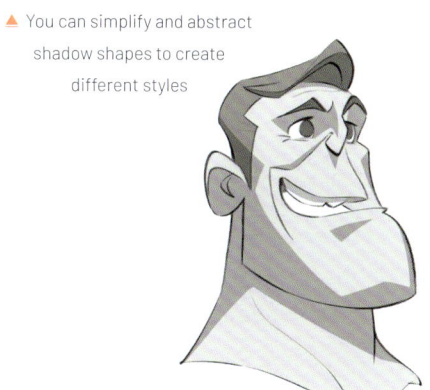

▲ You can simplify and abstract shadow shapes to create different styles

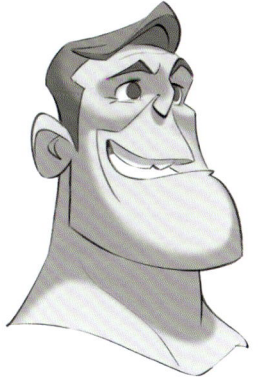

▲ One option is to play with how angular the shadow shapes are

STYLIZING FORM

There are various ways that light and shade can be used to stylize a character's form.

As detailed on page 23, the way light hits an object reveals the form of that object through the shadows it creates. As a character designer, you are in full control of how light hits a form. In other words, you can stylize forms by how you control your lighting and shading. This idea has already been somewhat explored on page 40, in the simple descriptive shadow pass and complex descriptive shadow pass – both are design decisions that inform the style of the character.

The aim is to make these design decisions consciously: making choices that have meaning, say something about the character, or create a style suitable for the story or the world to which a character belongs. On this page are some of the ways you may choose to stylize a character's form.

It's important to think about the actual shapes that light and shade create. Try to see them as shapes in their own right that can be manipulated and designed to make them pleasing to the eye.

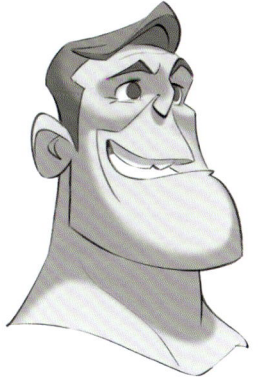
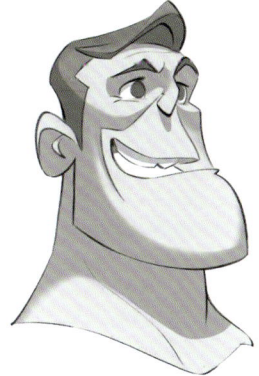
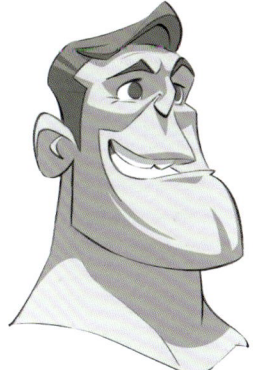

▲ Conversely, you can make the shadow shapes soft and rounded

▲ You can also experiment with mixing hard and soft edges

▲ You could also use the shadow shapes to really exaggerate the forms of a character's head

It can also help to think in terms of shadow grouping. For example, instead of drawing one shadow under the nose, then the shadow of one eye, then the other eye, and so on, you can group your shadow areas into one unified shape. This will give the design a feeling of unity and create a more appealing aesthetic.

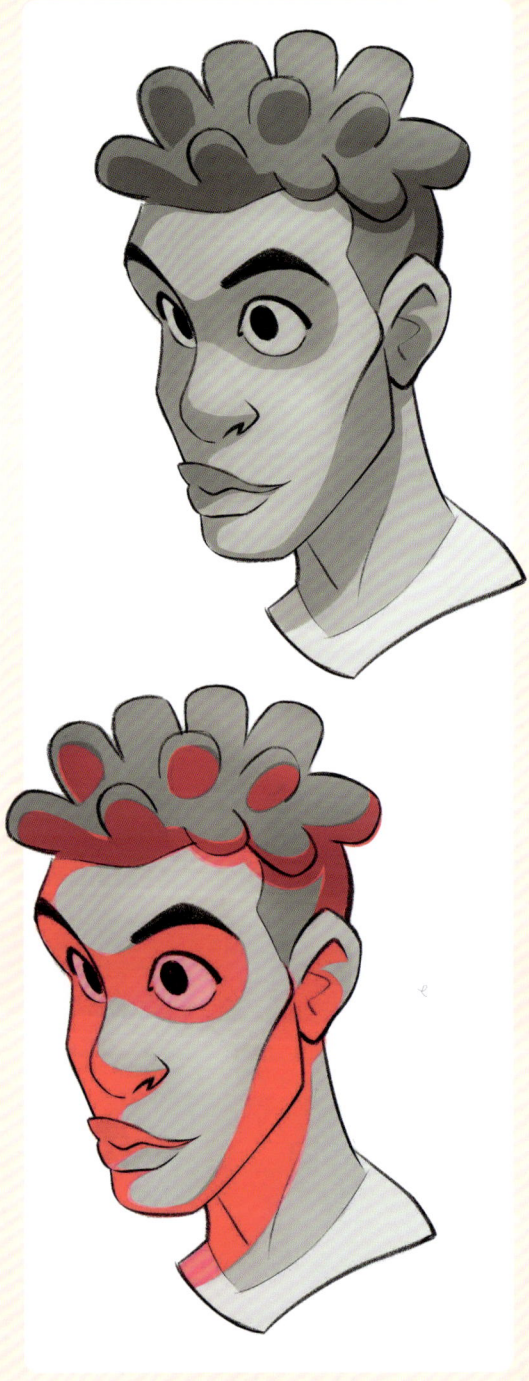

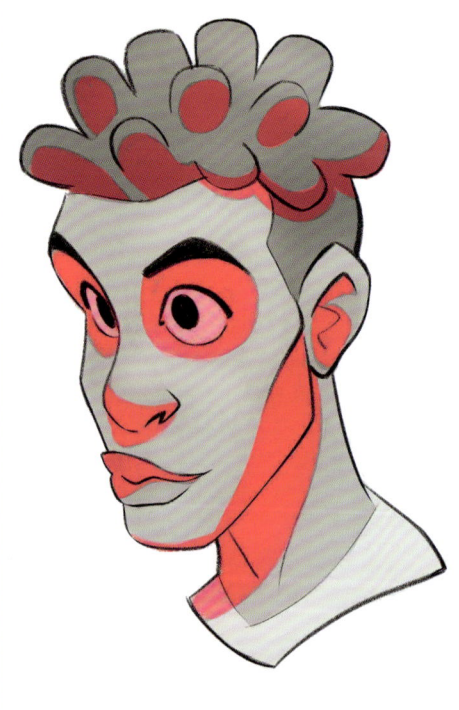

▲ Here the shadow shapes are disjointed and unconnected

▲ Here the shadow shapes are more unified, making for a more pleasing look

USING LIGHT WITHIN A DESIGN

Light itself can be a key design feature of a character design. A character could possess a flaming sword, or have glowing eyes, or be surrounded by swirling magic. Maybe they're an android and have glowing electrical circuits. Or maybe it's as simple as a character who carries an Indiana Jones-style torch.

Using light within a character design not only creates visual interest; it can also be used for storytelling purposes (this will be explored further on page 54). Any light element introduced should always align with the character's story and enhance their design, rather than overwhelming it.

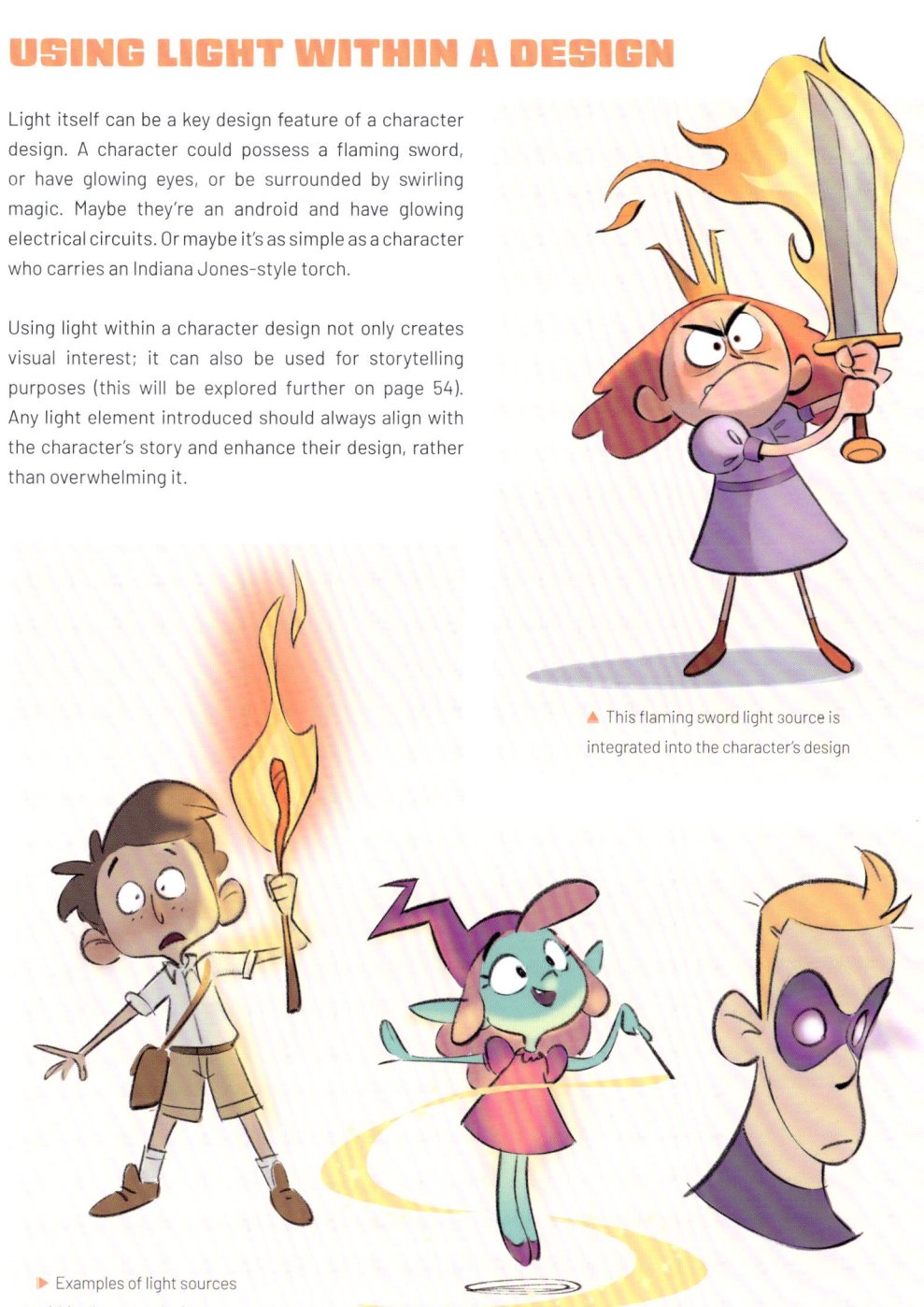

▲ This flaming sword light source is integrated into the character's design

▶ Examples of light sources within character designs

▶ The light source on the character's chest creates harsh shadows across the top of the design

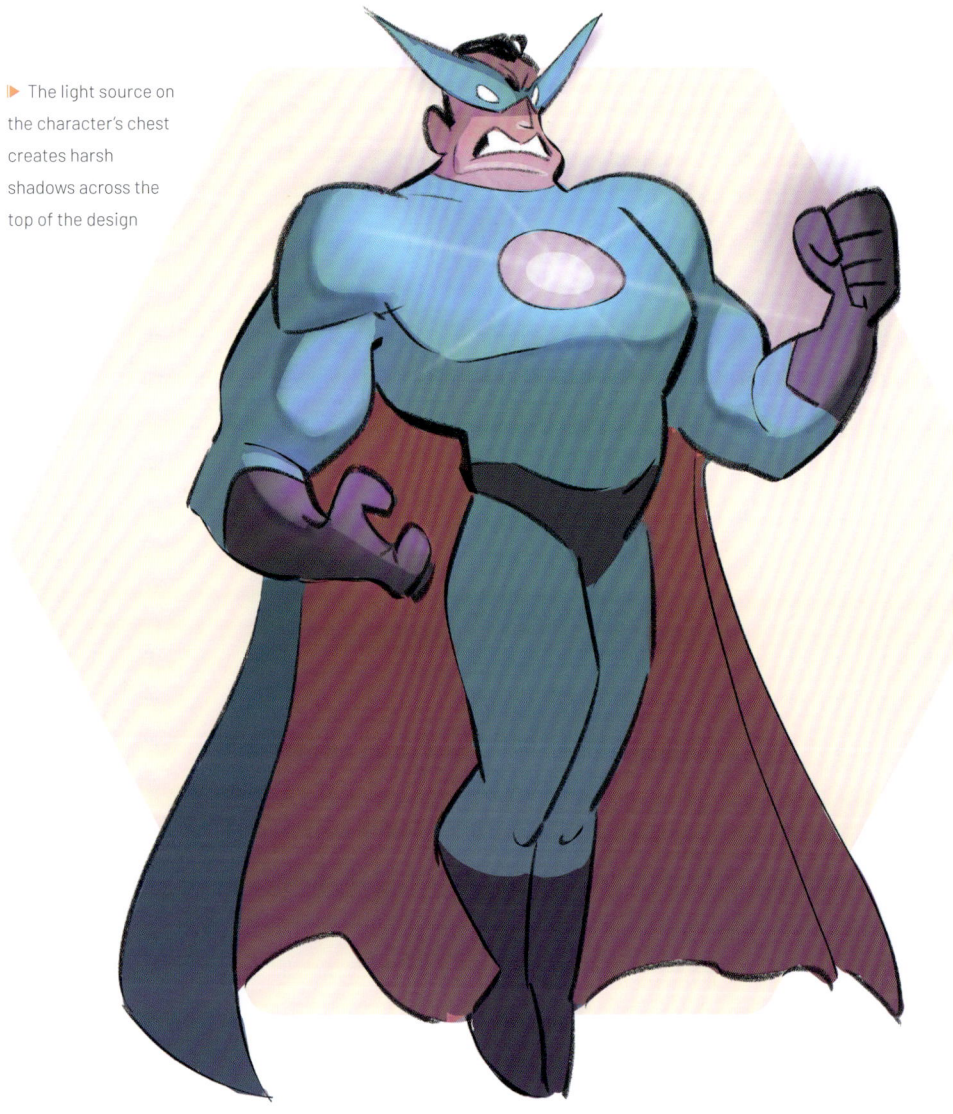

When introducing light within a character design, be mindful of how this affects form and cast shadows. This is less of an issue with simpler characters, where you can abstract reality enough that you don't need to worry about it. But in a more realistic character, consider how the lights affect the darks. For example, what shadows would bright, glowing chest armour cast across a design? Would these shadows aid or hinder readability of the character?

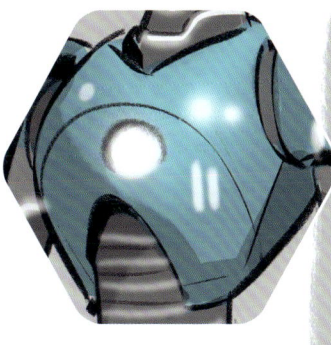

▶ Currently, the light on the robot's chest creates a strong focal point, drawing attention away from the face

Lights are typically the focal point of a design, as they're bright and usually high-contrast, drawing the viewer's attention. Use them to your advantage to ensure they don't become a distraction. In the example on the right, the number of lights incorporated into the robot's design affects its readability – it isn't clear where the viewer should look. This can be fixed by being more discerning about where the lights are placed, how many are included, and how bright they are relative to the rest of the design.

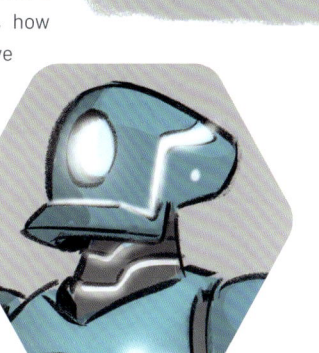

◀ Lowering the contrast on the chest and decreasing the overall number of lights moves the focal point to the robot's head

The character's face should be the focal point, unless there's good reason otherwise. In the example on the left, reducing the number of lights and arranging them in a way that enhances the design, plus softening the contrast in the chest area, helps to shift the focal point to the robot's face.

Of course, you may wish for the viewer's attention to be directed to another part of the design first and the face second. Whatever you decide, give the intended focal point the highest contrast.

ABSTRACTING LIGHT & SHADE

With stylized character designs, you don't need to represent light and shade realistically. There is endless potential for achieving unique styles – the only limit is the imagination. Here are a few ideas for how you can represent and abstract light and shade in your character designs...

▶ Screen tone combined with rim lights and graphic shadow areas can produce a visually impressive aesthetic

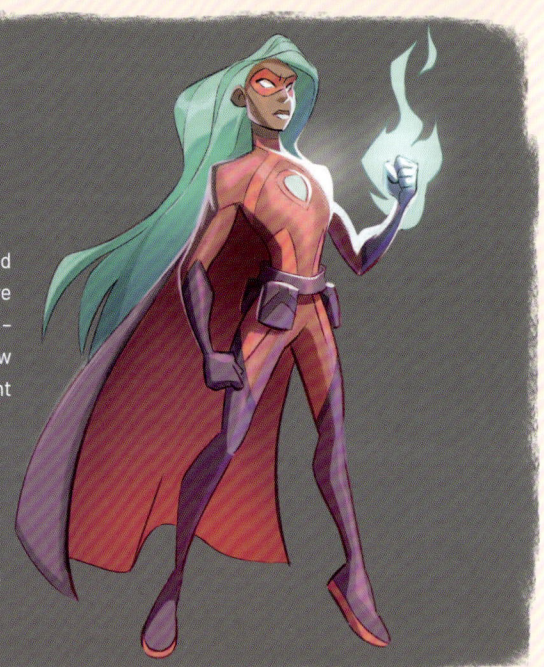

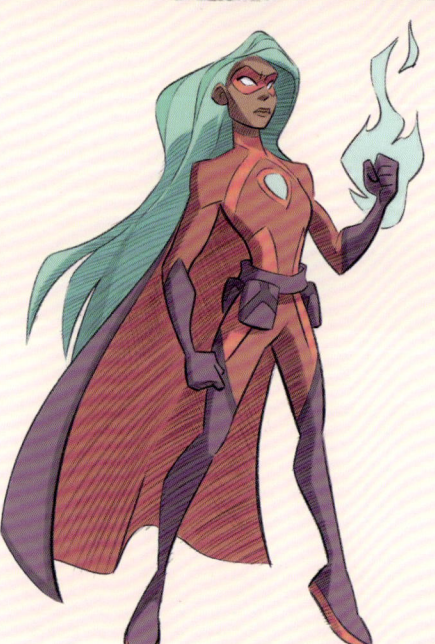

▲ A cross-hatching style can be used to represent shadows

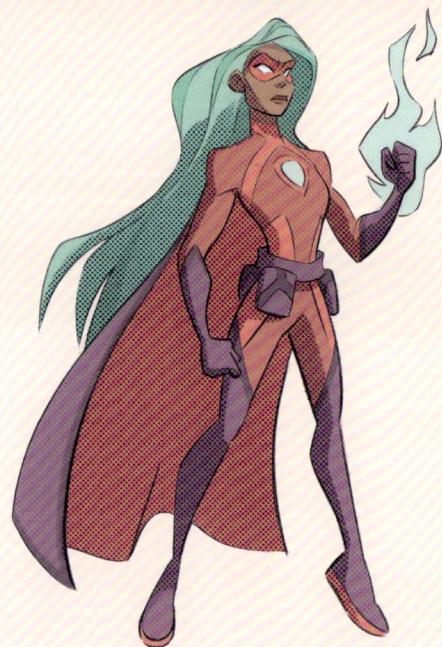

▲ A technique often seen in manga, screen tone is used on its own here to communicate shadow and light

Consider how each of these different approaches creates a different feeling or vibe, and how this should always support the character story. That said, 'cool' factor can also be a valid reason for a design choice. There is nothing wrong with adding a design element or treatment purely because it looks impressive.

This is particularly true for certain characters and genres of entertainment. If a design decision conflicts or distracts from the character story, however, then it may be a step too far. The perfect balance is a design that looks cool, with every element of the design serving the story.

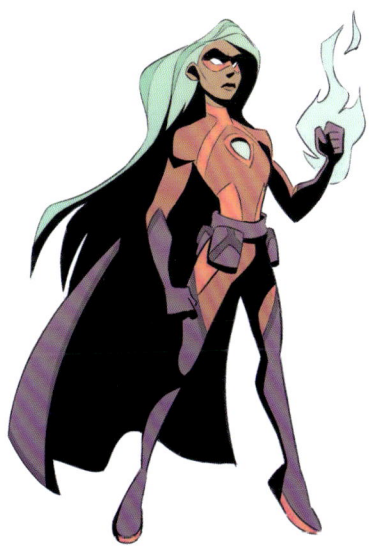

▲ A graphic comic style can be created by using large areas of black for the shadows

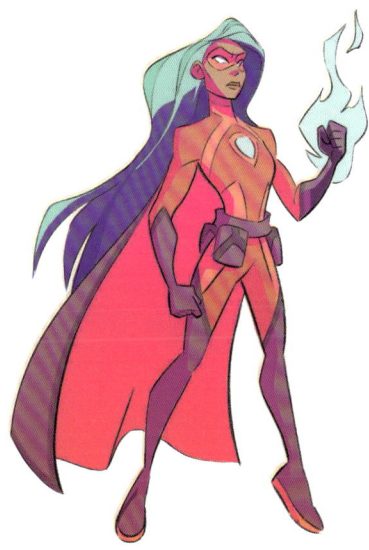

▲ Feel free to experiment with colours to represent lights and shades

ARTISTIC LICENCE

When it comes to stylizing characters, artists are allowed to break the laws of physics to experiment with weird and wonderful design choices. You can push boundaries and represent reality in ways that suit your character and the world they exist in, rather than perfectly reflecting the real world. In other words, you can use artistic licence, as long as the results are believable.

When moving away from reality and abstracting light and shade in more unique ways, it's important to remember that the fundamental rule of light and shade still applies: represent lights with brighter values and shadows with darker ones. This contrast is what will make your design choices believable. Without contrast, you lose the ability to represent light and shade at all.

Make sure you achieve clarity with every style decision you make. Finding the right style and choosing the right lighting is paramount, particularly with regards to storytelling. If you abstract too far or in unclear ways, you may confuse the audience and fail to communicate the character's story.

STORYTELLING

Light and shade are powerful tools that can be used to suggest mood and elevate storytelling in a character design. Everything covered so far has, in some way, been linked to storytelling. Story informs design; your style decisions depend on the story being told and, consequently, how you describe the form of a character depends on those style decisions.

All lighting choices have meaning. As a character designer, you want to make conscious design decisions to communicate the desired meaning and enhance the story being told.

STORYTELLING SCENARIOS

There are various ways to present a character for storytelling, each with its own strengths and weaknesses in terms of lighting. The previous chapters have shown characters on plain, abstract backgrounds, which works well for concept art as it allows you to clearly show a character's forms and design. However, when presenting a character in a way that focuses on storytelling, placing them in an environment can create a metaphorical stage on which they can perform. This environment doesn't need to be complex, but it should immerse the character in some sort of suggested or explicit world, hinting at the character's immediate surroundings, with all the story that can help conjure.

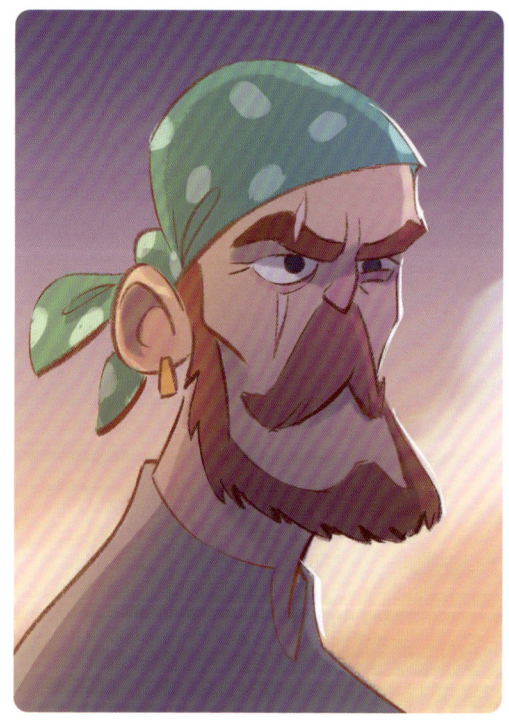

▲ This is an example of a character portrait; it focuses on the design of the character's head, while suggesting the world they exist in behind them

CHARACTER PORTRAITS

Offering a close-up of the eyes and facial expression, character portraits are great for capturing personality. In the portrait on the opposite page, the focus is on the character's head, while the background is subtle or suggested. A portrait also allows you to see the effect different lighting set-ups have on a character's face and how these might enhance expression and appearance.

HERO IMAGE

A hero image is ideal for showing the full body of a single character. Communicating pose alongside expression, it allows the character to perform in a way that sells their personality. With a hero image you can include some of the character's environment, including light sources and resulting shadows, and how these might influence a character and their immediate surroundings.

FULL ILLUSTRATION

A full illustration provides the most scope for storytelling. You can include a more realized background, opening up further possibilities for using light and shade to curate the story being told.

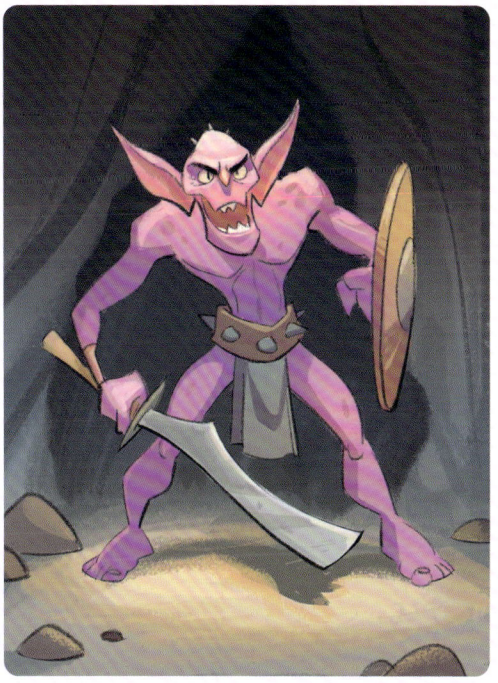

▲ Used for showcasing the full design, a hero image isn't just reserved for 'heroic' characters

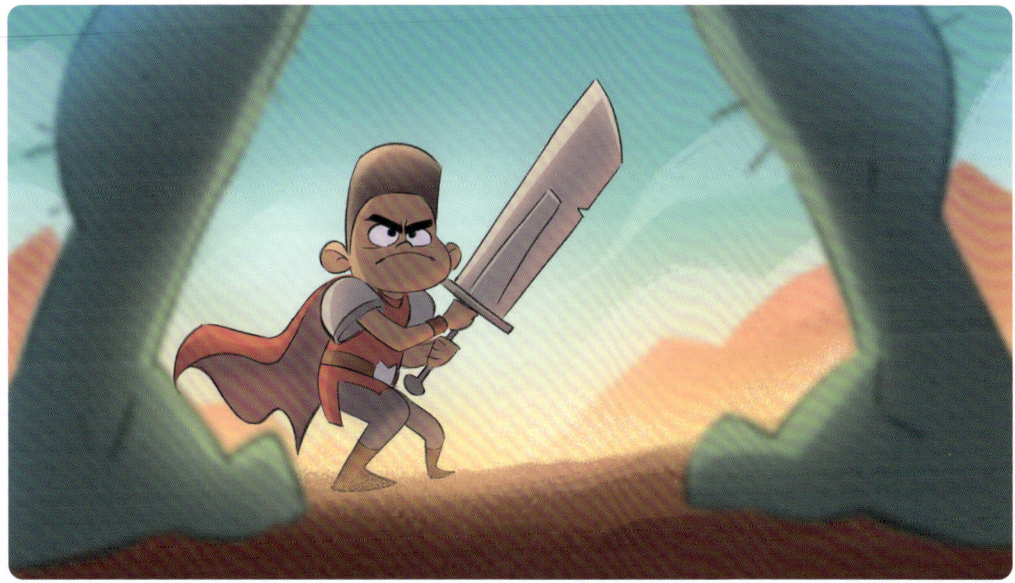

▲ Here a character performs in a full environment, with all of the storytelling lighting that entails

LIGHT SOURCES

Think about all of the possible light sources you could use to light your characters. The following list is by no means exhaustive, but is enough to build a picture of the types of light sources you can use to your advantage when telling stories with your lighting.

NATURAL LIGHT

Natural light is light found in nature. Sunlight, the most obvious example, is a versatile light source as it changes colour throughout the day. Depending where the sun is in the sky, it can create a range of shadows that can be adapted to your storytelling needs. The sun as a light source takes multiple different forms. A grey, overcast day is still an example of sunlight, just with the added element of clouds to diffuse the direct light. Other natural lights include moonlight, fire, lightning, lava, auroras, and bioluminescence. Though some of these are a little niche, they open up a realm of possibilities for lighting characters.

There are some limitations to using natural light. For example, you can't use sunlight in a deep cave and still have a believable lighting set-up. In this scenario, bioluminescence or lava might be a more suitable light source. Additionally, sunlight is generally always above a subject, or above and to one side. Unless a character is upside down, it would be impossible for sunlight to light them from below. You can bend the rules in fantasy settings, as long as the light source is still somewhat believable and fits the story being told.

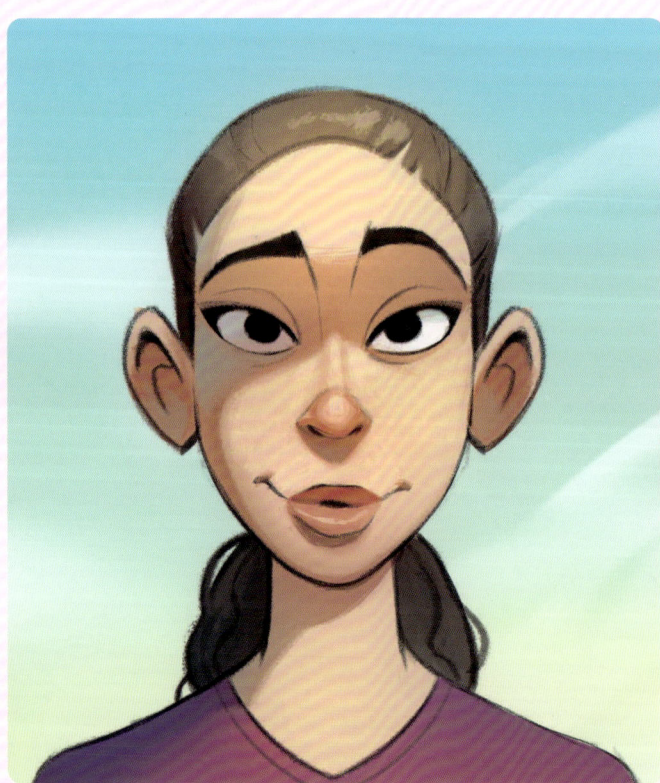

▲ This character is lit by natural light

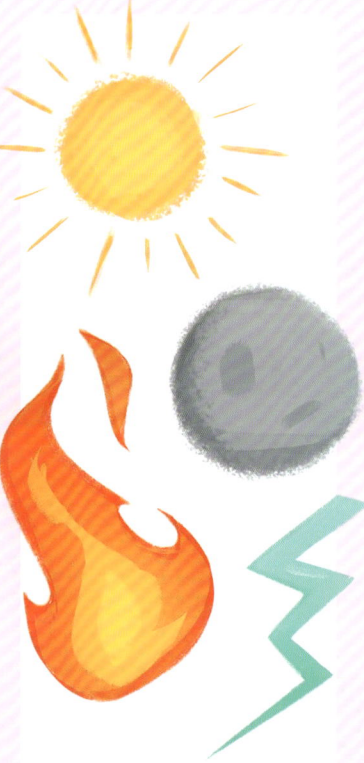

▲ Examples of natural light

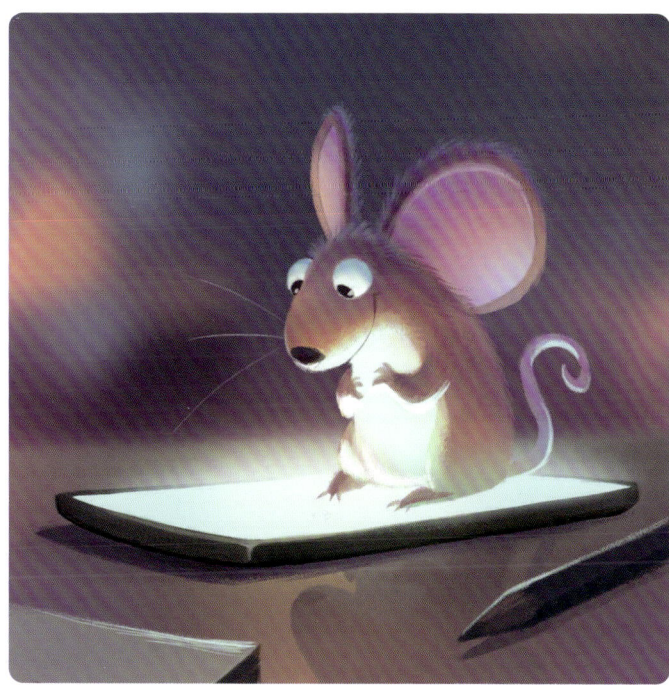

▲ Here the character is lit by the light from a phone screen

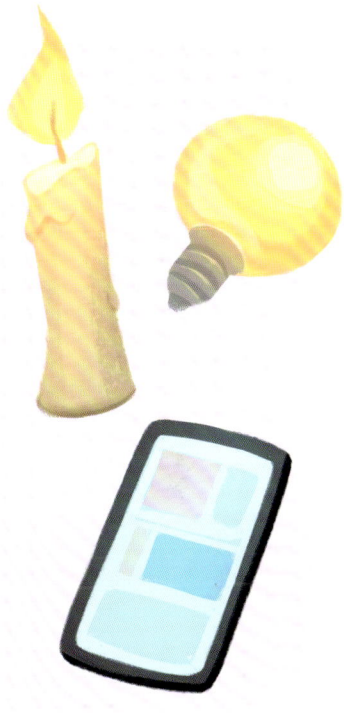

▲ Examples of human-made light

HUMAN-MADE LIGHT

Artificial, human-made light sources generally fall into a few broad categories. The main type is light bulbs, which come in various shapes and sizes, and can create different brightnesses and colours. Old incandescent bulbs emit light from the warmer end of the light spectrum, whereas modern bulbs often produce cooler or bluer wavelengths of light.

Electronic light sources – such as televisions, smart phones, and computer screens – can provide a distinct feeling or mood when used in a character design. Similarly, neon lights and lasers have their own distinctive properties and can be suggestive of futuristic or sci-fi themes. Fire could also be considered an artificial light source when referring to controlled varieties, such as a candle, fireplace, or open-flame torch.

The benefit of using human-made light sources is that, within reason, you can move them wherever you like. There are fewer constraints on where they can be placed, though it might look odd to have a table lamp outside on a sunny day. Artificial lighting also gives you full creative control over how you light a character, including the intensity and colour of the light, plus the direction it's coming from. You can use it to light a character in any way you like to suit your storytelling needs, while still making a believable set-up.

A human-made light source will, however, lock your character in a particular time and place. Candles, for example, may suggest the character is from a past era, while light from a screen or hologram implies a present-day or futuristic character.

CHARACTER LIGHTS

These are light sources that are integrated into a character's design. They can be natural and ethereal, such as a magical aura surrounding a character, or artificial, such as lights on a cyborg.

Character lights have the potential to enhance storytelling. For example, if your character has glowing eyes, you could make their eyes glow red when they're angry to enhance that emotion. Or perhaps a character is in the middle of conjuring a spell, with magic swirling around them. This could be an effective and interesting light source that also says something about the nature of the character and their abilities.

Character lights may not be able to fully light a character, however, so using them in conjunction with environmental lighting can prove effective.

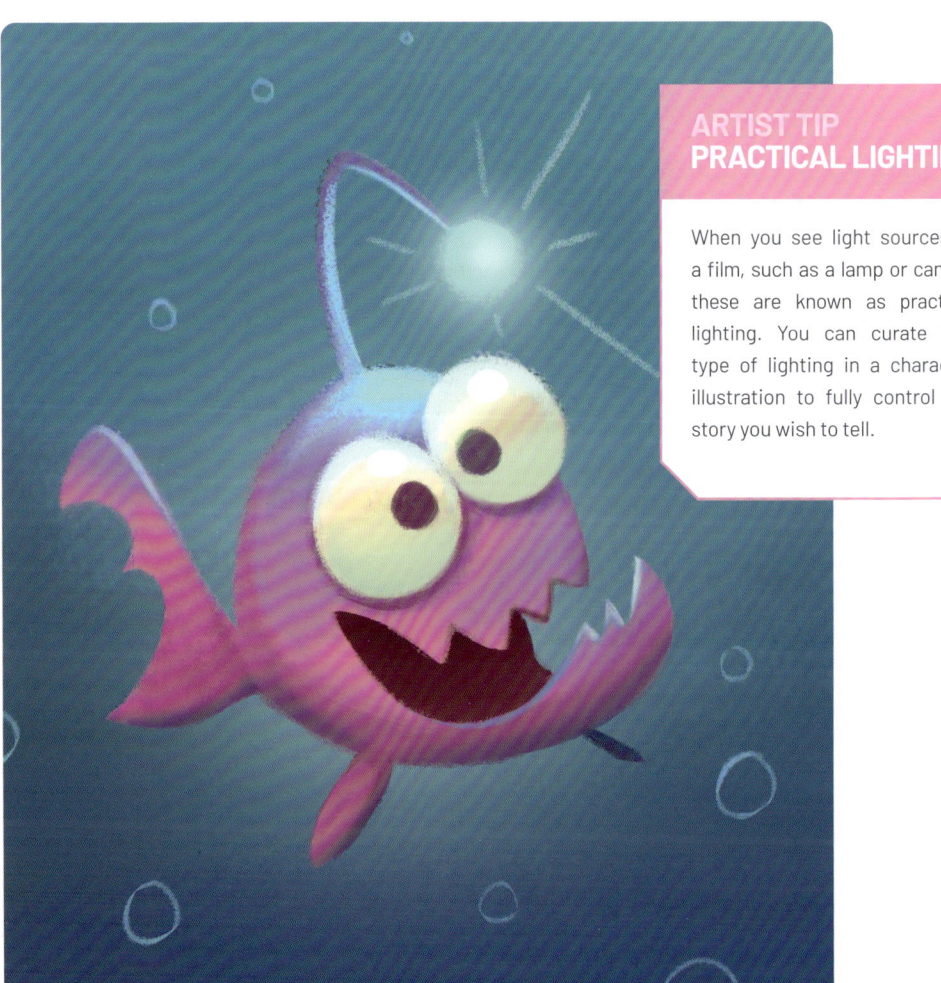

ARTIST TIP
PRACTICAL LIGHTING

When you see light sources in a film, such as a lamp or candle, these are known as practical lighting. You can curate this type of lighting in a character illustration to fully control the story you wish to tell.

▲ The light source is part of the character's design

BASIC LIGHTING SET-UPS

NATURAL/AMBIENT LIGHTING

This is lighting you might find outdoors in nature, away from human-made light sources. It can include a sunny day, moonlit graveyard, or a landscape of molten lava.

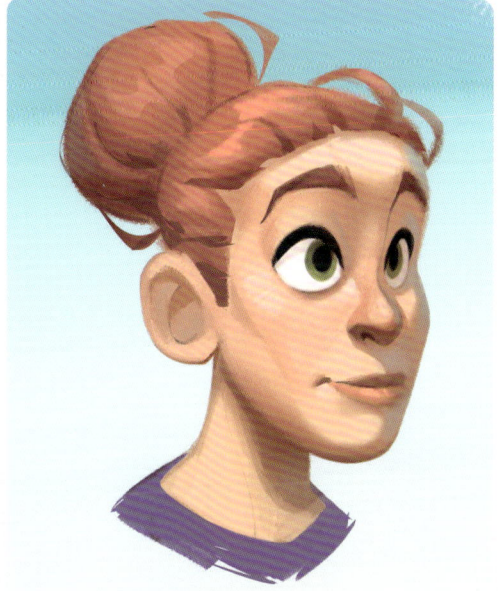

▶ Ambient lighting will vary depending on environmental factors – here there is the suggestion of strong sunlight with blue bounced light from the sky in the upward-facing shadows

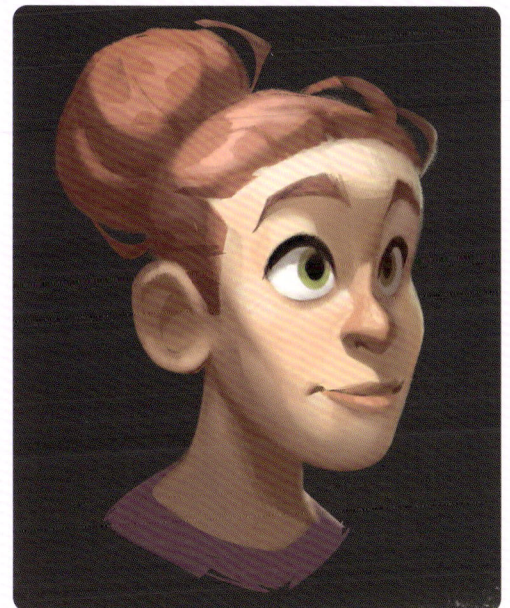

▲ Three-point lighting is a great set-up for showing a character clearly while maintaining visual interest

THREE-POINT LIGHTING

This classic lighting set-up is often used in photography and film. It is particularly useful for character portraits, as it can help show the dimension and form of the character clearly, while also looking quite natural without dramatic hard shadows. Three-point lighting consists of:

- **A key light:** the main light source that illuminates the subject, usually from the side and slightly above the subject's eye level.

- **A fill light:** positioned opposite the key light, softening any harsh shadows created by the key light. It is usually a weaker light source.

- **A backlight:** a source that lights the back of the subject, separating them from the background by creating a glow or rim light effect around them.

HIGH-KEY LIGHTING

This type of lighting is bright and even, with soft, or no, harsh shadows. It can be used to create a positive, upbeat vibe.

LOW-KEY LIGHTING

The opposite of high-key, low-key lighting is high-contrast and uses minimal fill lights to create deep shadows. It can be used to create drama or mystery.

RIM LIGHTING

Rim lighting occurs when a light hits a character from behind to create an outline or glowing edge of light around them. It works well with character portraits and can help to separate a character from a background and emphasize their silhouette.

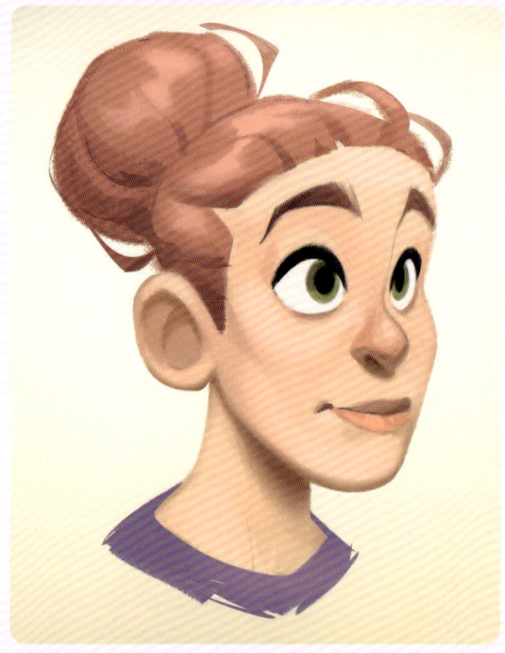

▲ With high-key lighting, the shadows are minimal and soft

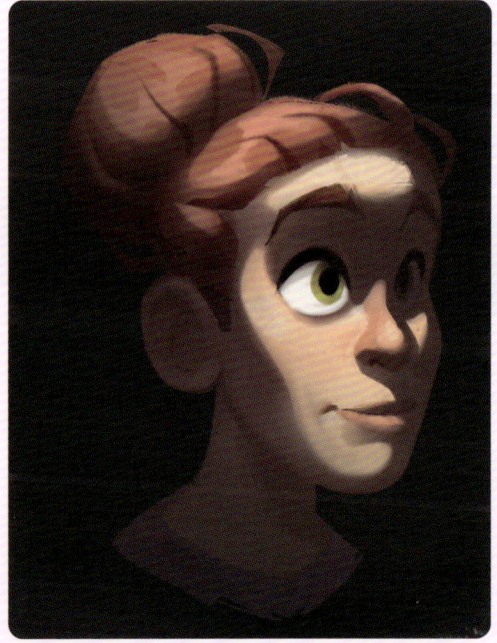

▲ In this low-key set-up, note the strong directional light that creates dramatic form and cast shadows

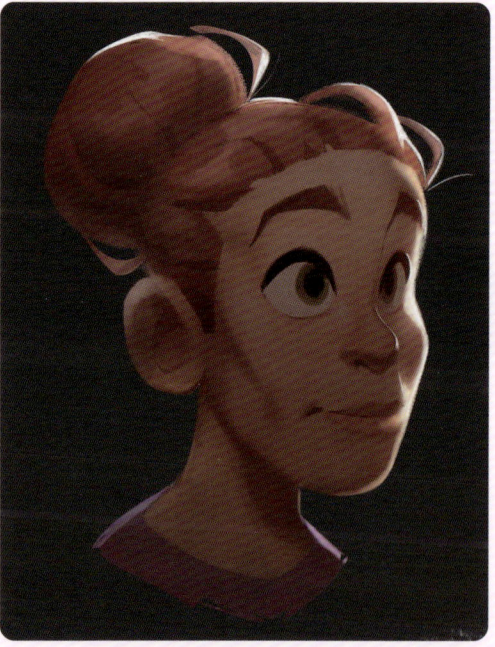

▲ Rim lighting catches the edge of a character – the edge light varies depending on the forms being hit

STORYTELLING WITH LIGHT

You can build on these simple lighting set-ups to start telling stories with light and shade. Here are some common moods or themes and how you can use light and shade to create them.

UPLIFTING LIGHTING

To create an uplifting or happy lighting effect, opt for high-key lighting. Minimizing shadows and bathing characters in soft, diffused light will produce a feeling of cosiness. Backlighting can also be used to create a soft glow behind them.

The aim is to avoid creating strong areas of light and dark, prevent harsh shadows, and instead soften the whole scene. Filling the scene with light will ensure there are no areas of heavy shade, as shadows can have symbolically negative connotations. Sunlight and warm light colours work well to create a happy, cheerful vibe.

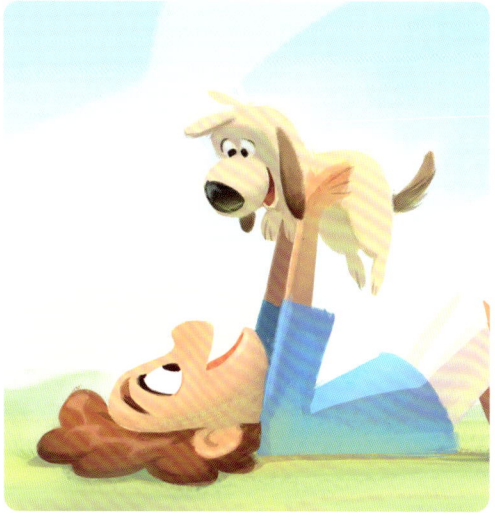

▲ The soft, diffused light and lack of harsh shadows capture the boy's happiness

ROMANTIC LIGHTING

Reducing the intensity of the light and employing warm colours, such as reds and pinks, can create a romantic mood. Soft glows and slightly blurred backgrounds convey a feeling of intimacy between characters. Similar to uplifting lighting, the aim is to create soft, gentle, diffused lighting to help minimize harsh shadows. You could also use candles or fairy lights as a light source.

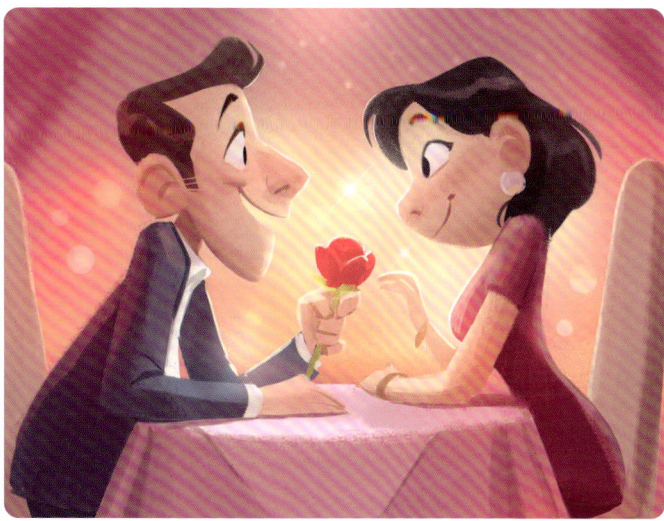

◀ The soft, glowy lighting and blurred background create an intimate, romantic vibe

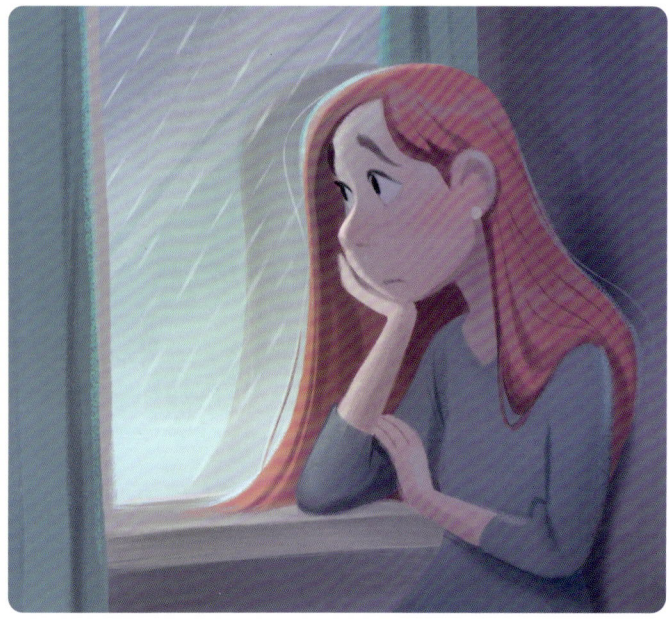

SAD LIGHTING

Sad lighting is the opposite of high-key and romantic lighting. Low-key lighting will create deeper shadows and convey a moody atmosphere. Using cooler, desaturated colours can help to sap any joy from an image. You can then use light and shade to isolate the subject in the composition.

◀ Overcast lighting from the window on a rainy day pushes the sad, melancholic mood of this character

DRAMATIC LIGHTING

To create dramatic lighting, aim for high contrasts in your light and shade to convey visual tension. Using a strong key light will produce bold and well-defined form and cast shadows. You could also frame the character half in and half out of the light, or create strong silhouettes and rim lighting. Experiment with the composition of light, using it to make interesting and dynamic angles in the light and shadow shapes. Bold, intense, or contrasting colours will also increase the feeling of drama.

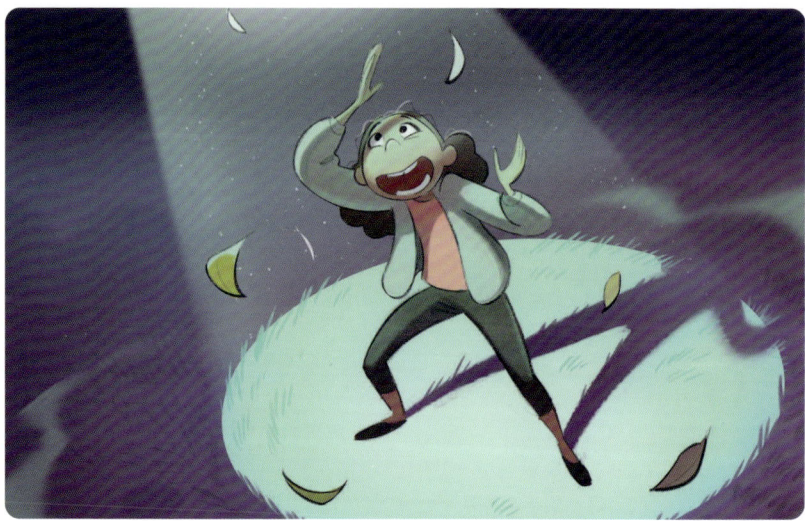

▶ Intense directional lighting can enhance the drama of a scene

ADVENTURE LIGHTING

Natural light is preferable when creating adventure lighting, as it conjures feelings of being outdoors or on a quest. Introducing elements of dramatic directional light will produce striking shadows, as will beams of light passing through cracks in a jungle canopy or cave roof.

Golden-hour lighting refers to the period of time just after sunrise and just before sunset. The angle of the sun in the sky at these times of day makes sunlight more diffused, slightly redder, and particularly flattering. Golden-hour lighting can suggest a feeling of triumph or grandeur, often associated with adventure. The soft, warm glow of the sun can make a scene feel cinematic.

Alternatively, low-key lighting could be used to create more mystery or drama, with some practical light sources – such as torches or lanterns – helping to create an adventure vibe.

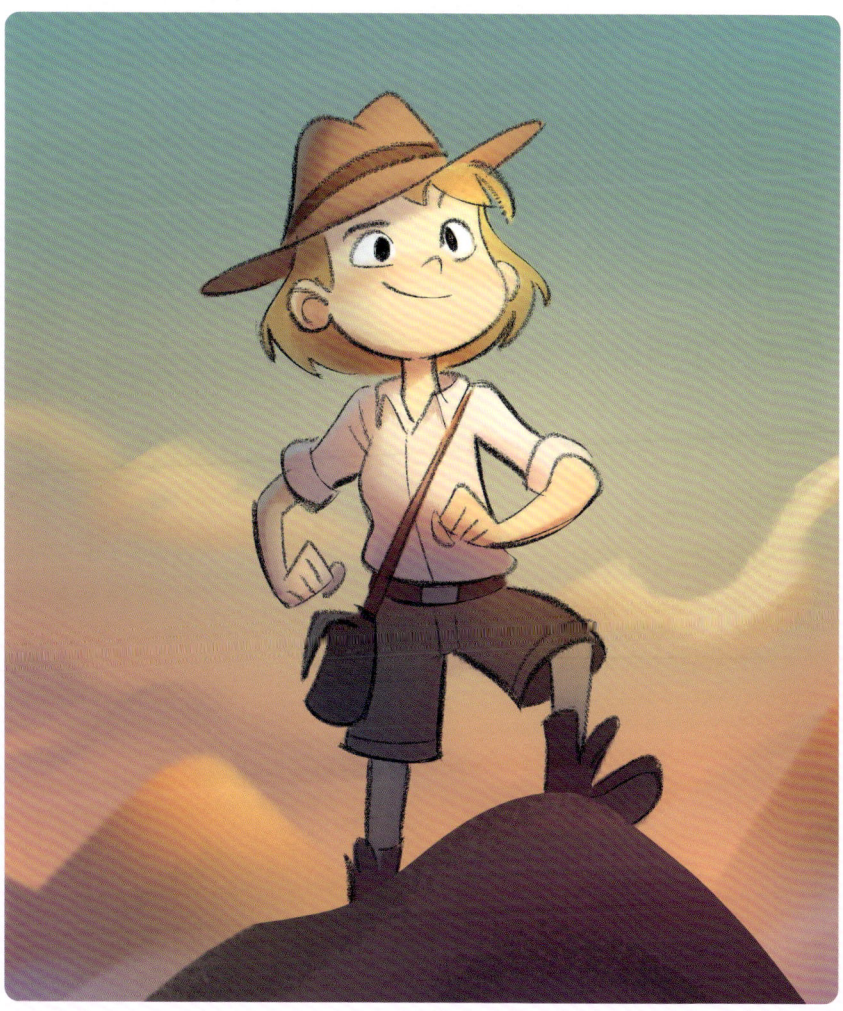

▲ Golden-hour lighting is just one way of conjuring the idea of outdoor adventure and triumph

MYSTERY LIGHTING

Mystery lighting benefits from a low-key lighting set-up. Creating hidden areas in an image, with plenty of shadow areas for things to hide in, can elicit a feeling of suspense and mystery. Any form of fog or atmosphere will also contribute to this, as well as positioning light sources out of view. Such lighting techniques are often found in film noir, a film style popular in the 1940s and 50s that was associated with crime dramas and thrillers.

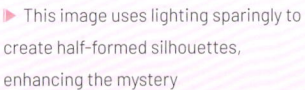 This image uses lighting sparingly to create half-formed silhouettes, enhancing the mystery

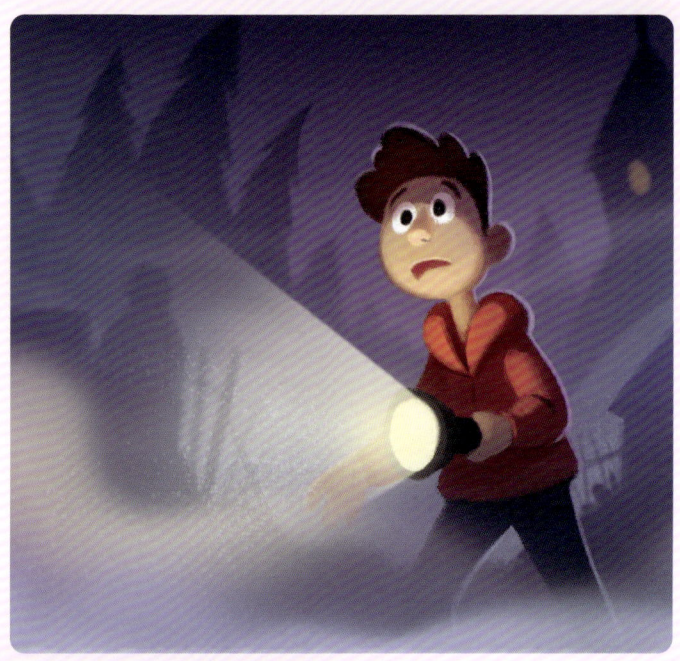

HORROR LIGHTING

Similar to low-key and mystery lighting, horror lighting creates areas of shadow on the character or in the scene. Unusual lighting set-ups, such as up-lighting (where the light source is placed below the subject), can be used to suggest an unnatural feeling. Certain light colours can also help to instil unease, as can using lights and darks to isolate a character, making them feel more vulnerable.

◀ Low-key lighting, up-lighting, and unnatural colours enhance this character's horror vibe

COMPOSITION

Consider how light and shade can affect the composition of an image and the effect that will have on the story. Your lighting choices, and consequently your compositional choices, should always enhance a character's story rather than detract from it.

▶ Light and shade can lead the eye to the focal point

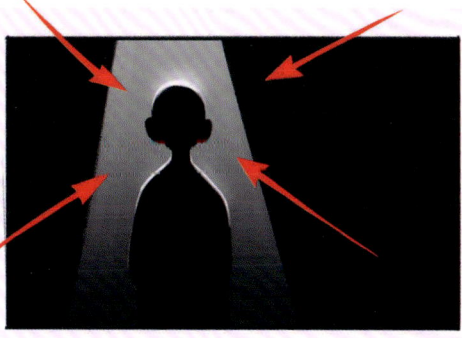

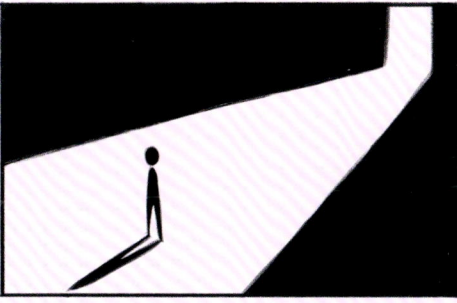

▲ Light and shade can be used to frame a character to make them feel small or isolated

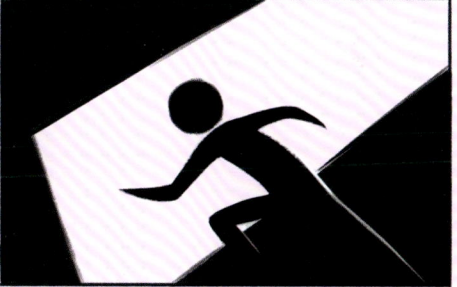

▲ Angled directional lighting can enhance the drama of a character's pose

SYMBOLISM

When deciding how to light your characters, always ask yourself: what do these light and shade choices mean? Bringing symbolism into your design decisions will allow you to convey ideas effectively using visuals alone. While this isn't too dissimilar to the different types of storytelling lighting, the following examples will enable you to push symbolism even further.

You can also use symbolism in your colour choices. While there is no universal meaning associated with colours, as every culture assigns their own meaning to them, as a character designer you can still create meaning within the context of your artwork.

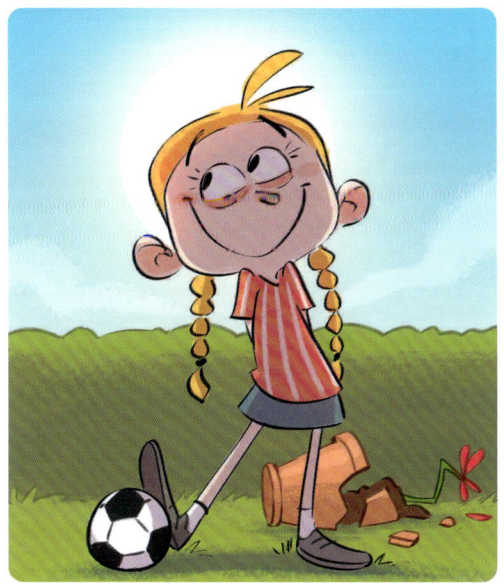

◀ The light of the sun is used to create a halo effect behind the character, suggesting that they are acting innocent

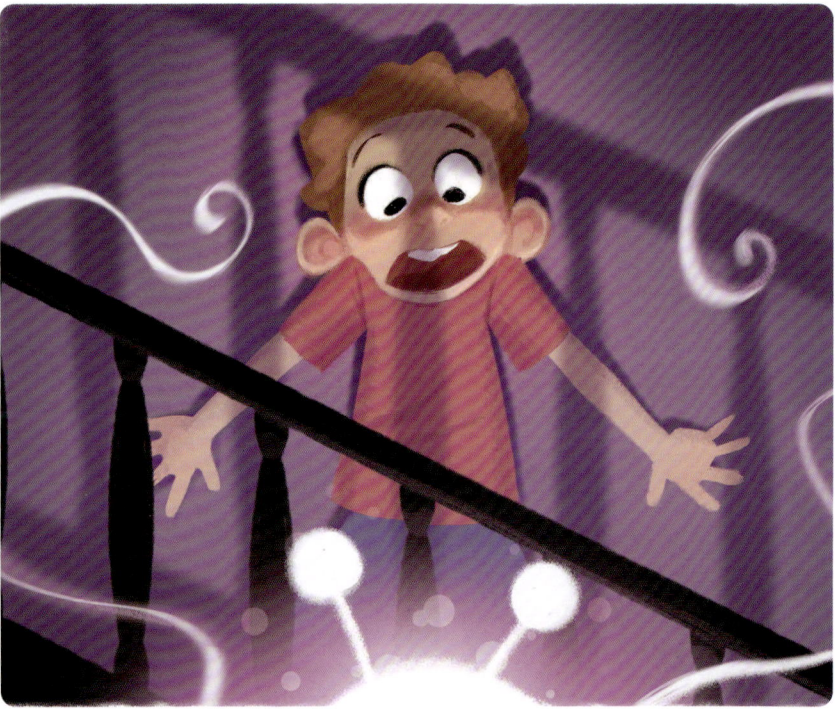

▲ The vertical cast shadows on the character and environment symbolize prison bars, suggesting that the character is trapped

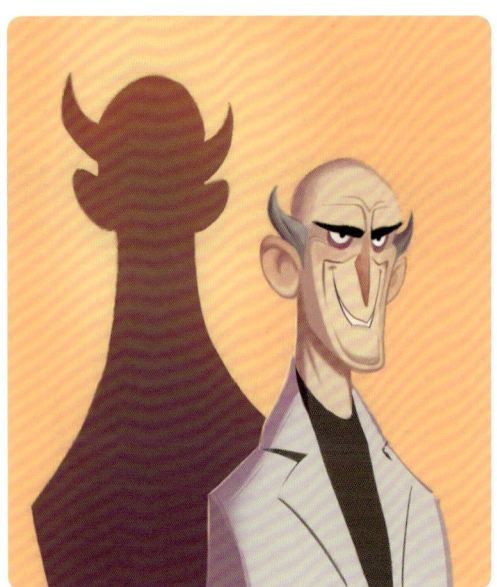

▲ The character's cast shadow is suggestive of devil horns, hinting at their malevolent personality

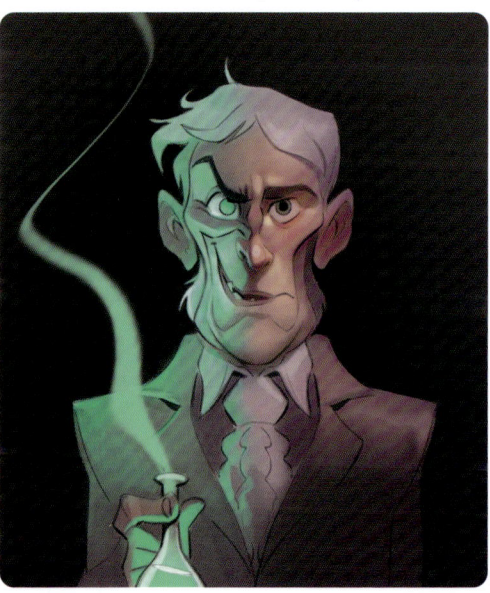

▲ Using a complementary colour in the lighting emphasizes the character's two opposing personalities: one good and one evil

MAKE CONSCIOUS CHOICES

These are just some of the ways you can use light and shade to enhance the storytelling in your character artwork. There is so much potential here, only limited by your imagination! The key thing to remember is that your lighting choices have meaning and, as a character designer, you want to make conscious choices to convey the desired meaning and tell the intended story.

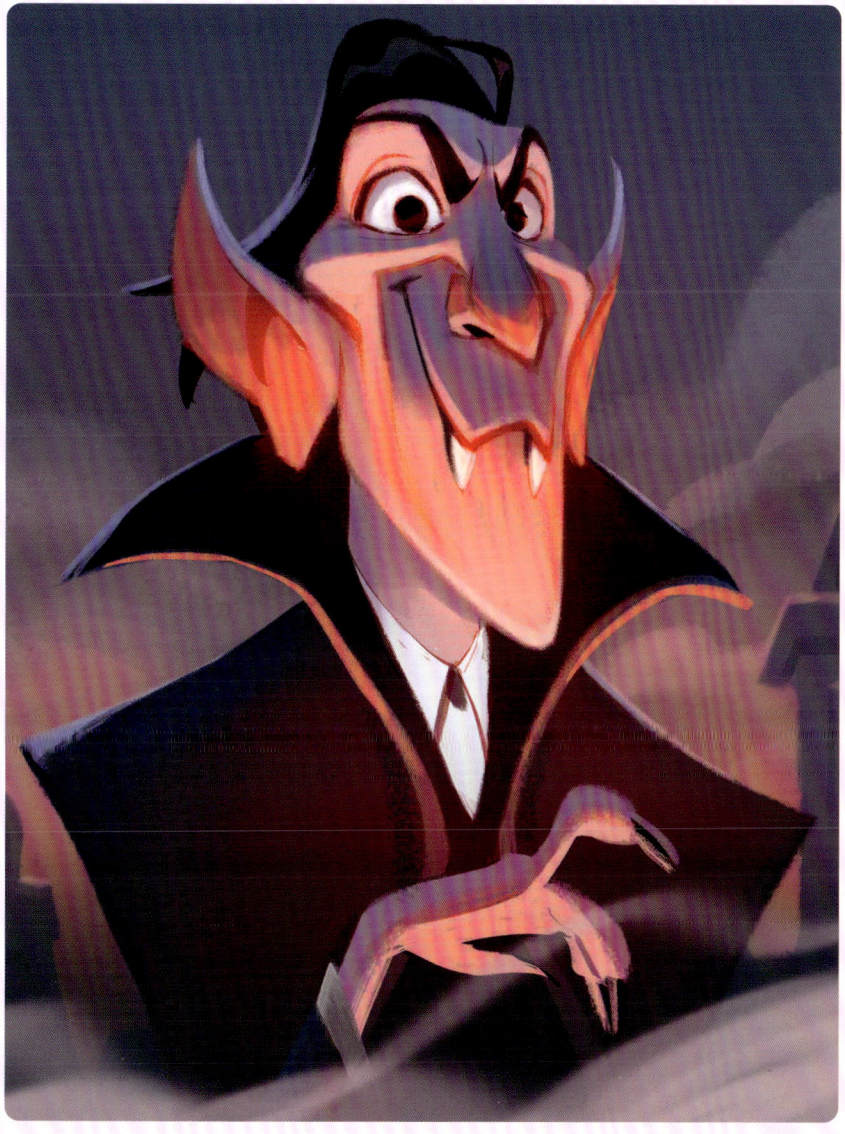

▲ Red is used here to symbolize danger and this vampire's obsession with blood

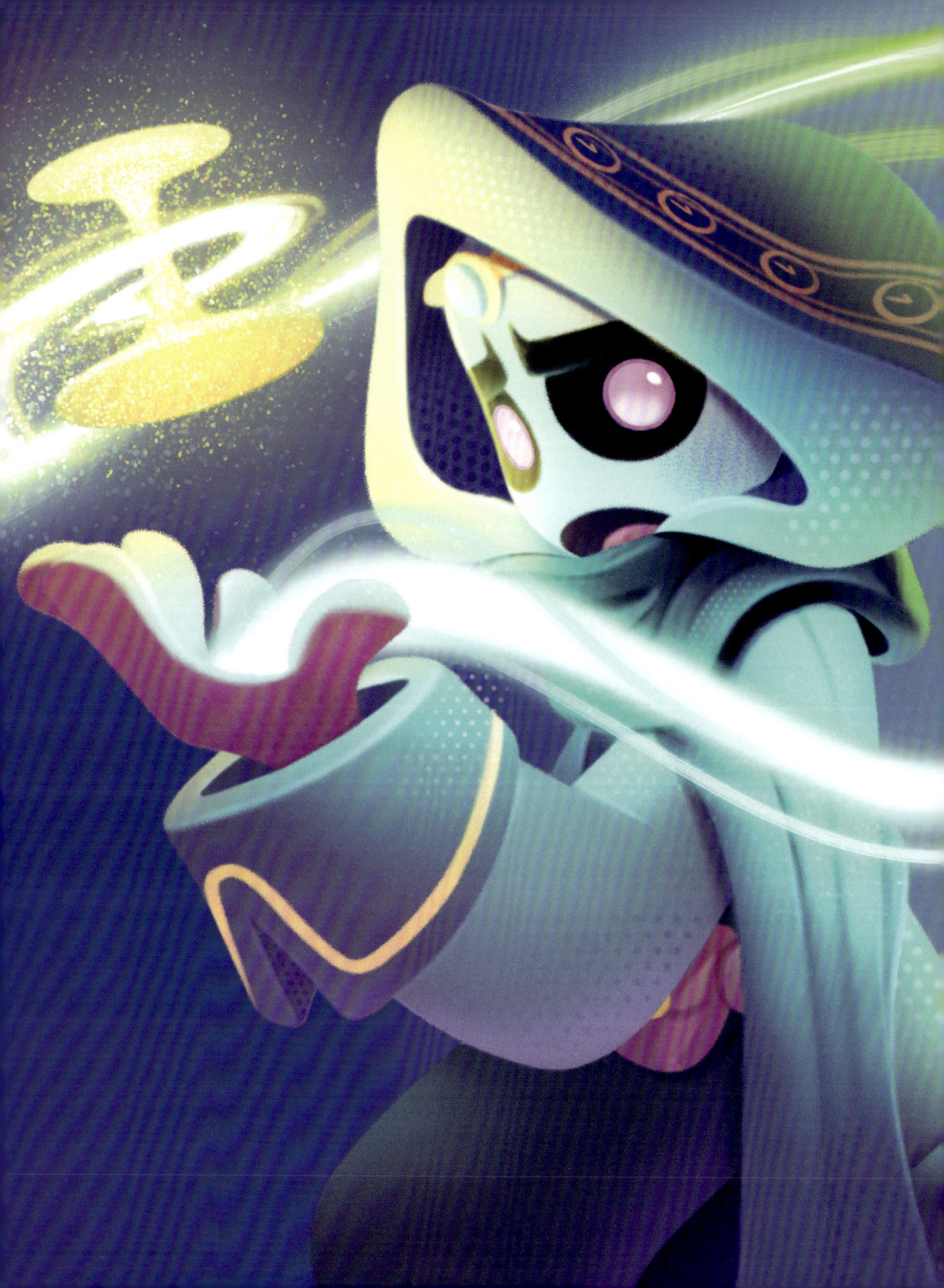

TUTORIALS

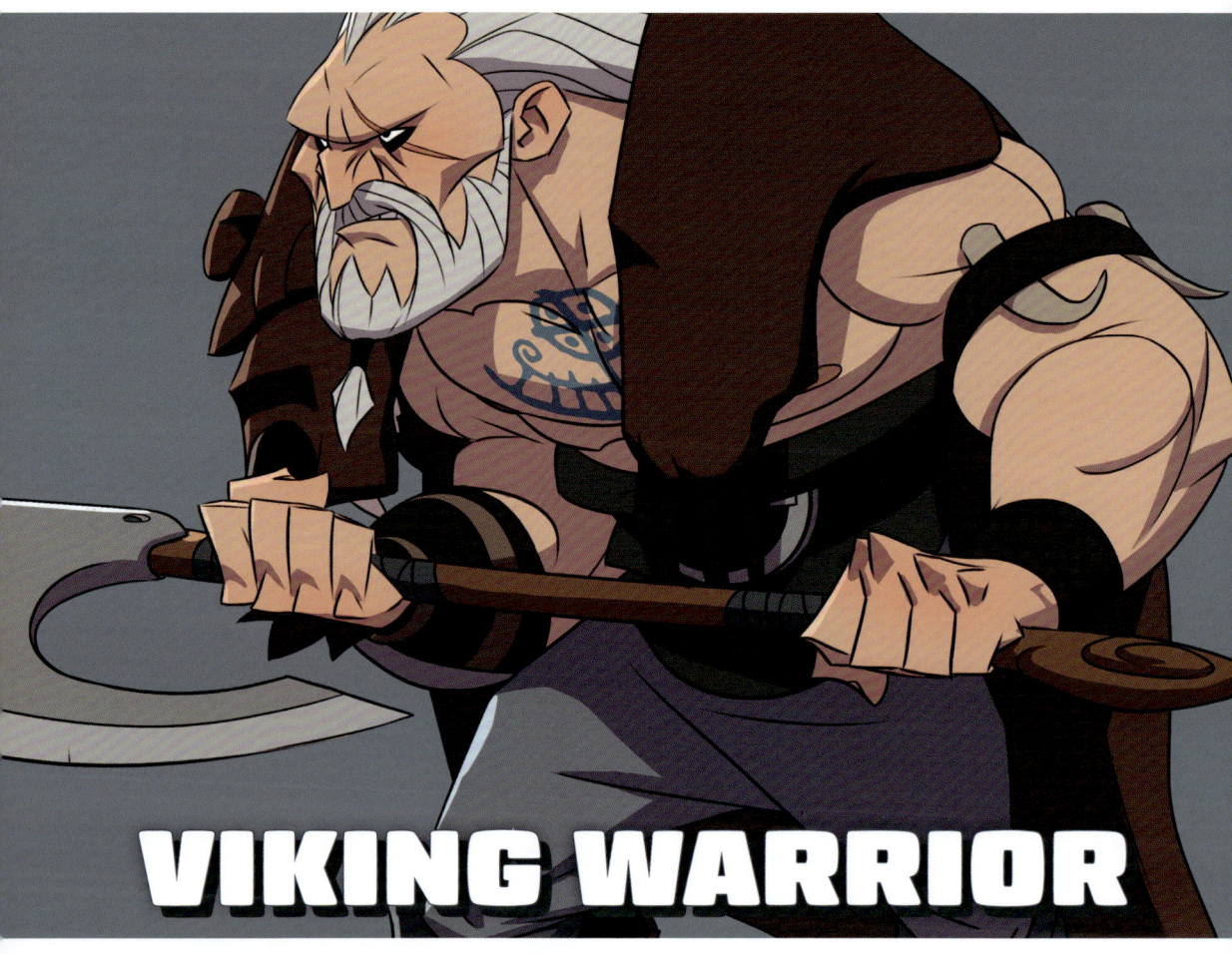

VIKING WARRIOR

DESIGNING A CHARACTER WITH SIMPLE LIGHT & SHADE

There is no better place to start than with the basics. This tutorial will teach you how to design a fierce Viking character, using simple but effective cartoon-style shading techniques to create an engaging final image as well as a three-angle turnaround. After the initial sketches and introduction of colour, the steps will guide you through an example workflow for shading and lighting a character. By the end of the chapter, you will have a better understanding of how simple shading can be used to shape the volumes of a character and bring it to life.

This tutorial uses Adobe Photoshop, but you can follow along with whatever digital-painting software you like.

By Gabriel Gómez Almenzar

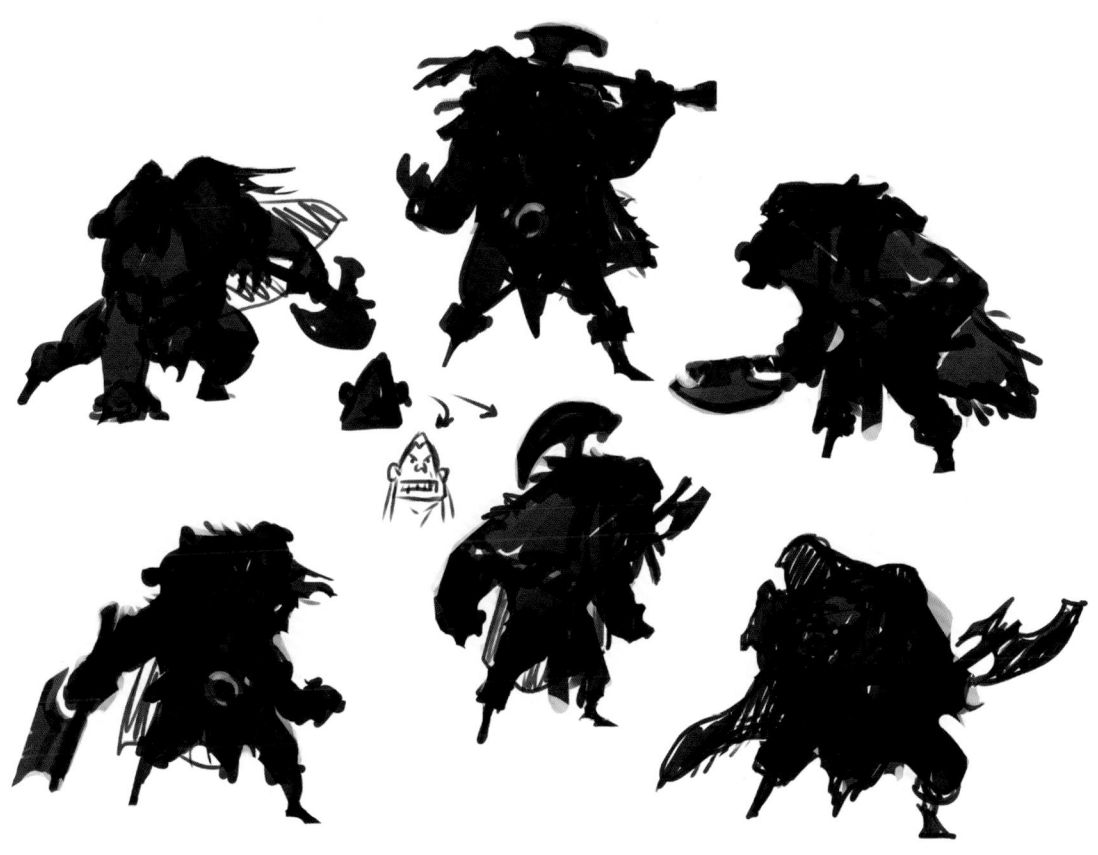

▲ Draw various character sketches to explore ideas and visualize the design

01 SKETCHES

Start by sketching out different ideas for a Viking character. As the aim of this tutorial is to understand shadows, look for a fun, interesting design with a range of shapes that you can add shadows to in later steps. When considering volumes and shapes, think about the highlights and shadows these could create. As this character will have simple cartoon-like shading, the process will involve using two main types: attached shadow and cast shadow.

02 FINAL POSE SKETCH

After sketching out a few different options, choose the pose you wish to develop further. This sketch depicts a stocky figure leaning slightly forwards and holding an axe. Next, decide on the direction of the light source. The light source here will be overhead. Any part of the character facing the light will be illuminated, while any hidden areas, such as on the underside of the body, will be in shadow. Sketching in some basic shapes can help you to work out which areas will be in shadow and which will be hit by light. Here the rectangular blocks map out the overall shapes of the character's body. Due to the overhead light source, the top rectangle casts a shadow over part of the lower rectangle.

▶ Choose a design to continue with, then create a quick study of lights and shadows

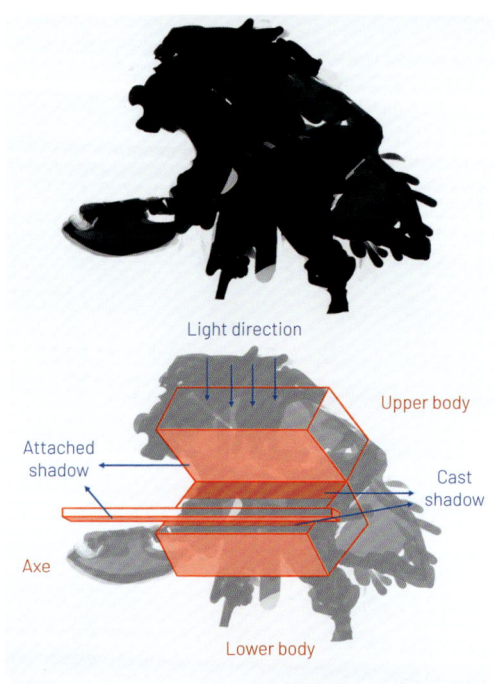

Light direction

Upper body

Attached shadow

Cast shadow

Axe

Lower body

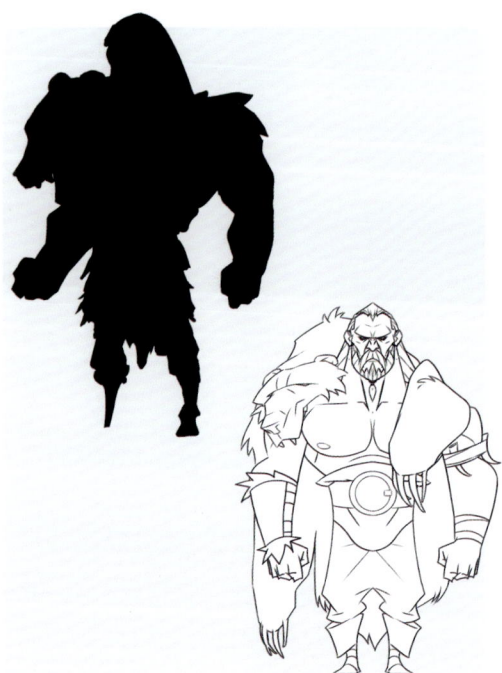

03 SILHOUETTE & LINES

Define the Viking's shapes and volumes. Draw simple line art for the front view of the character. This will help you to understand where to place the shadows for each body part, plus any external elements, such as props or clothing. Next, create a simple silhouette study to check if the character's overall shape reads clearly.

◀ Create a silhouette of the Viking to check readability, as well as front-view line art

04 COLOUR

Experiment with a few different colour options to find the tones that best fit the style and design of the character. As he is a Viking, the brown of the bearskin, dark greyish colours of the belt, and greyish blues of the trousers are a good fit. Consider the tone of each colour before you move on to shading to ensure the colours don't become too dark in the process.

▼ Introduce colour to the front view of the turnaround, selecting tones that fit the character

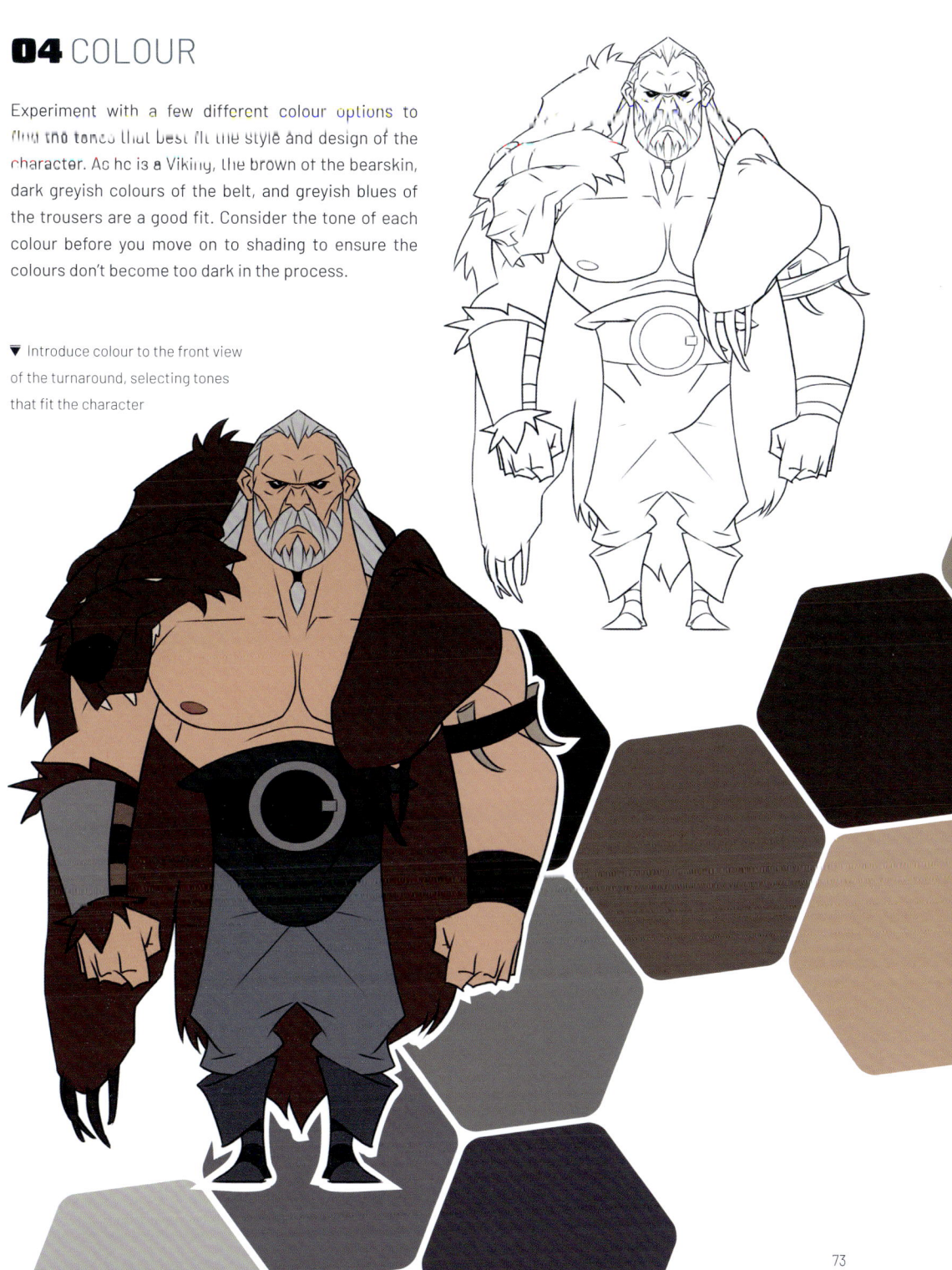

05 FRONT-VIEW SHADING

Now it's time to introduce shading. If using a digital-painting software, try using one layer for the line art, another for the colours, and another for the shadows. (If using complex shading, you could use multiple layers for the shadows, but one layer should suffice for this simple cartoon-style approach.) Set the shadow layer's blending mode to Multiply, position it above the colour layer, then select a slightly purple tone to ensure the shadows don't appear too cold. Using a hard-edged brush, start to shade any areas that don't receive light from the overhead light source.

▶ Use Multiply mode to shade the front view of the character in a simple cartoon-like style

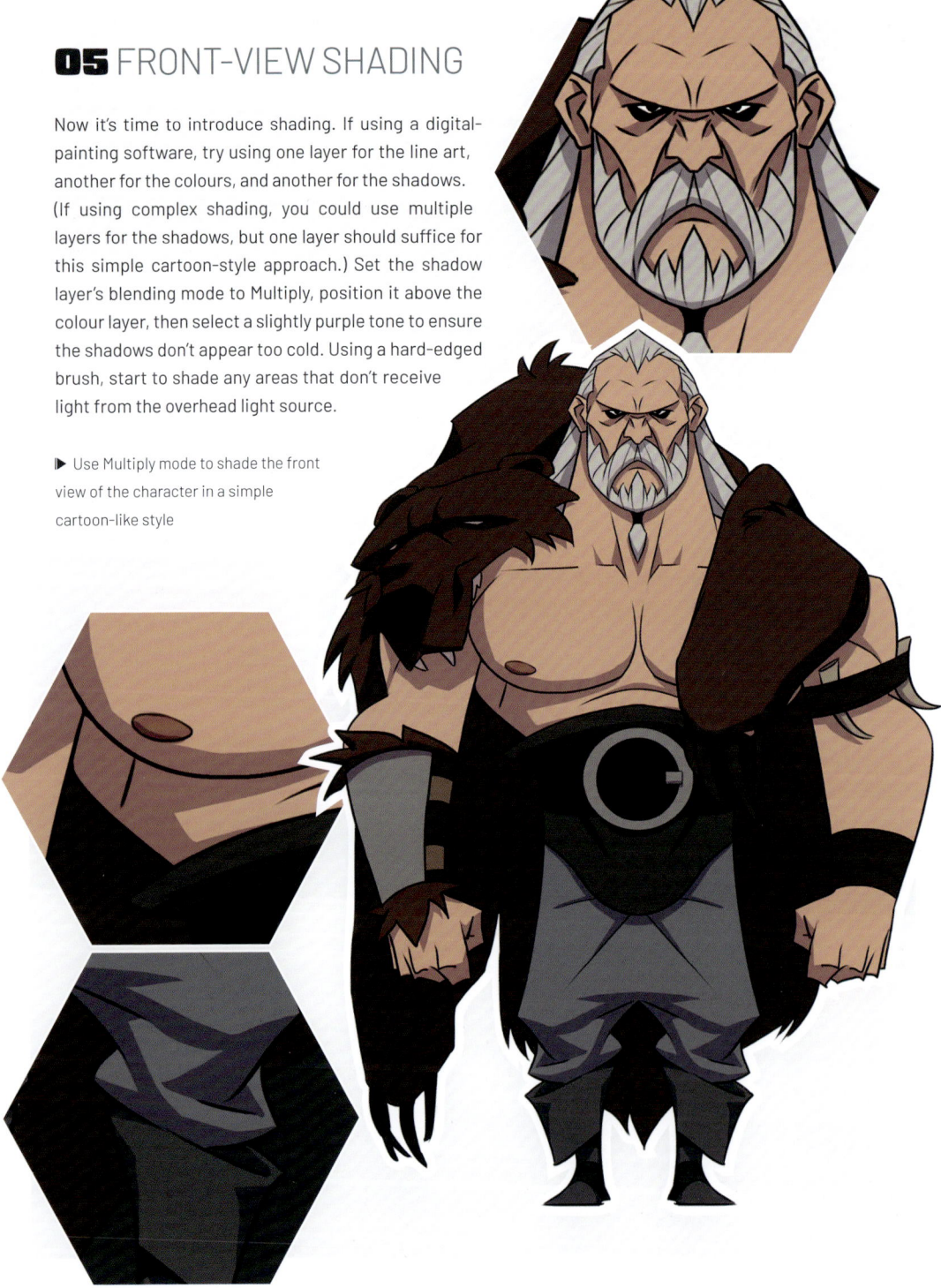

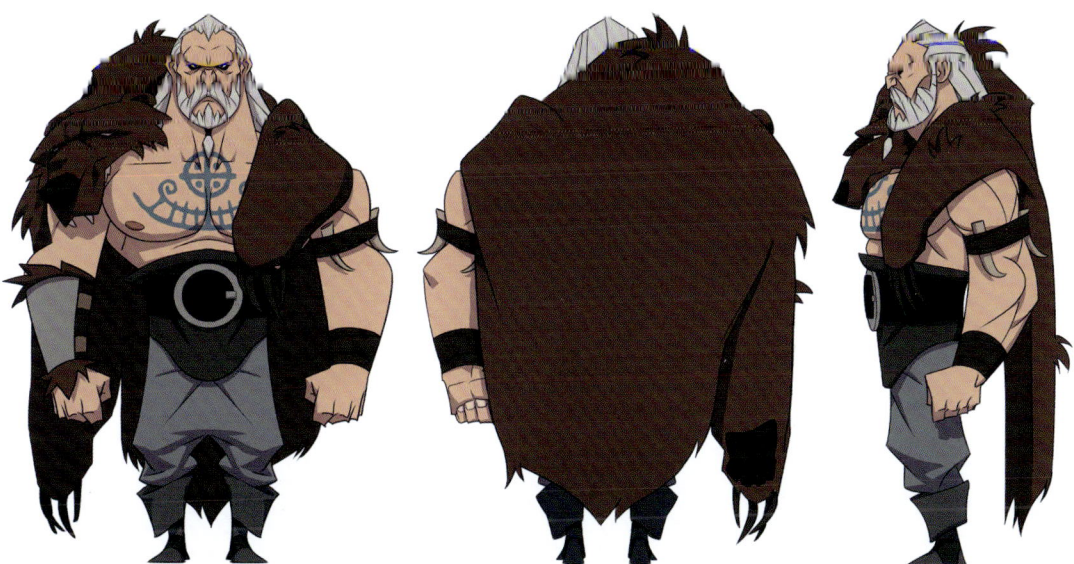

▲ Cartoon-style shading of the remaining views of the turnaround

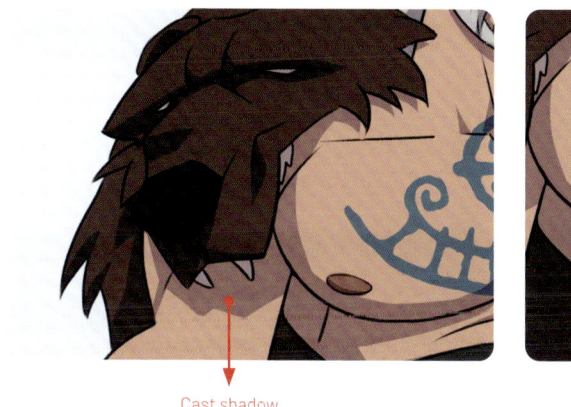

Cast shadow

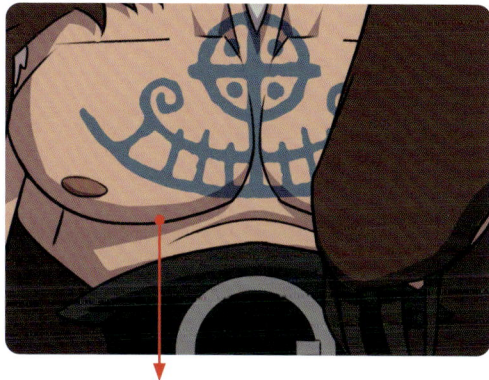

Attached shadow

06 TURNAROUND SHADING

Follow the previous steps – line art, colour, shadows – to complete the side and rear views of the character turnaround. When painting in the shadows, consider the direction of light and how it will hit the different volumes and shapes. As with the previous step, any areas that are not in direct reach of the overhead light

source will be in shadow. For example, the lower part of the character's pectoral muscle should be shaded. This is known as 'attached shadow', created on the form itself. Superimposed elements, such as the bear's paw, project a shadow onto the character's chest. This is a 'cast shadow', as it's cast by a different form.

07 FINAL POSE

Once the turnaround is finished, begin work on the final pose. While the turnaround provides a clear view of the character's design from various angles, the final pose will be more dynamic, capturing the Viking's ferocity and grit. When creating the line art, you can tweak the design slightly to better tell the character's story. For example, here the character has a facial scar and wooden leg after a fierce fight with a bear. Next, paint in colour, considering how this can develop the character, illustrating his persona and the world he inhabits.

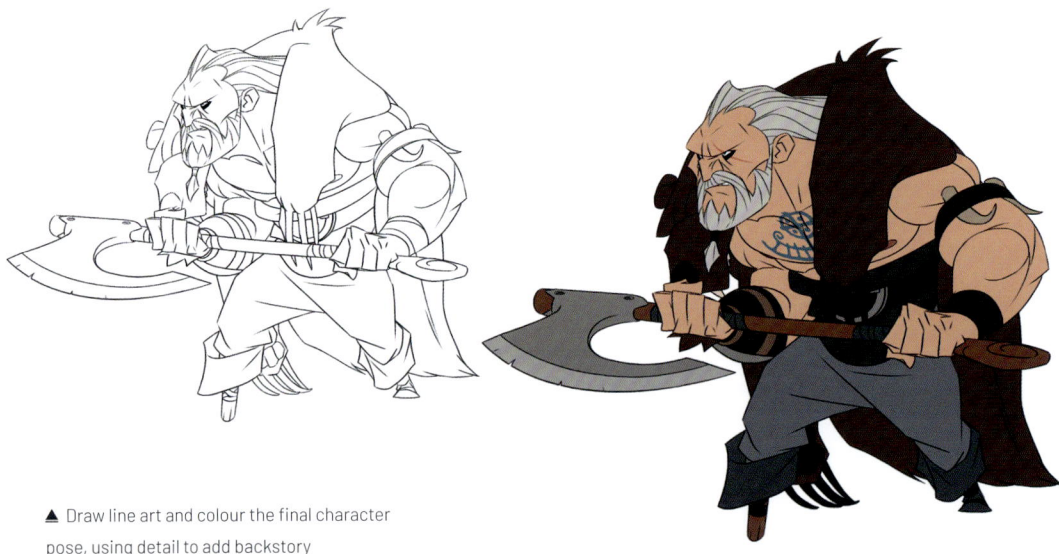

▲ Draw line art and colour the final character pose, using detail to add backstory

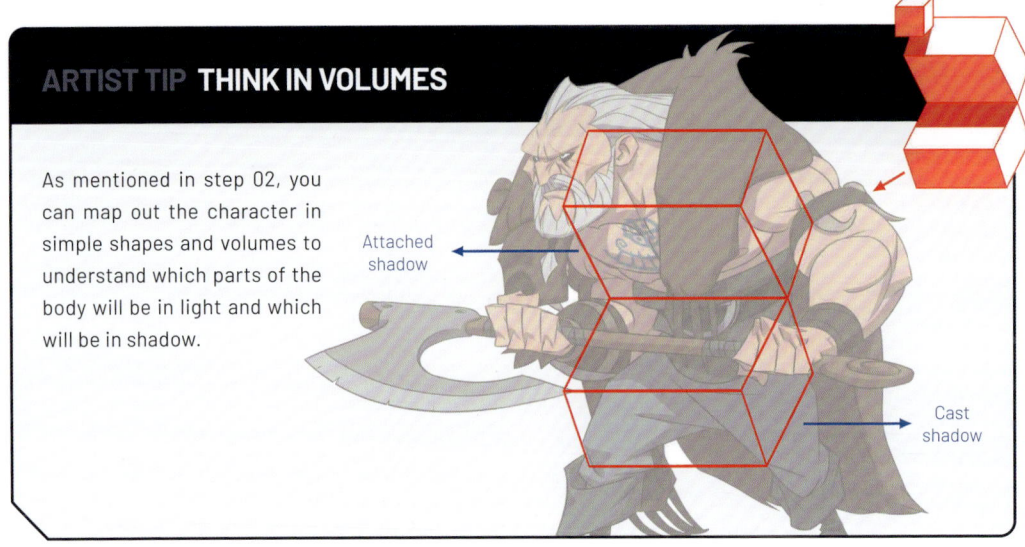

ARTIST TIP **THINK IN VOLUMES**

As mentioned in step 02, you can map out the character in simple shapes and volumes to understand which parts of the body will be in light and which will be in shadow.

Attached shadow

Cast shadow

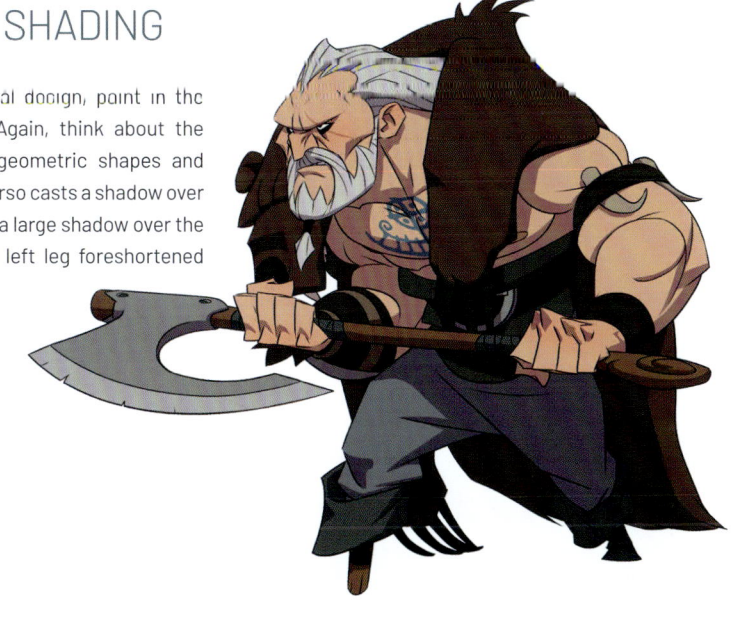

08 FINAL POSE SHADING

Once you're happy with the final design, paint in the simple cartoon-style shadow. Again, think about the character's pose in terms of geometric shapes and volumes. The upper part of his torso casts a shadow over his trousers. The bearskin casts a large shadow over the back of his body, including his left leg foreshortened behind him.

▶ Paint in shadows on any areas of the Viking's body that are hidden from the light

09 FINAL POSE HIGHLIGHTS

Keeping the overhead light source in mind, paint highlights on any planes that directly face the light. For example, the top of the head, top of the leg, and the axe. Next, paint any final details, such as giving the hands, face, and ears a slight reddish tone. Darken the character's facial scar to make sure it's clearly visible.

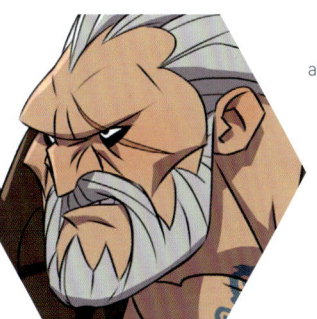

◀ Paint a highlight on all upward-facing planes, then add any final storytelling details

10 ALTERNATIVE SHADING OPTIONS

Experiment with a few different shading options to see how this can affect the design. For example, choosing a lower angle for the direction of the light source – as if the character were approaching a bonfire on the ground – will create completely different shadows and alter the overall mood of the image. Here the colours are darkened and the shadows are intensified and extended. The character's eyes and chest tattoo are then illuminated, creating a more sinister and eery mood.

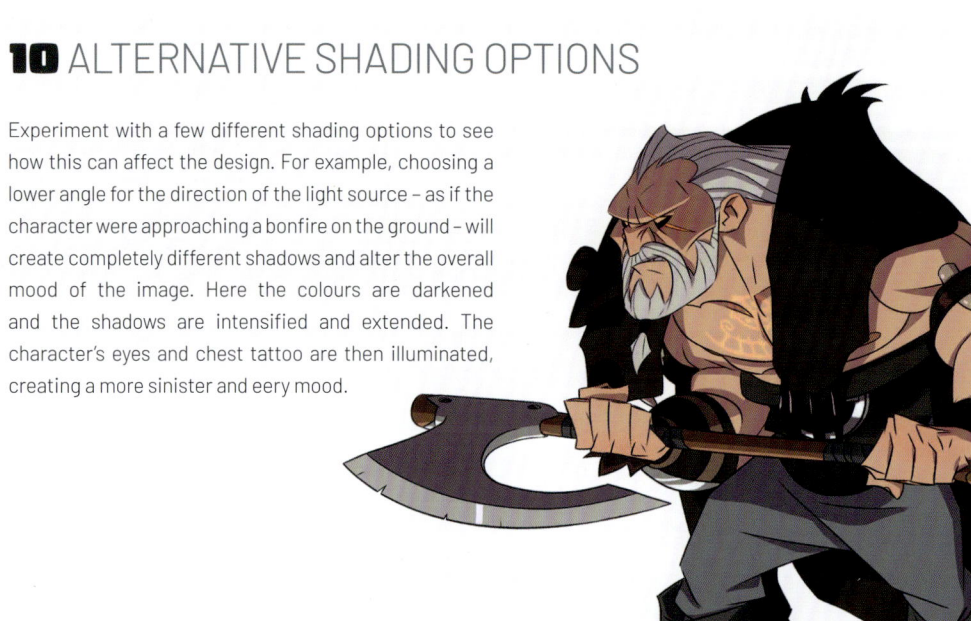

▶ Change the direction of the light source to experiment with the different kinds of shadows you can create

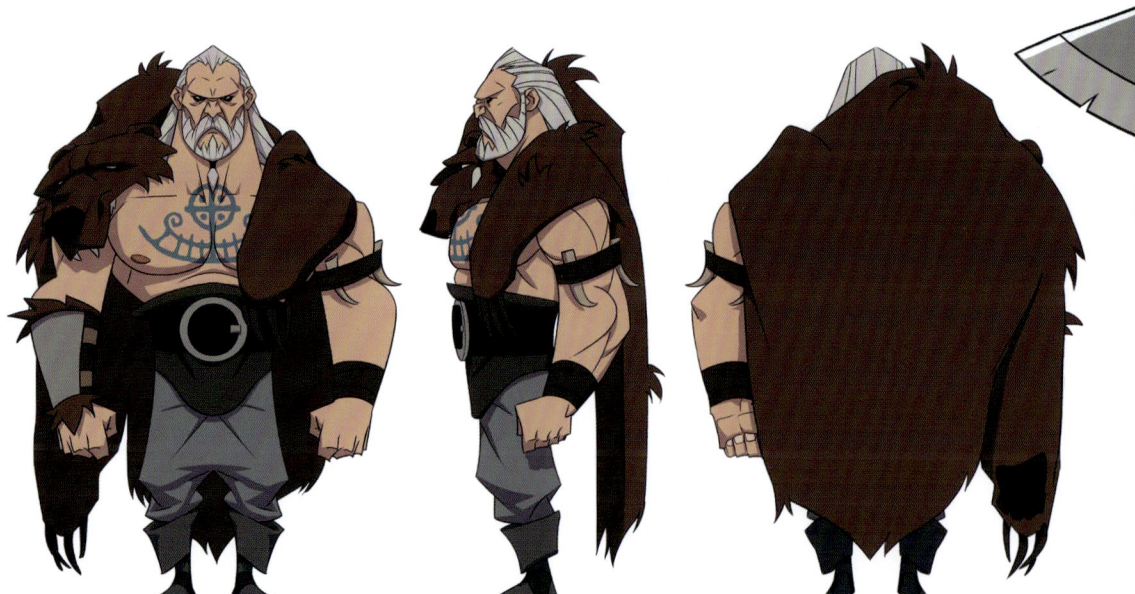

▲ Final character turnaround showing shading from multiple angles

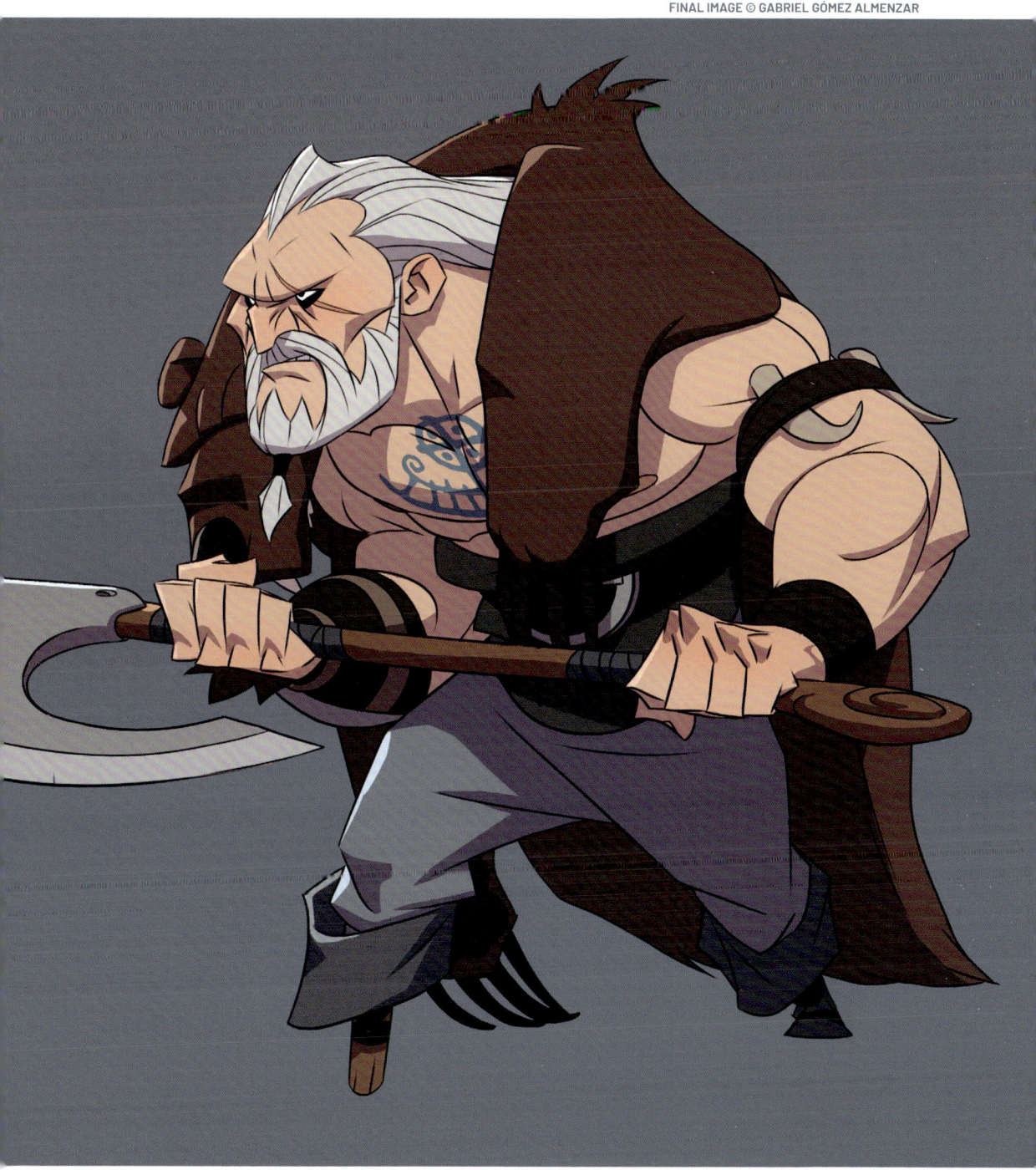

▲ Final pose of a bloodthirsty Viking warrior, ready to strike!

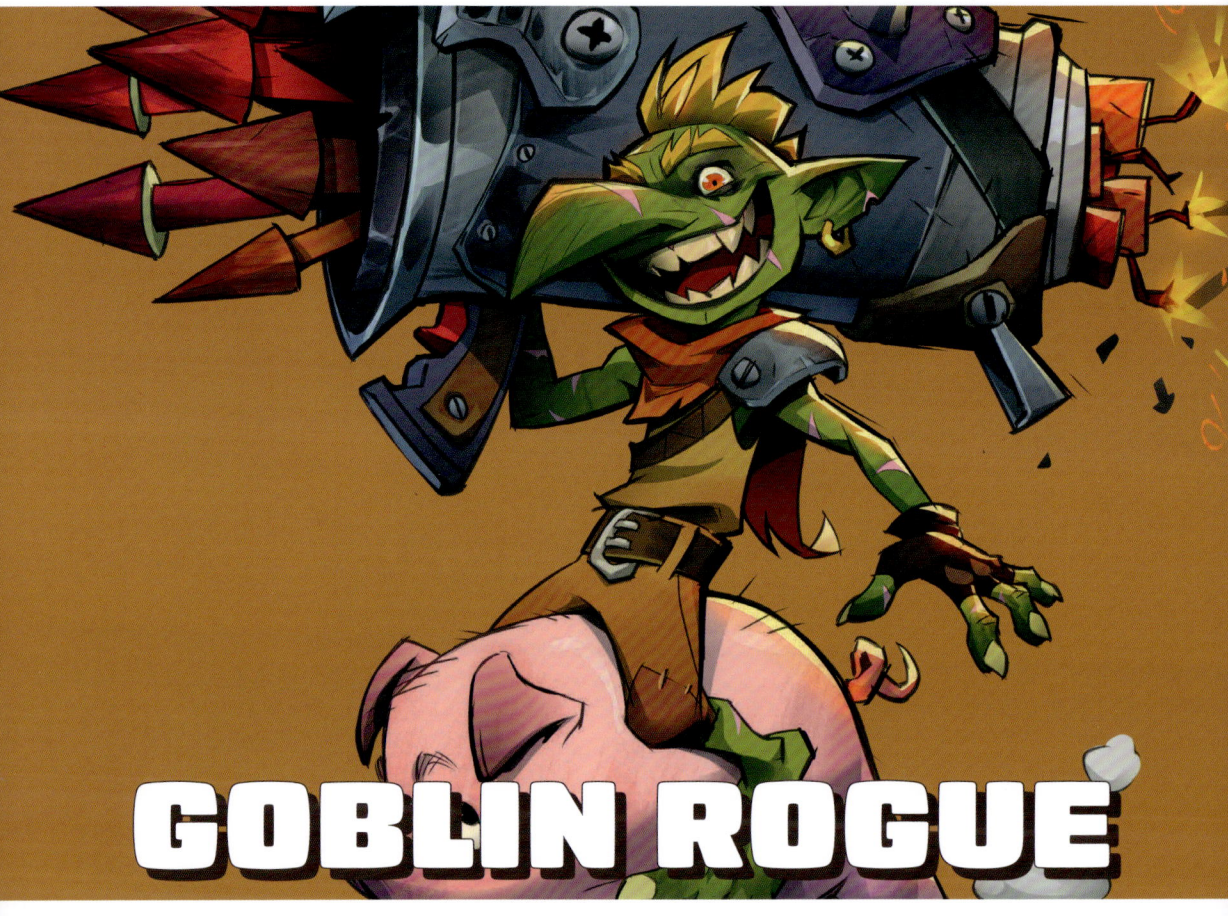

GOBLIN ROGUE

STYLIZING A CHARACTER WITH LIGHT & SHADE

Applying shadows to a character can make the design more visually appealing, as well as helping the audience to understand its forms. This tutorial will provide a step-by-step guide on how to create a character from initial concept to final image, with emphasis on using light and shade to define the design's three-dimensionality. The goal is to create a heavily stylized character that still has believable shapes and forms determined by the dynamics of light and shadow. This is especially important if you're part of a production line and your character will be modelled in 3D.

This tutorial is completed using Adobe Photoshop, but you can follow along with any digital-painting software available to you.

By Guilherme Franco

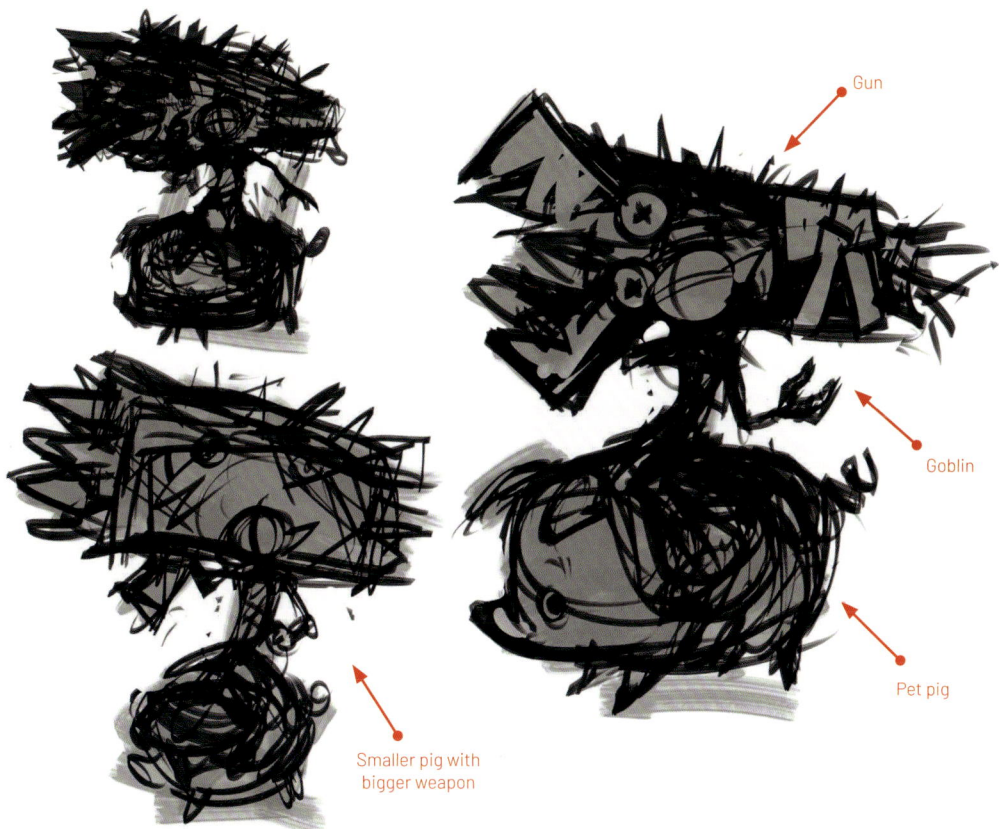

THUMBNAIL STUDIES

Gun

Goblin

Pet pig

Smaller pig with bigger weapon

01 THUMBNAILING

To bring a character to life using light and shade, start by considering the different forms that can overlap to create a sense of depth. Create quick loose sketches to test out different ideas. These thumbnails roughly depict what will become a fun goblin character riding a pig and holding a large explosive weapon. These three main elements will need to work harmoniously together to create a good balance. Inside the main elements will be smaller details, ensuring a visually pleasing ratio of large, medium, and small shapes and more opportunities for cast shadows.

▲ Sketch out exploratory thumbnails for a character

02 REFINEMENT

Select a thumbnail to progress with, developing it into a slightly clearer drawing. It doesn't need to be too clean at this stage, as you are still testing out the balance and rhythm of the design. Aim for a good contrast between the shapes – not too even but not too exaggerated either. Establish a humorous relationship between the elements: a large, spiky shape at the top and a cute, rounded pig as the base, with the main character in the middle, steering both. Visual tension can make a design funnier and more interesting. Outlining the silhouette can also help to create a stronger design that can be understood on first glance. Additionally, the silhouette will serve as the base on which you will mask the colours and shadows in later steps.

▶ Refine the chosen thumbnail, ensuring it reads clearly and has a good visual rhythm

Refinement

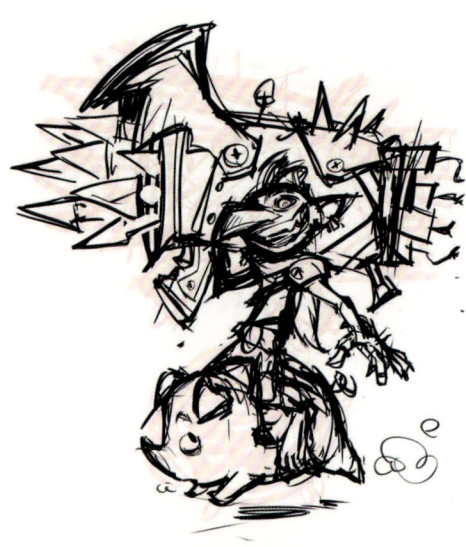

Size contrast

Silhouette

Menacing

Cute

03 COLOUR COMPS

Test out some quick colour comps on your sketch. Be mindful of the values to ensure each element has strong readability. Giving the weapon a darker value and the character a lighter value will create a good contrast. Here are four colour-palette options, but you can create as many as you like. By trying out some unusual choices, you might end up with a surprisingly good alternative you hadn't previously considered. You can also use this step to test various lighting scenarios. Experiment with different light-source directions and the shadows they create, defining the forms of the character. You could go for a neutral set-up, or a more dramatic set-up with focused light sources.

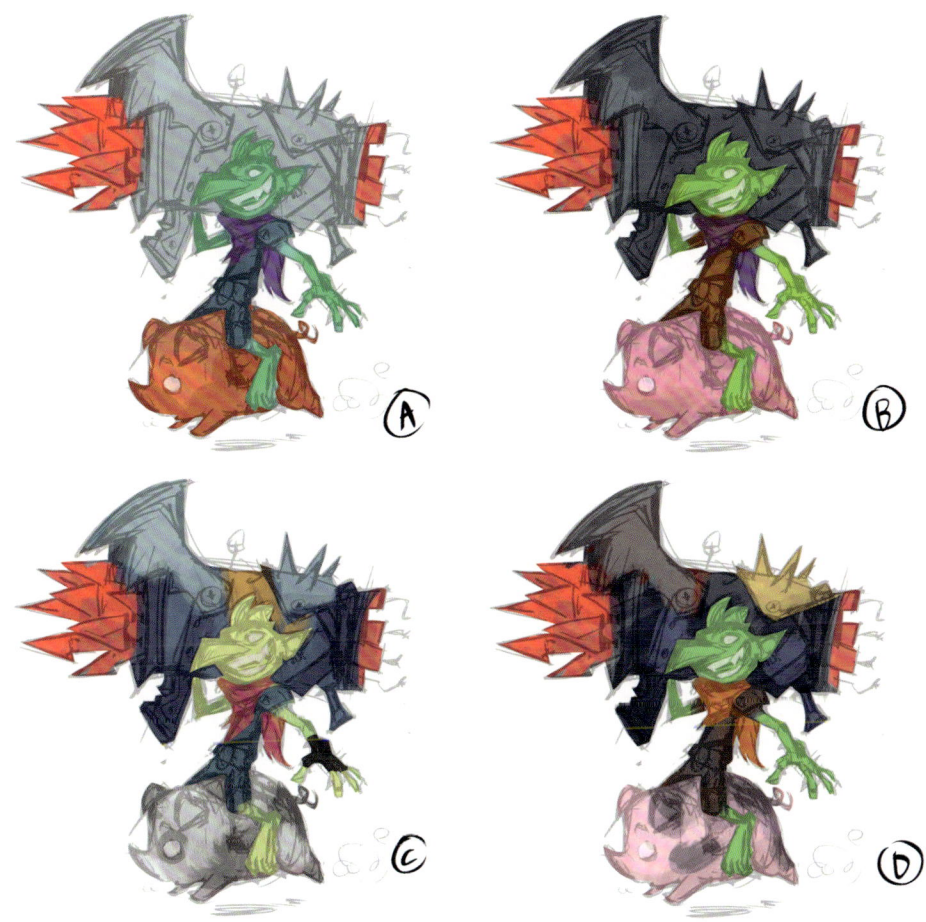

▲ Experiment with unusual colour palettes and several lighting scenarios

04 LINE ART

Now you have a direction for the character, create the final line art. Take your time to define every detail, as this will form an important guide when adding colour and shading later in the process. Applying notions of real anatomy to stylized characters is a good way to make them more believable. Even though this character is cartoony and exists in a fantasy world, his muscles, expressions, and movements are physically possible in reality. This will be reinforced by the light and shadows in later steps.

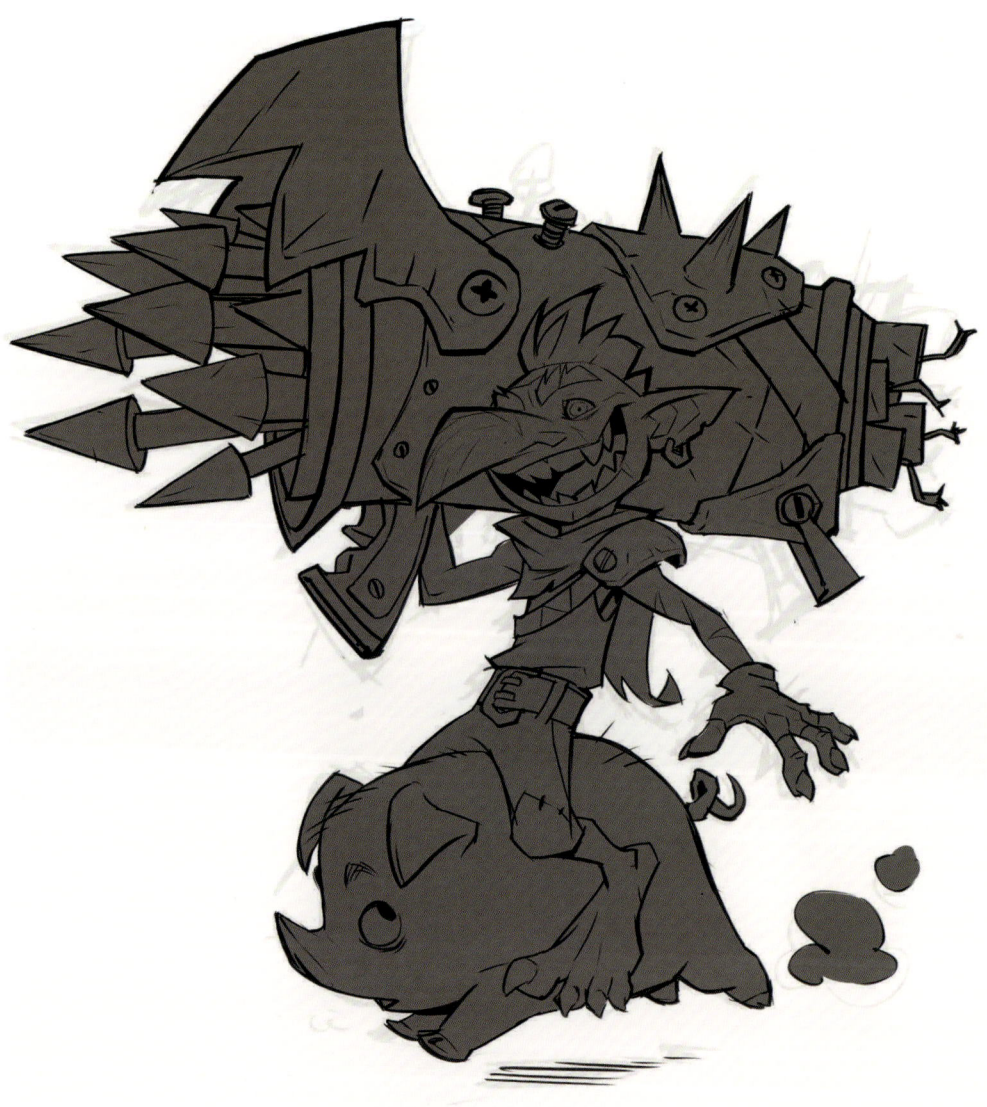

▲ Create clear line art, defining the different elements

05 BASE COLOURS

Choose a colour palette from one of your colour comps (step 03), or combine the strongest elements of your favourite comps, then paint in the local colours on a layer underneath the line art. These are the default colours of each element without any influence from the light. They should appear flat for the time being, but will be affected by ambient and artificial lights later in the process

▼ Paint in the local colours without any lighting influence

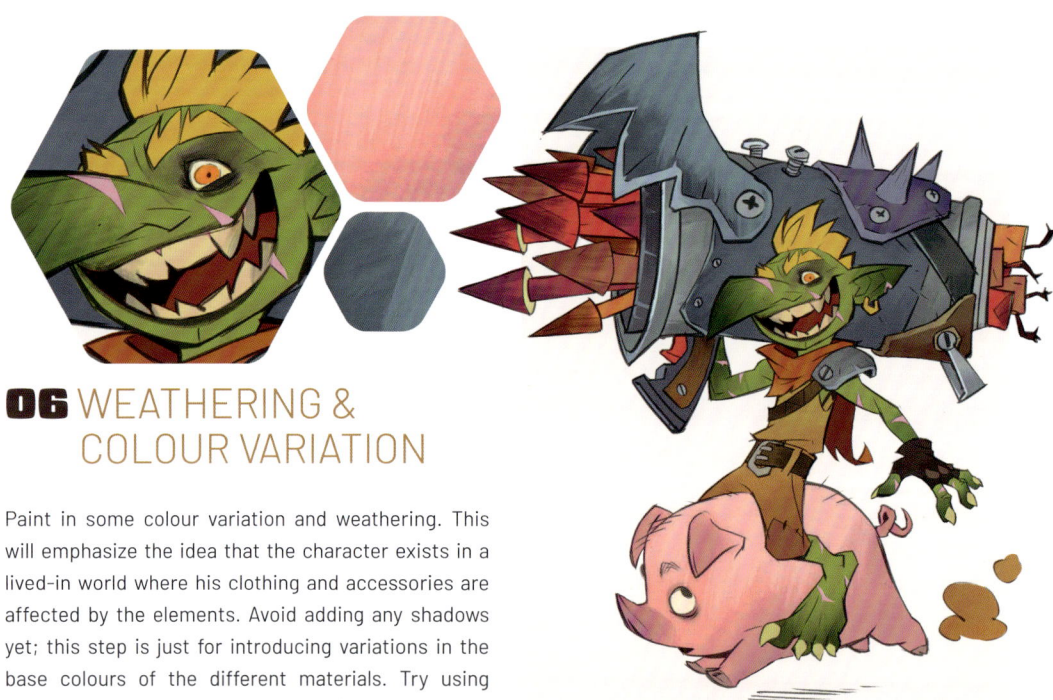

06 WEATHERING & COLOUR VARIATION

Paint in some colour variation and weathering. This will emphasize the idea that the character exists in a lived-in world where his clothing and accessories are affected by the elements. Avoid adding any shadows yet; this step is just for introducing variations in the base colours of the different materials. Try using analogous colours, as keeping everything in the same hue can lead to muddy colours in the final image.

▲ Add some variation to the base colours to make the design feel more believable

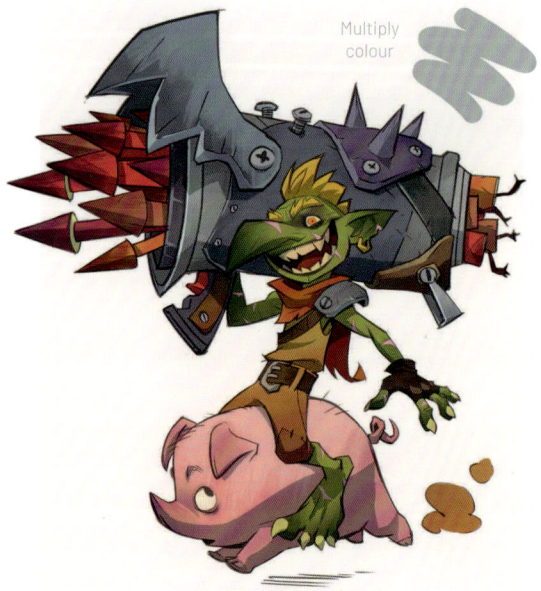

07 SHADING

Before introducing shading you must first decide on the light source. This will dictate how you apply shadows to each element. Here a fairly neutral light is shining down from above, so shadows will form on the underside of the design. Create a Multiply layer, as this will blend with the base layers to make a darker value, ideal for shadows. Use a slightly blue colour and a hard round brush to define big shadows where the light doesn't directly hit. Blue is used here as the sky above is blue and, since light bounces, it usually influences shadows in a neutral environment. Try to view the 2D drawing as a 3D object. This will help to create a three-dimensional look. You may need to lower the opacity of the Multiply layer if the shadows appear too bold.

◀ Create volume using shading in Multiply mode

08 AMBIENT OCCLUSION & SOFTER SHADOWS

Use a soft-edged eraser to soften the shadows on rounder objects and surfaces. Leave a hard edge on any shadows cast by sharper objects, such as the big jaw-like weapon or the goblin's shoulder pad. As this is a stylized character, you can paint what looks good rather than what's more realistic. While a design does need to be grounded in some kind of form and function, it doesn't need to represent light in the most precise or physically correct manner. Next, using the same colour, create a new Multiply layer on top of the first one. Paint in ambient occlusion: smaller areas that are obscured from the light source inside the big shadow areas. Use the Lasso tool to make the selections and a soft brush to fill them. This will give the shadows some nuances, making them less simplistic and more three-dimensional.

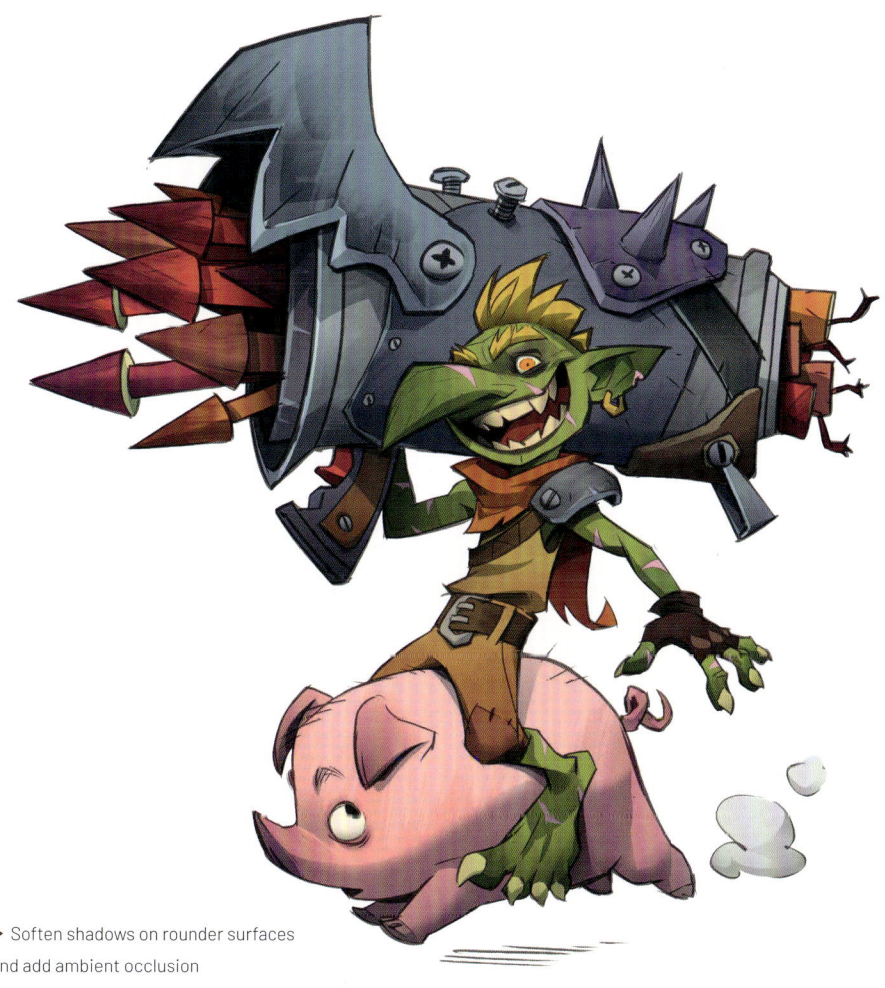

▶ Soften shadows on rounder surfaces
and add ambient occlusion

09 RIM LIGHT

At this stage the forms are well defined and there is a clear separation of each main element: weapon, goblin, and pig. Rim light – often thinly present on the edges of objects closer to light sources – can now be added to strengthen the shapes directly affected by the light. This is not something you commonly see in everyday neutral lighting scenarios, as it's the result of a direct focused light source, usually artificial. However, as this is a heavily stylized character, rim light can be employed to improve the sense of depth by separating even more elements of the image. Take care not to add too much rim light, as it can become distracting. To make it even more appealing, add an Overlay layer on top of the rim-light layer and airbrush some analogous colour.

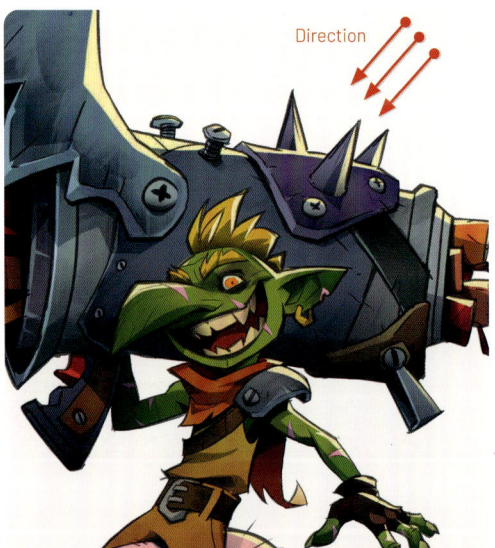

Direction

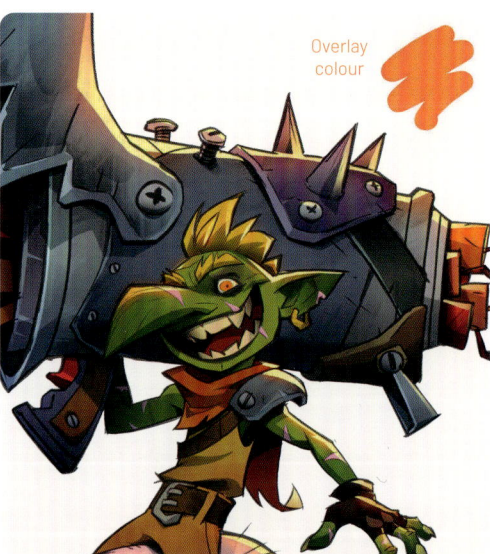

Overlay colour

▲ Paint rim light on areas close to the light source, such as the top of the weapon and the character's hair

10 FINAL DETAILS

Use the final step to add extra details and effects. To make the design more dynamic and to improve the sense of movement, add fire and smoke on the fireworks' fuses, as well as screws and nails flying off of the machine. As the goblin built the weapon himself, it's not particularly well constructed and parts keep falling off as they move. Paint darker shadows into areas such as the character's armpit and inside the weapon's barrel. Finish by making any small fixes and drawing in any additional line work you feel is missing.

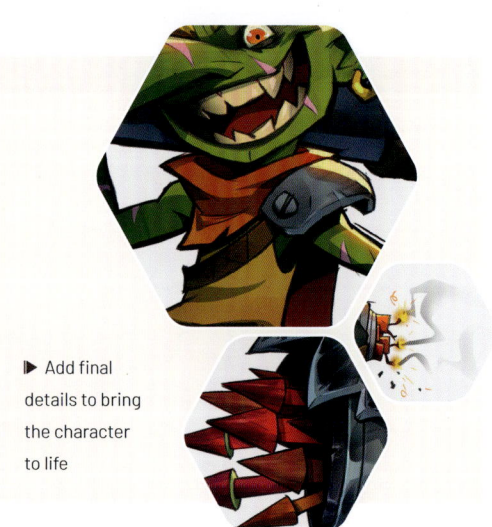

▶ Add final details to bring the character to life

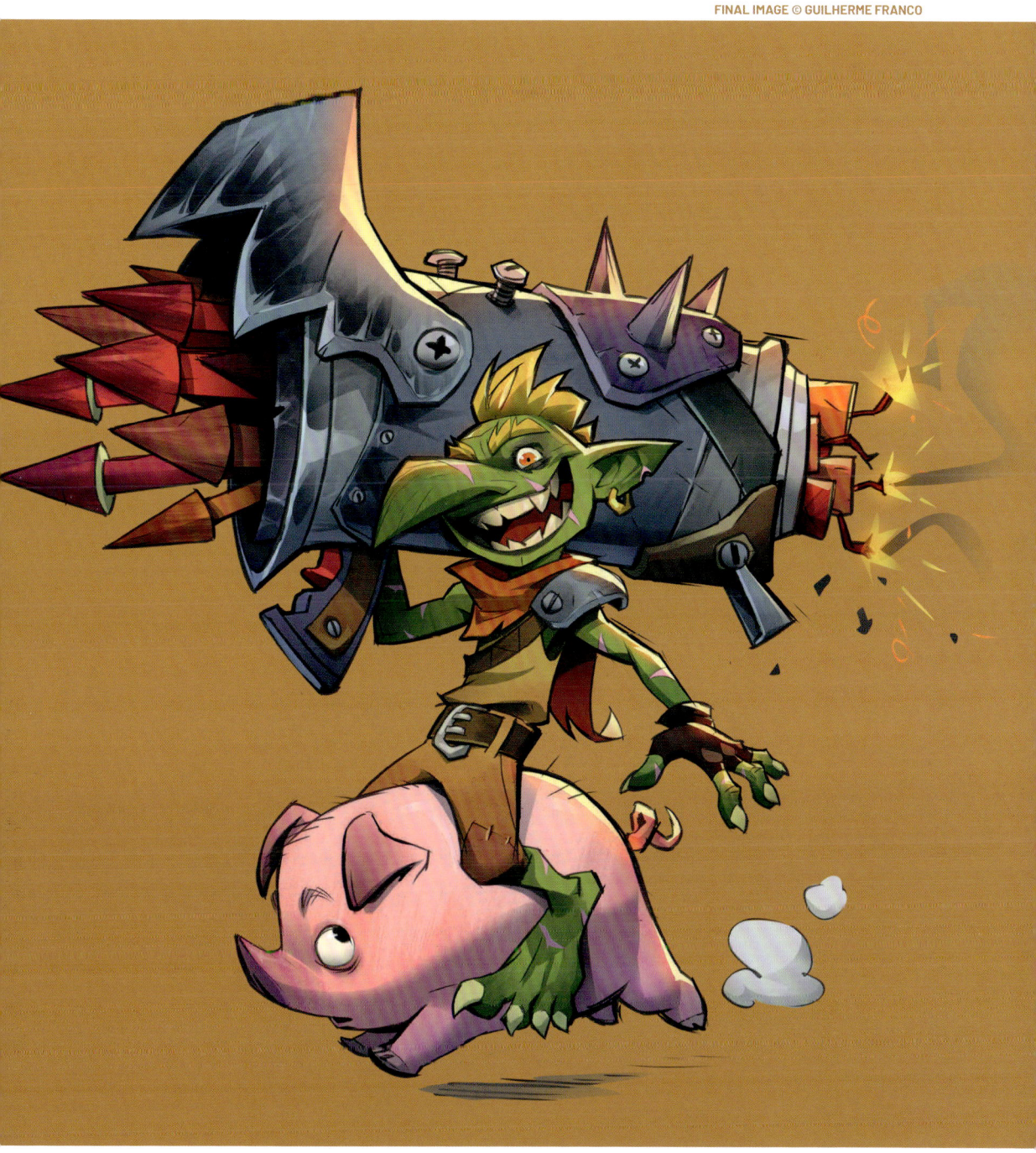

▲ The final stylized character, showing how various types of shadow and light can be used to add volume and a sense of three-dimensionality

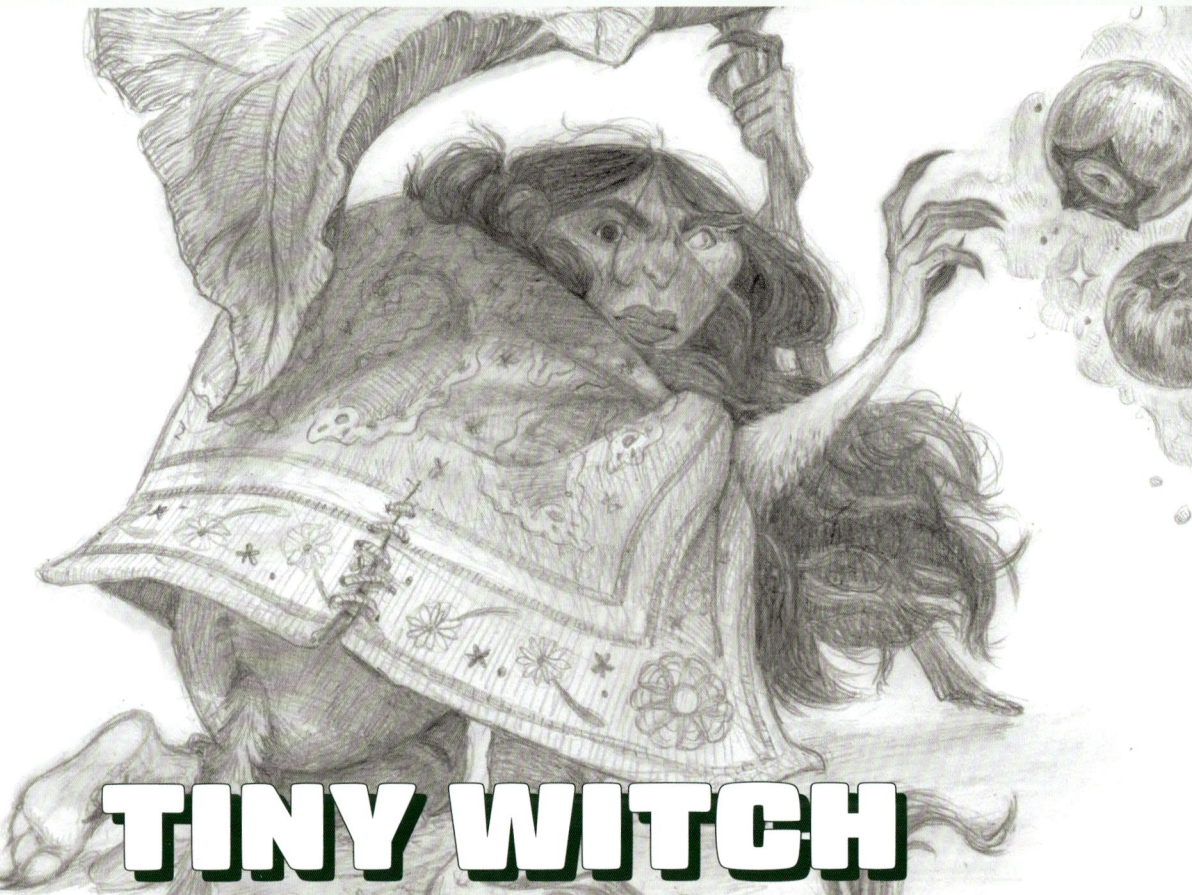

TINY WITCH

CONTROLLING THE TONAL STRUCTURE OF A CHARACTER WITH LIGHT & SHADE

There's something almost magical about creating a character and bringing them to life with just pencil and paper. To make a character appear believable, there are a few ways to trick the eye into seeing depth without it actually being there. Using traditional pencil, this tutorial will focus on how to control the tonal structure – the range of grey tones created by pencil marks – and how to recreate shadow and light.

By Rachelle Joy Slingerland

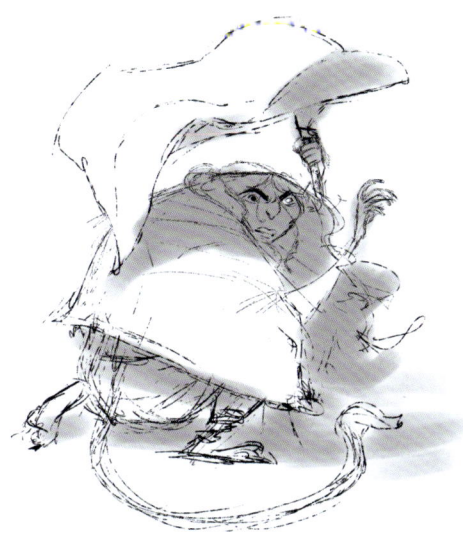

01 INITIAL SKETCHES

Start by doodling ideas for a character. Once you have a sketch you wish to explore further, create a thumbnail to draw the character's body in full. Decide where the light source will be – in this case, overhead – and block in the big shadows. A thumbnail can help to develop your idea, especially if you're not sure what you plan to do with shadow and light. Here the big cast shadow, created by the leaf, will give the witch a more mysterious look and emphasize her ethereal light eye.

◀ Create a loose character sketch and roughly block in the shadows

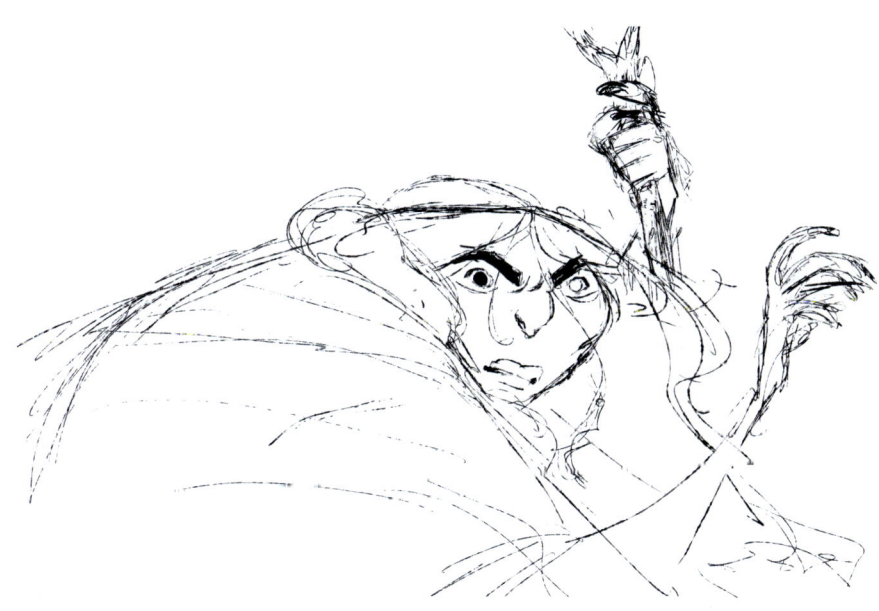

02 SCULPT THE FRAME

Think of this step as sculpting: building the frame, or skeleton, of the character you're going to draw. Using light, soft strokes on paper, sketch out the larger shapes first: the leaf, cape, long hair, and mouse-like tail. Try to see the outer shapes of the character as big flat blocks. Keep your pencil pressure light so it's easy to erase – paper is not always as forgiving as you might think. Feel free to pencil in a few details on the face; it's the spirit of this little being, after all!

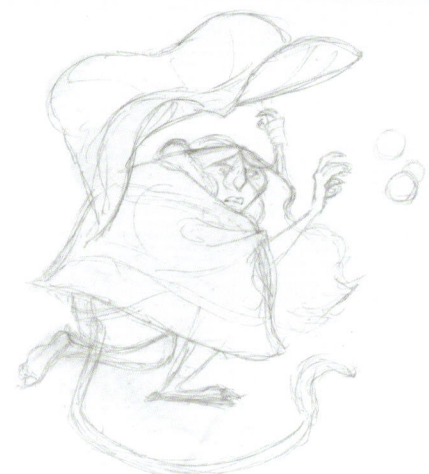

▶ Build up the character using light pencil strokes

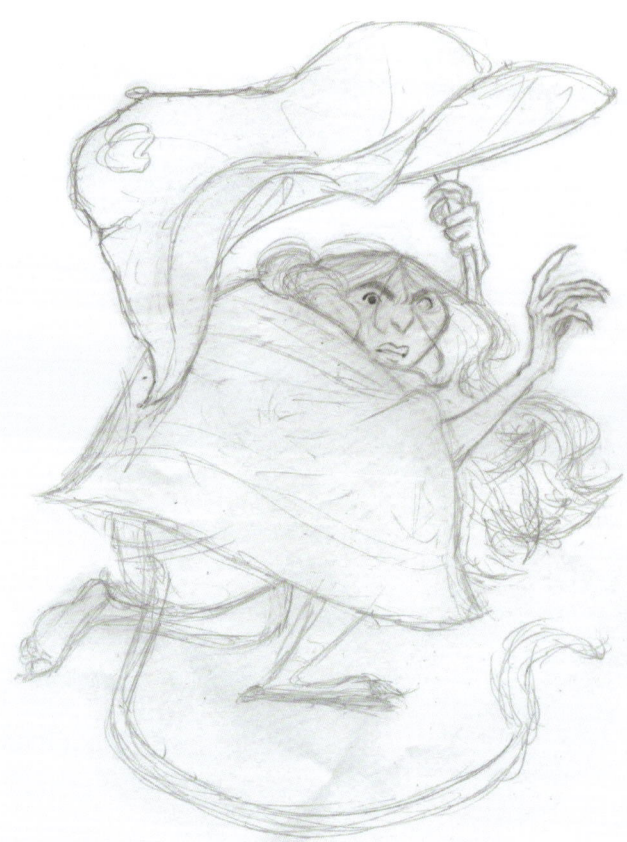

03 FLESH IT OUT

Once you're happy with the base, develop the witch's expression and pose, as this will determine the tone of the rest of the drawing. Choose a clear point of focus – here it is the face and hand area – then give this a little extra time and attention. The rest of the drawing will hinge on this.

◀ Decide on the focal point

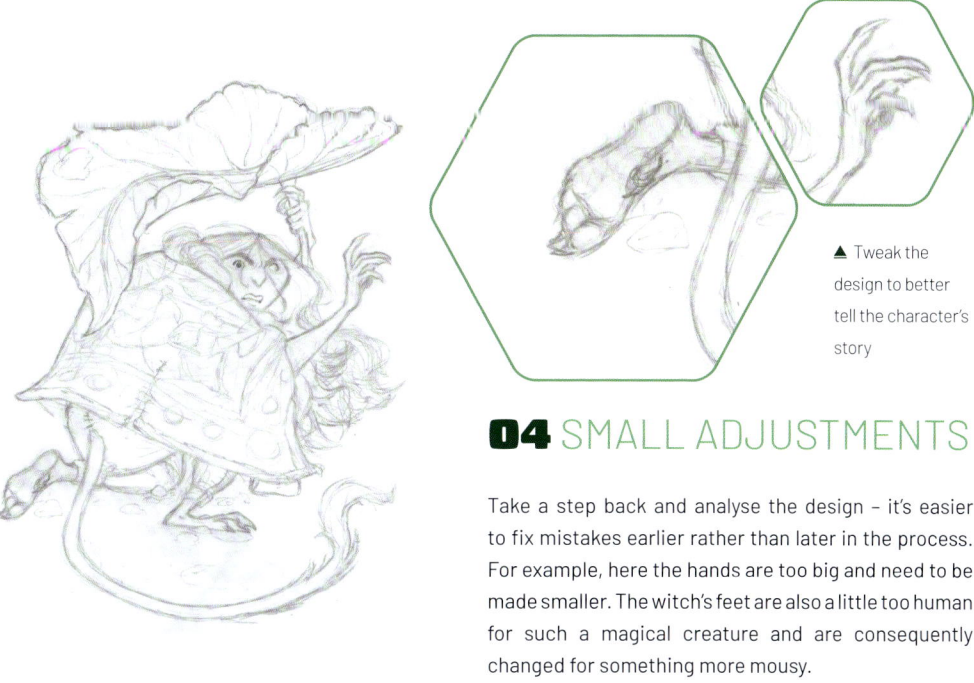

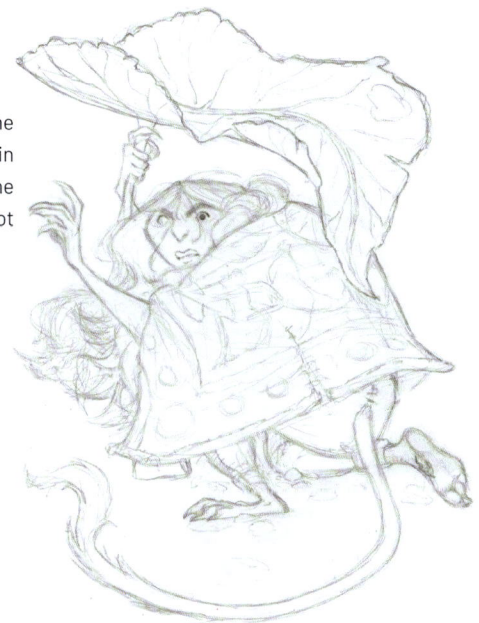

▲ Tweak the design to better tell the character's story

04 SMALL ADJUSTMENTS

Take a step back and analyse the design – it's easier to fix mistakes earlier rather than later in the process. For example, here the hands are too big and need to be made smaller. The witch's feet are also a little too human for such a magical creature and are consequently changed for something more mousy.

05 FLIP & CHECK

Once you're happy with the design, take a photo of the drawing and flip it horizontally or vertically, or hold it in front of a mirror. This tricks your brain into seeing the image as if for the first time and will allow you to spot any elements that need fixing.

▶ Flip the drawing to check for inconsistencies

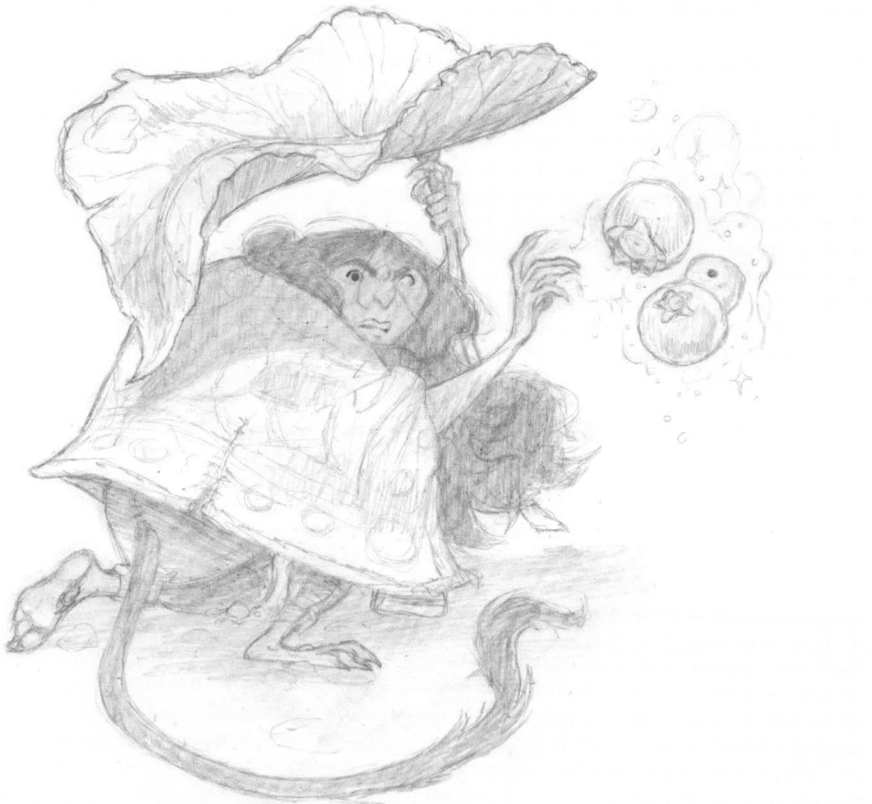

06 SET THE TONE

It's easier to build shadow in layers than it is to apply too much too soon and have to erase it later. Referring back to your thumbnail, lightly block in the big areas of dark and shadow. This includes cast shadows – cast by the leaf and her body – as well as the witch's mass of dark hair. This will not only create visual distinction between objects, but also starts to trick the eye into seeing volume. Using large differences in values between elements can make your character more readable, as well as letting you see if any areas of the design appear off balance. In this case, the witch needs a few magical berries.

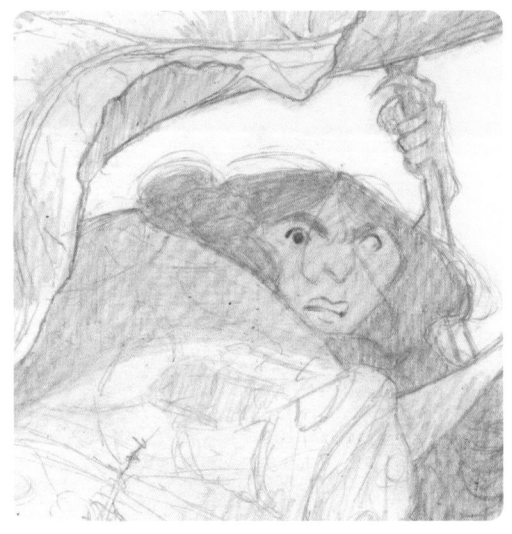

▶ Build up areas of dark and shadow to create a sense of volume

07 DETAIL & CONTRAST

Your focus and patience may loosen over time, but this is something you can use to your advantage. If you look at the work of master painters, you will notice that the focal points of their paintings (typically faces) are highly detailed, whereas coats, hats, and background elements are often painted with rougher strokes. With the fresh enthusiasm you still have, develop the part of the design with the most detail and contrast. This is the most important part of the character, as it's where you want the audience to look.

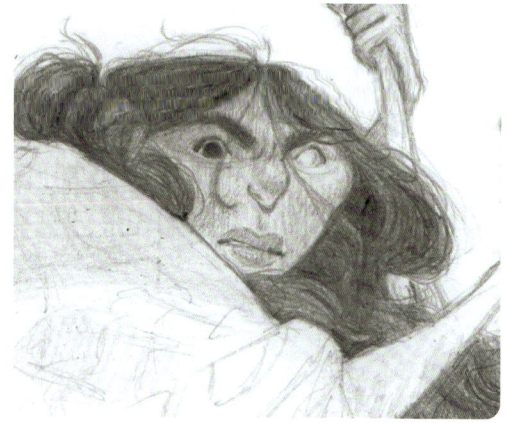

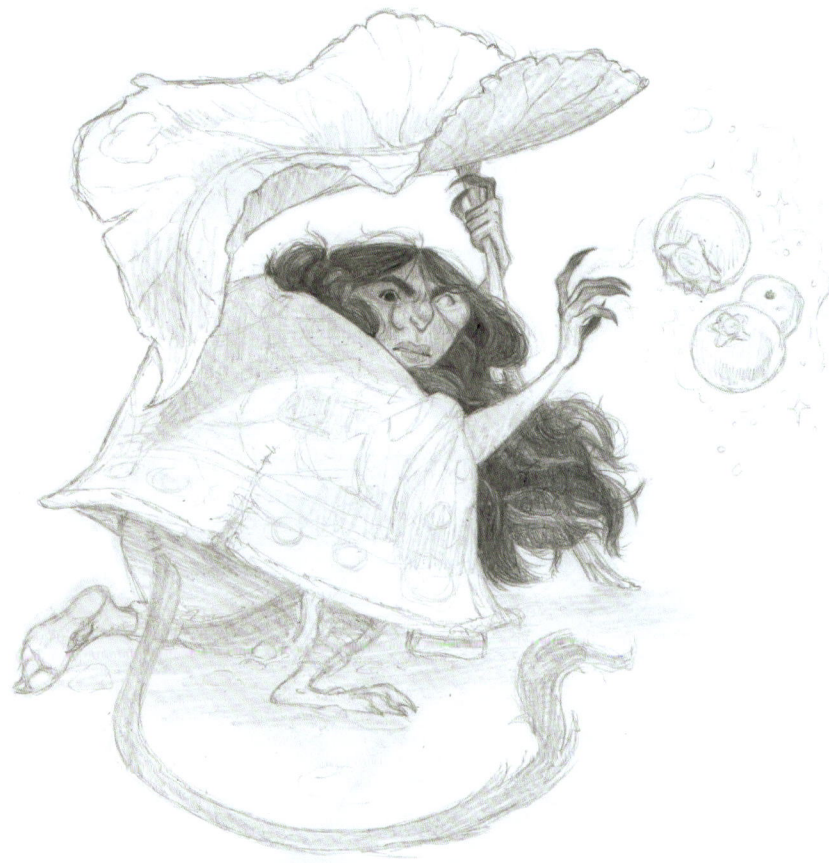

▲ Refine the witch's face and surrounding area to ensure it attracts the viewer's gaze

08 DIRECT THE EYE

When developing the drawing, make sure all of the little details point to the witch's face. The leaf's veins and etchings not only accentuate its shape, but also steer the viewer's eye towards her head, as does the little knick in her cape. The pattern on the cloth suggests that this mousy witch has stolen a bandana or scarf, which emphasizes her small size. The fur on her arms illustrates that she's not entirely human.

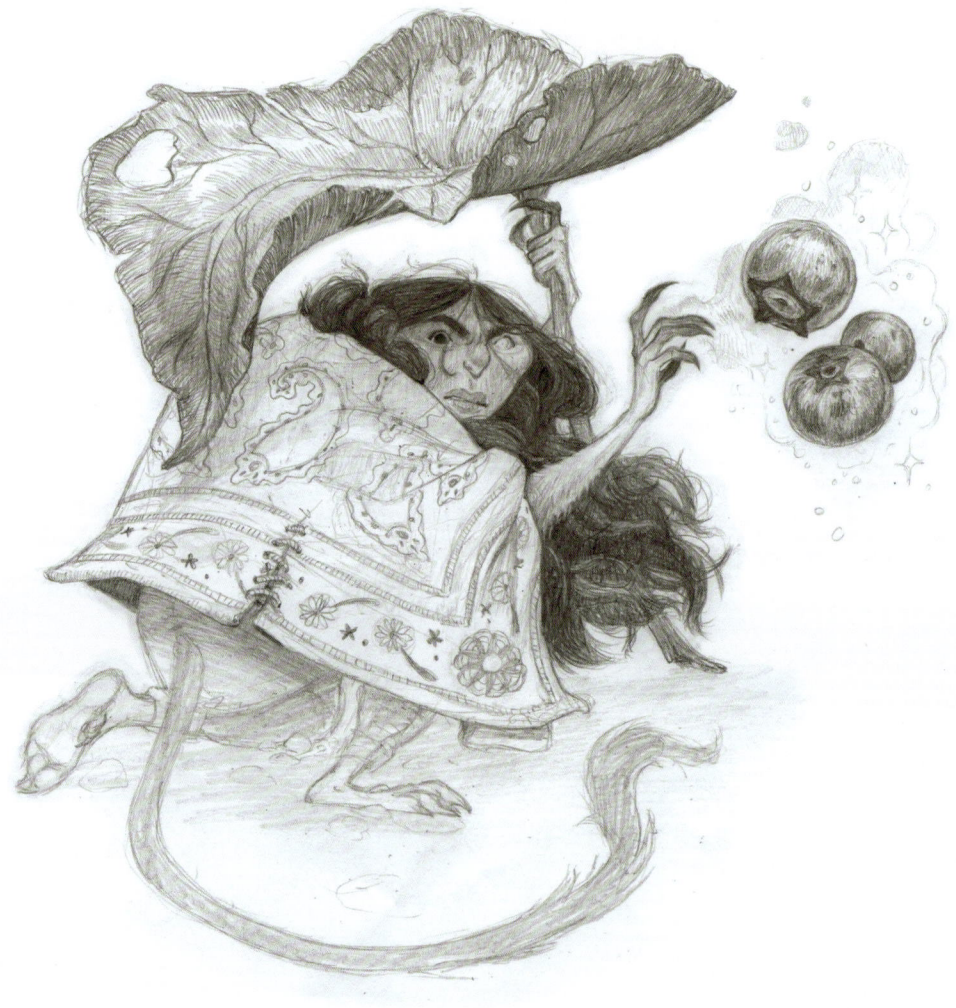

▲ Use details to guide the viewer's eye to the focal point

ARTIST TIP PENCIL PRESSURE

It's easy to develop hand cramps from holding the pencil too tightly or with excessive force. A mechanical pencil can help to train you out of this bad habit, as the lead will snap as soon as you apply too much pressure. After a while, you will learn to be a little less aggressive.

▲ Use shading to increase the tonal variation

09 ADDING SHADE

With the patterns and important details in place, you can now incorporate more shade. When in the light, the bandana details are more obvious and have a wider range of values. In the shade of the leaf, the details appear less defined and the values are more 'pulled together'. The same occurs on the underside of the leaf – the difference in values is smaller and they are darker overall.

10 THE TAIL END

As in the previous steps, add shadow, patterns, and texture to the tail end of the witch's design. The deep dark of her hair will attract the viewer's focus, so make sure not to go too dark with the remainder of the image. Keep the contrast highest where you want the audience to look first. A character with a range of different values will make for a more visually interesting design.

▼ Add pattern, texture, and shadow, taking care not to distract from the focal point

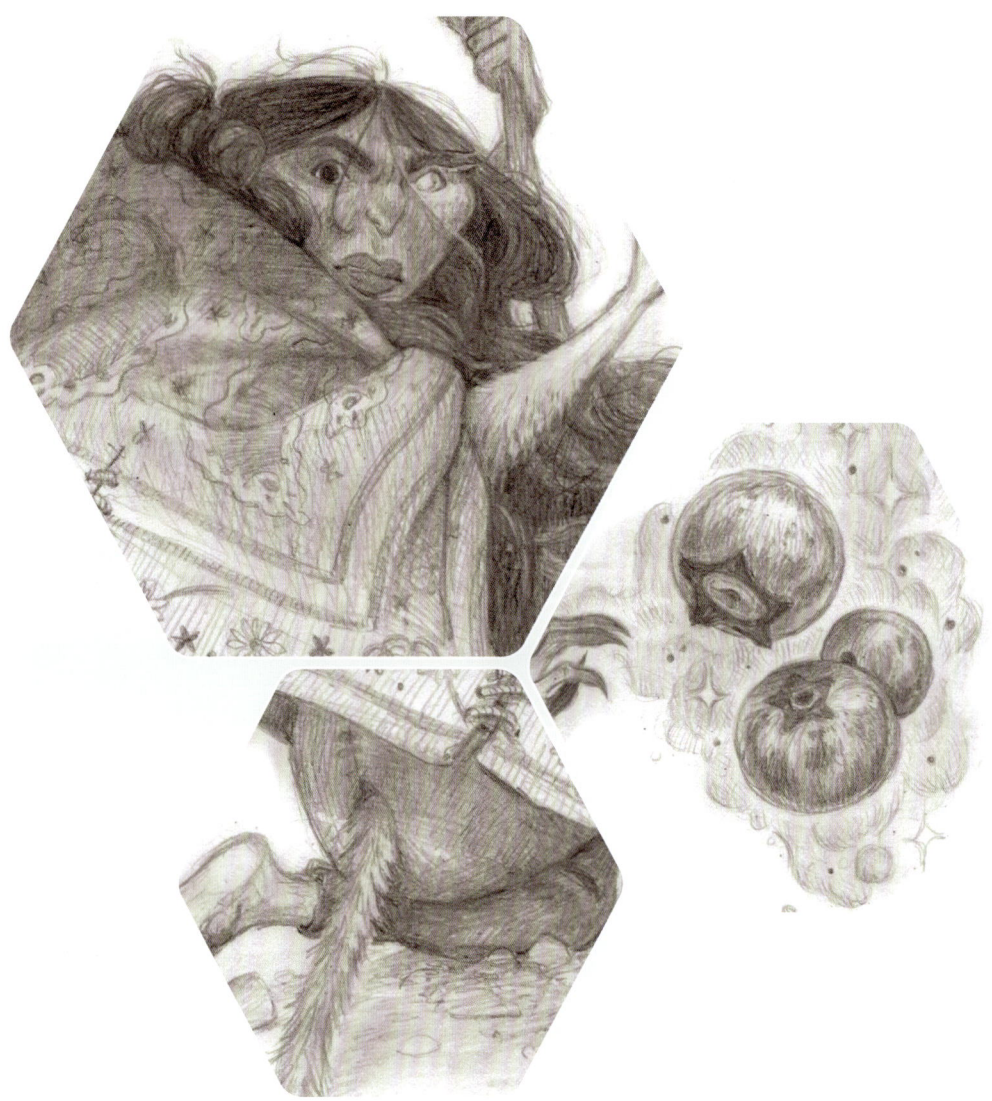

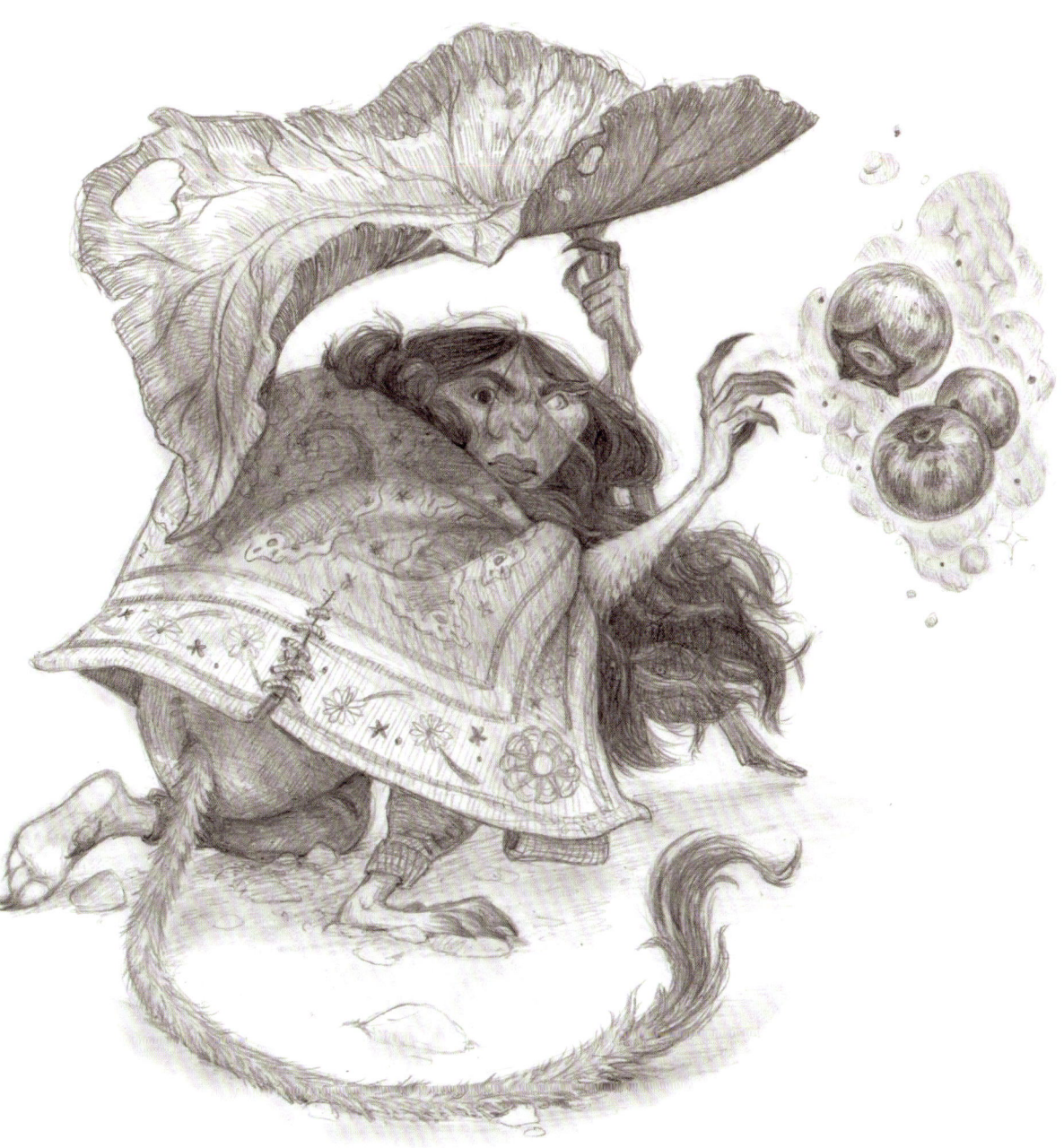

▲ The finished design of this tiny witch shows great depth of value, all achieved with pencil alone

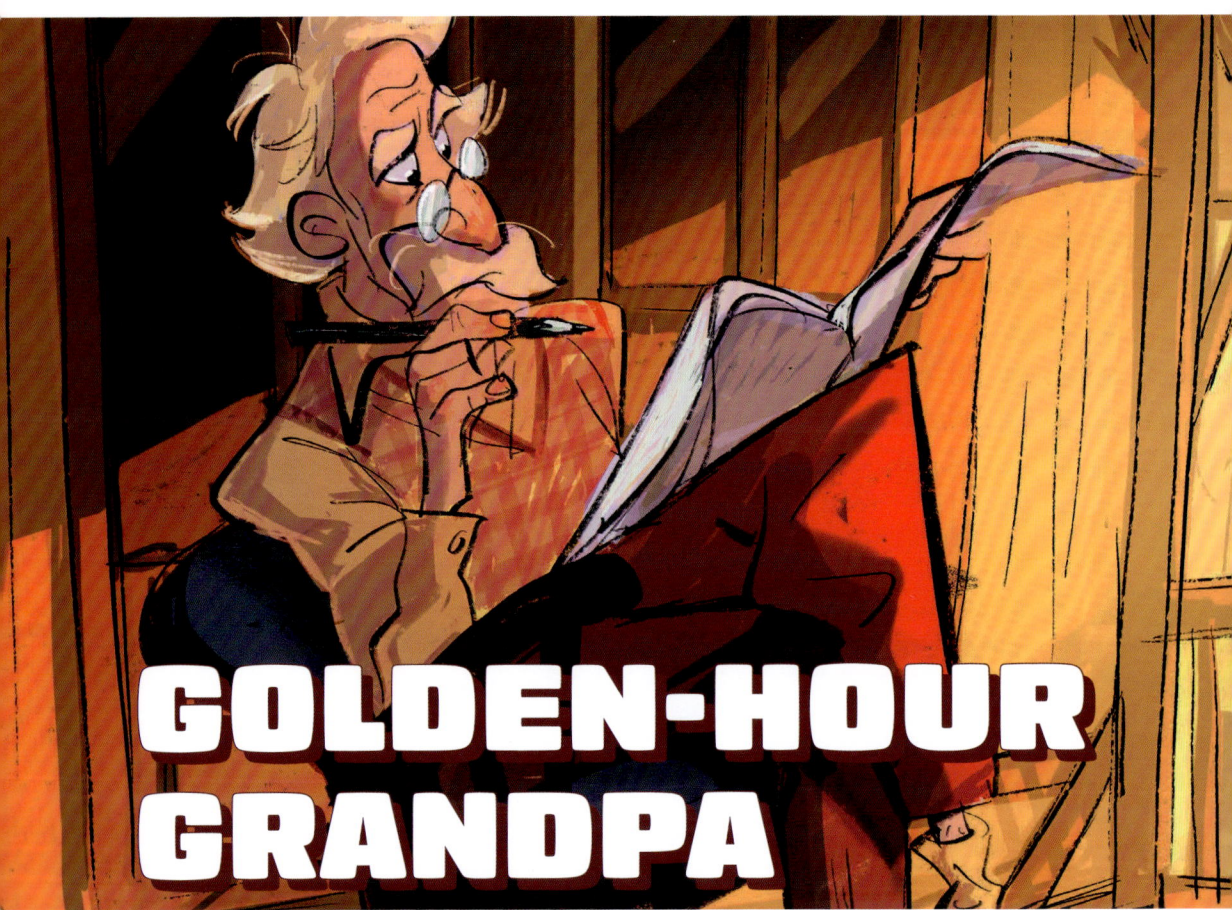

GOLDEN-HOUR GRANDPA

CHARACTER, COLOUR & LIGHTING IN A SCENE

One of the most effective ways to grow in skill as a character designer is to explore different moods, lighting set-ups, and stories within the same frame. Reworking a character or scene allows you to focus on how lighting alone can change the vibe – whether it's a warm, inviting glow or harsh, cold shadow. By keeping the concept the same, you can experiment with how light affects mood and storytelling without the distraction of changing details. It's a great way to familiarize yourself with how lighting can make a scene feel totally different, while keeping the core elements consistent.

This tutorial is created in Procreate, but you can follow along in a digital-painting software of your choice.

By Taraneh Karimi

01 DESIGN YOUR CHARACTER & SIMPLIFY THE SET-UP

Start by designing your character with just enough detail to capture their essence. Focus on creating expressions and posture that reflect their feelings, while planning for a simple lighting set-up that will let the emotions shine through. Consider the scene as a whole. Placing a character in a familiar setting can add to the vibe of the story, with space to explore different moods. At this early stage, keeping it simple will help to highlight these contrasting feelings without distraction.

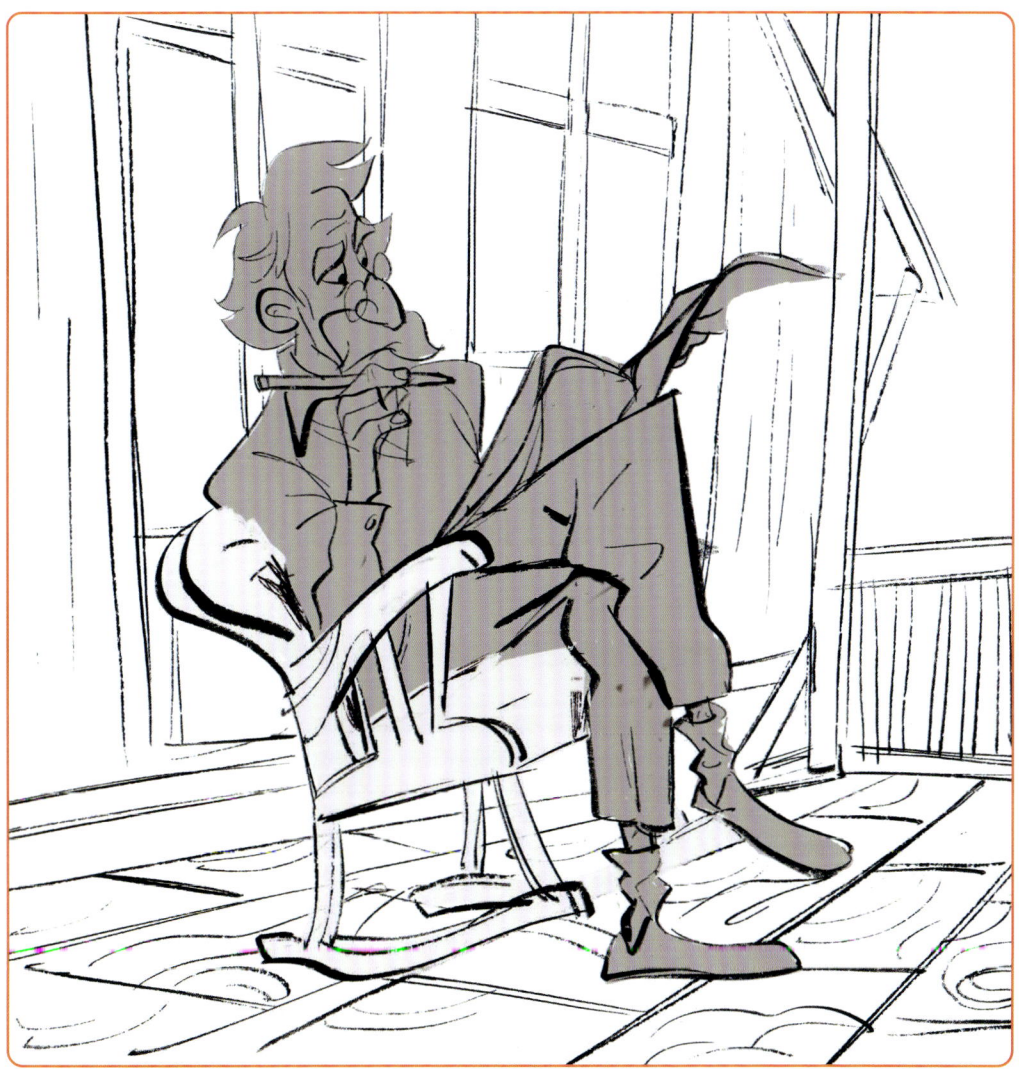

▲ Create rough, loose sketches for the initial steps – this will allow you the freedom to make changes without the fear of losing the 'perfect' look

02 ADD LOCAL COLOUR

Start adding local colour on a layer below the lines – basic, flat colours without any shading or depth. This step is about establishing the natural colours in the scene. Think about your character and setting – if your character has warmer tones and the background feels cooler, keep that contrast in mind. You want to create enough difference to separate the character from their environment, but not so much that the image feels disconnected. This base layer will provide you with a simple road map of colours to build on as you start exploring lighting and mood.

▼ To create a perfect balance between colours, try to use higher contrast and values for the areas that serve the subject and story, while keeping the rest of the image more monochromatic

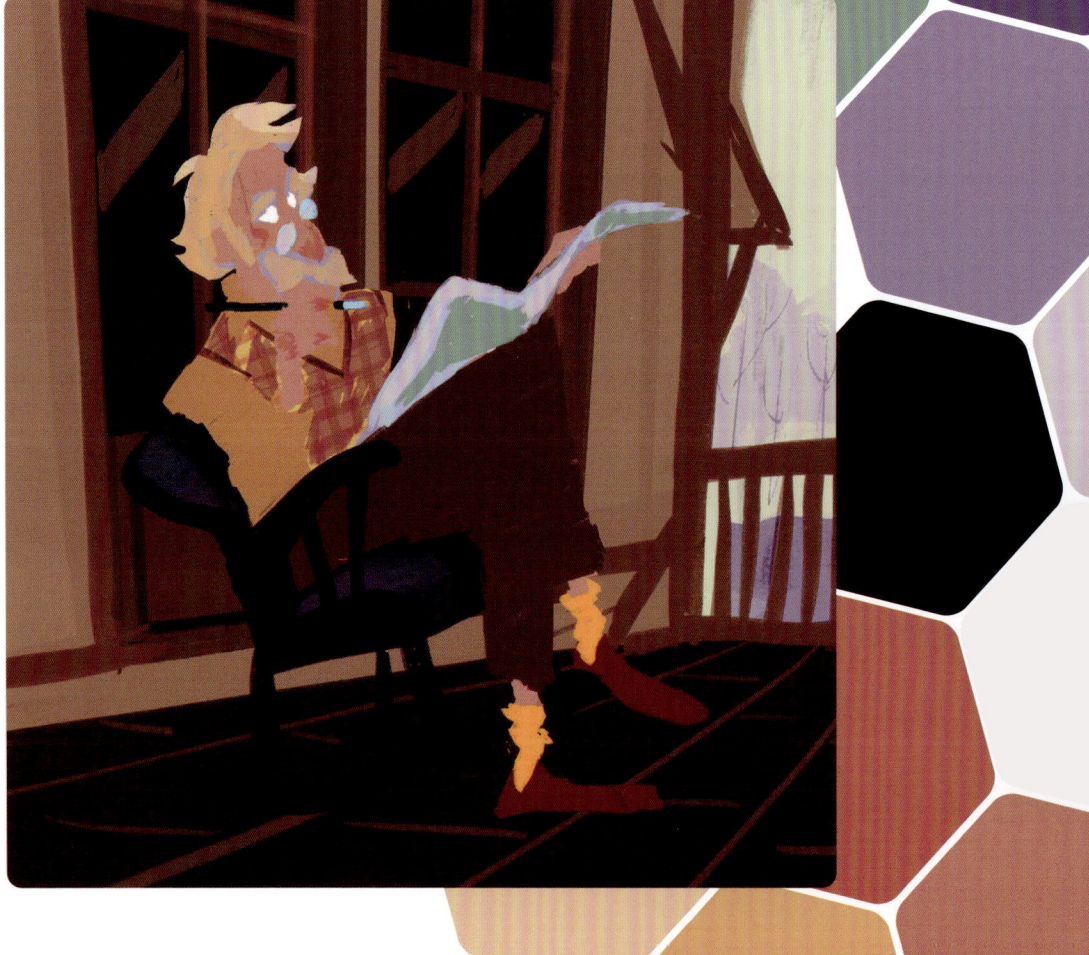

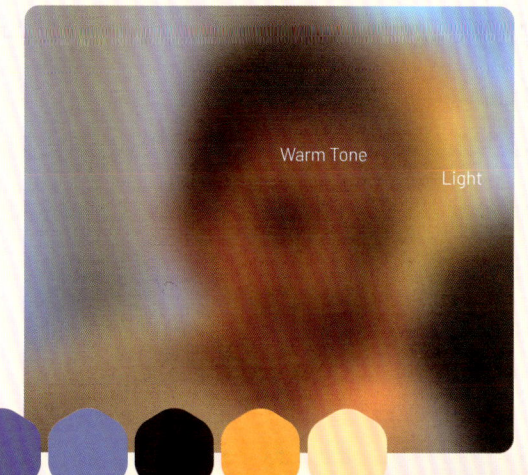

Warm Tone

Light

◀ This photo has some interesting elements that inspire the lighting set-up below; the emotion in the warm lighting directly on the subject, paired with a toned-down cold palette in the background, can give life to a character

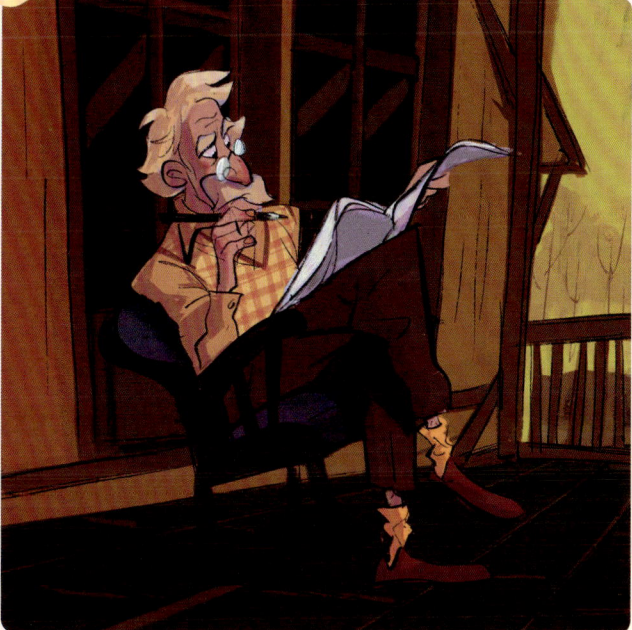

03 SET THE MOOD WITH REFERENCES

Choose a mood that best conveys the emotion you want the character design to impart. Look for references that align with your vision. These will help you to avoid guessing and keep your focus sharp. Whether you're aiming for a cosy, curious vibe or a quiet, sad tone, establishing a clear direction will make your references more effective at guiding you to create the right atmosphere.

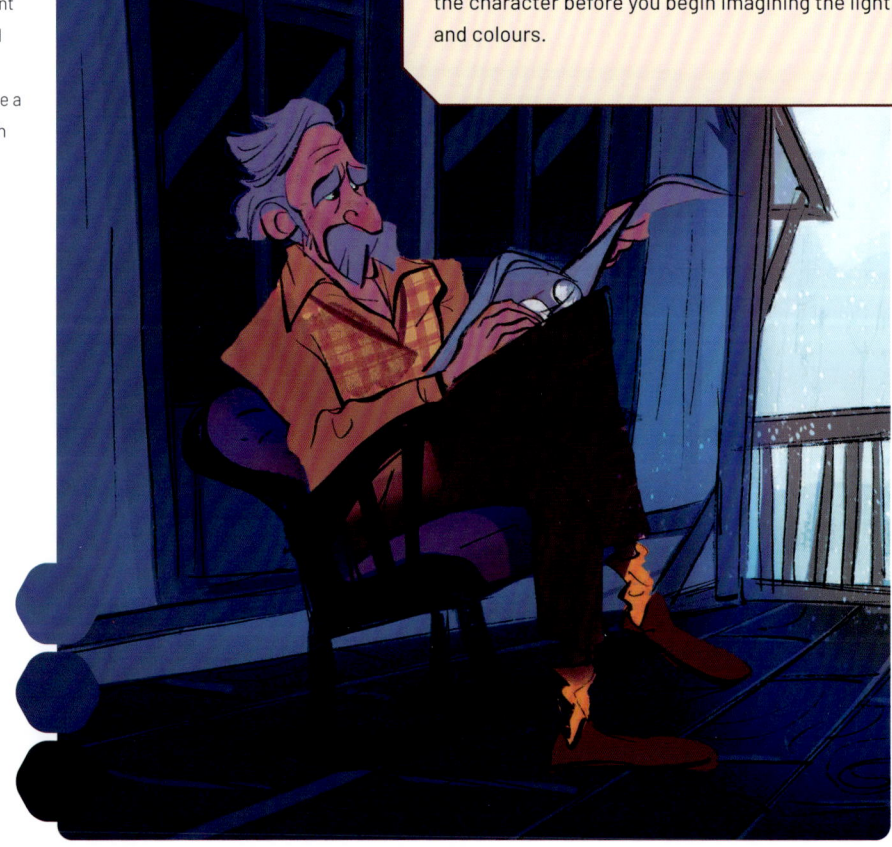

04 TWEAK THE DESIGN FOR DIFFERENT MOODS

Adjust your character and environment to reflect the different moods you're exploring. Minor tweaks, like slightly changing the pose and expression of a character, can make a big difference in conveying the desired feelings or story. Small adjustments can significantly impact how the mood is communicated.

ARTIST TIP EMOTION & MOOD

Decide the emotions you want to convey through the character before you begin imagining the light and colours.

▶ Try a different expression and mood; for example, create a sad feeling with blue lighting

05 BLENDING MODES

When it comes to colouring a scene, using layer blending modes is quick and easy, and can yield great results, especially if you're new to working with colour. Don't hesitate to use them as you refine your palette. Try laying orange brushstrokes on a new layer over your local colours. Cycle through the different blending modes available, and raise or lower the layer's opacity, until you find a warm sunset glow that you like.

▶ The fun experimental nature of blending is that you can accidentally stumble across a colour palette that makes the concept richer, replacing your original reference palette

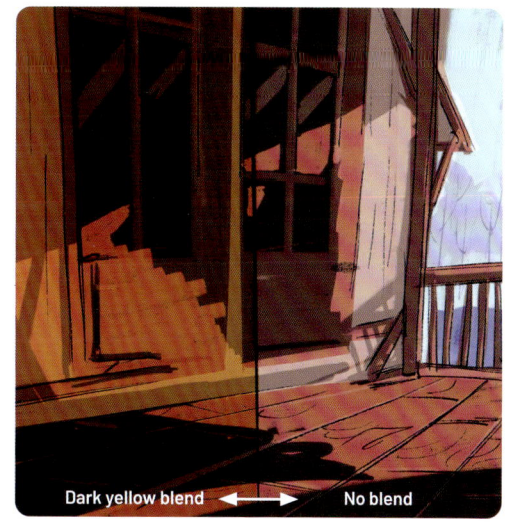

Dark yellow blend ◀——▶ No blend

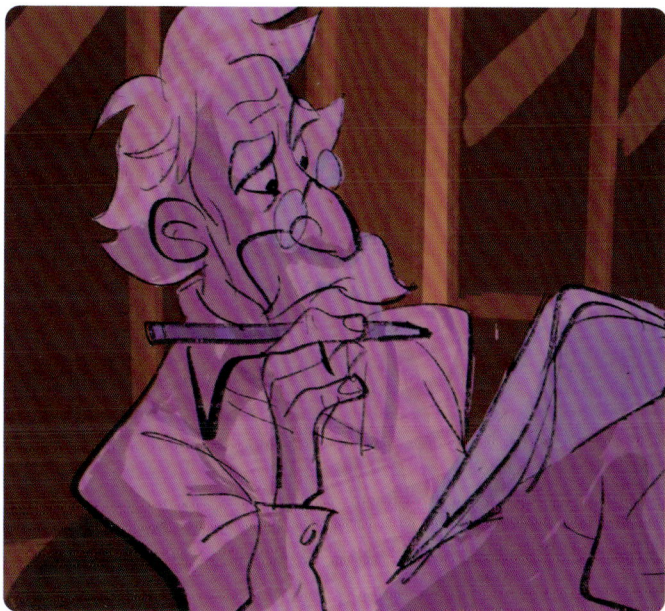

◀ Experiment with one or multiple blending layers

06 BLENDING OPTIONS

Try painting on different blending-mode layers for the background and foreground, before adding a final blended layer on top to unify the overall feel of the scene. Keep it simple and harmonious, but don't be afraid to experiment with different blends. There is no formula for which, or how many, blending options work best. And remember, this is only the first step – there's still more to refine before reaching the final look.

07 ADD SHADOWS & LIGHT

Now you've chosen your base colours and mood, it's time to add shadows and light. Start with shadows, considering the direction and number of light sources in the scene. To create a richer look, aim to use colourful shadows instead of just black and white; purple is a good complement to the warm orange light. Keeping all of your layers separate will make it easier to adjust as you go along, helping you to maintain a clear and dynamic interplay between light and shadow.

▶ For this warmly lit scene, try using purple and maroon-toned shadows, and lower the opacity to around 30% to make them blend more subtly

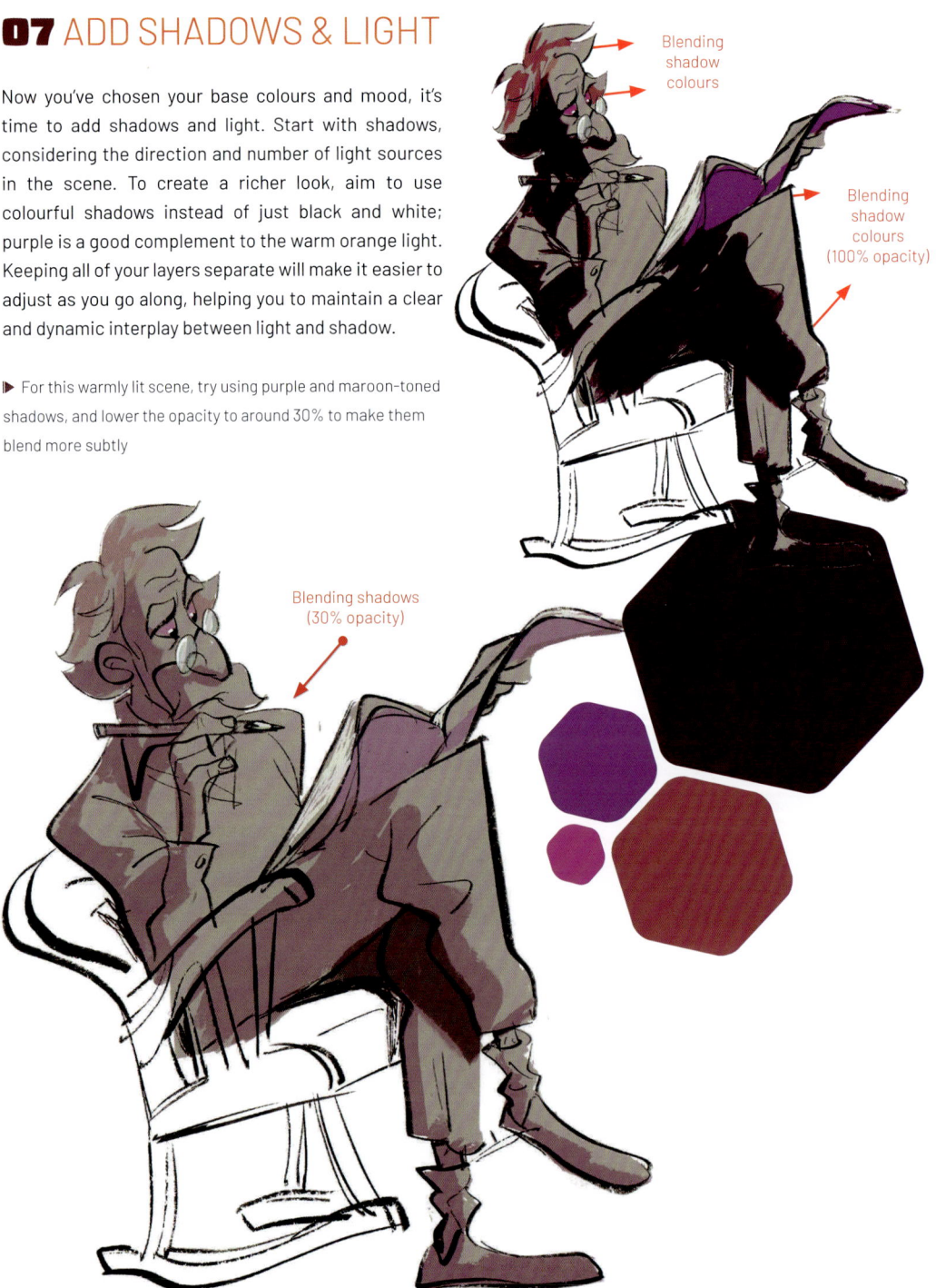

Blending shadow colours

Blending shadow colours (100% opacity)

Blending shadows (30% opacity)

08 PLAY AROUND WITH COLOURS

Now it's time to add more depth and interest by incorporating multiple light sources. Consider using a cold bounce-light colour from the background alongside a warm light from another point. This contrast can create a focal point, guiding the viewer's eye through the story. For example, in the warm version, the glass, pencil, and newspaper share the same tones, linking them as elements of the narrative. Experiment with colour relationships to enhance visual storytelling.

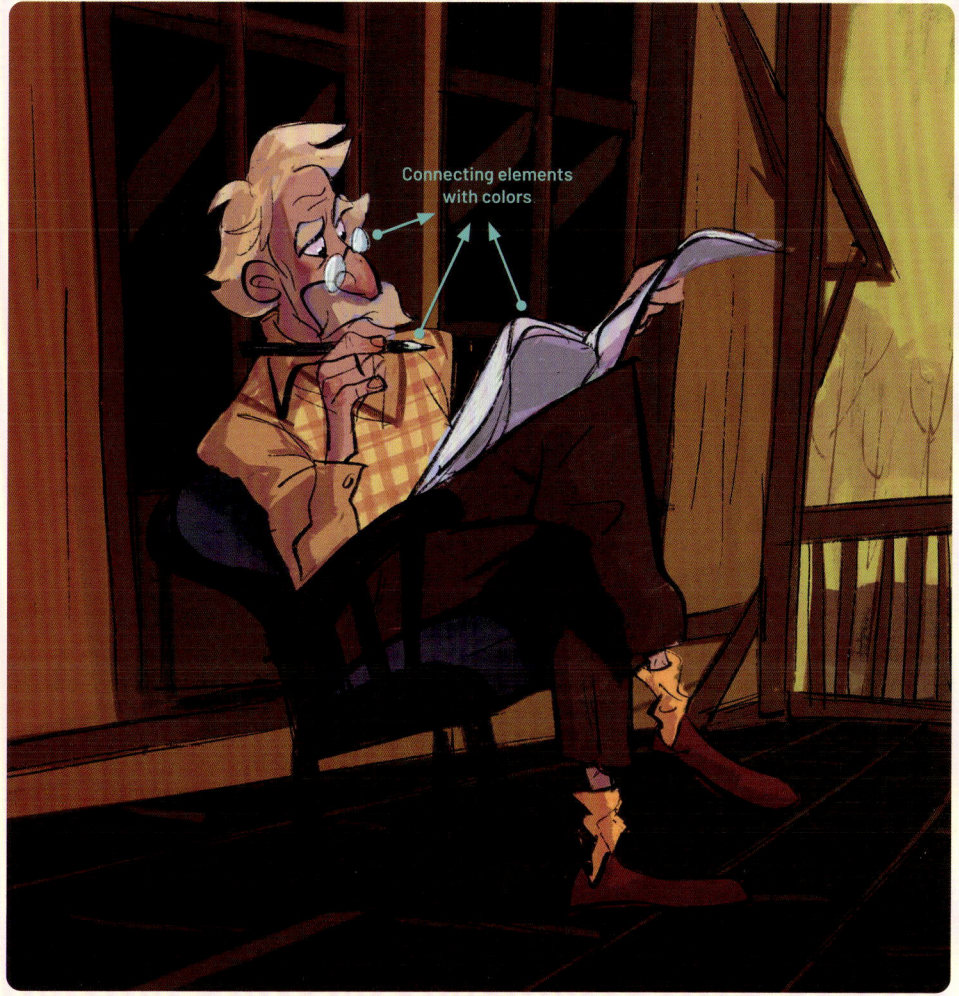

Connecting elements with colors

▲ Experiment with the use of colour to connect story elements (such as props and clothing) and guide the viewer's eye through the image

09 BLEND MODES & SATURATION

Be cautious with blend modes as they can easily lead to oversaturation, causing many colours to get lost in the process. To avoid this, consider using a soft brush to add atmospheric effects, creating extra shadow or light. This technique helps maintain clarity in both the background and foreground, while allowing for effective blending without overwhelming the scene. Balance is key to keeping your colours vibrant and harmonious.

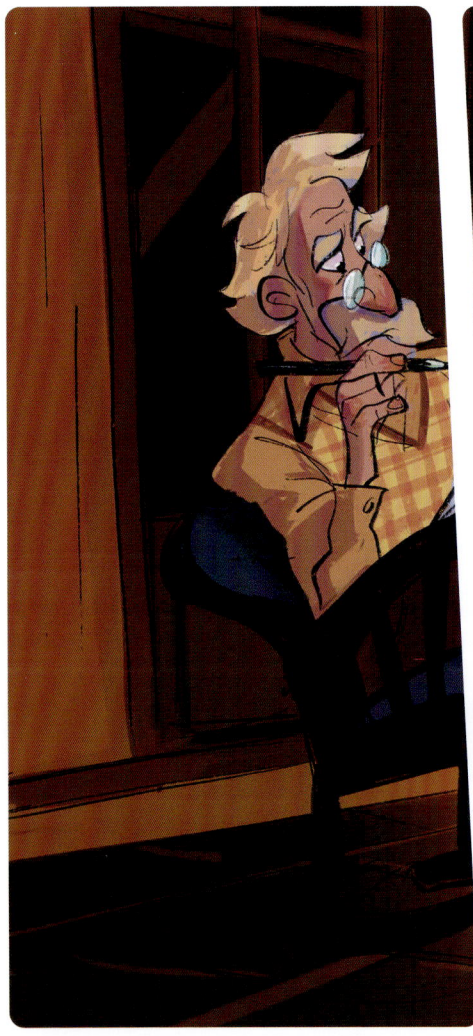 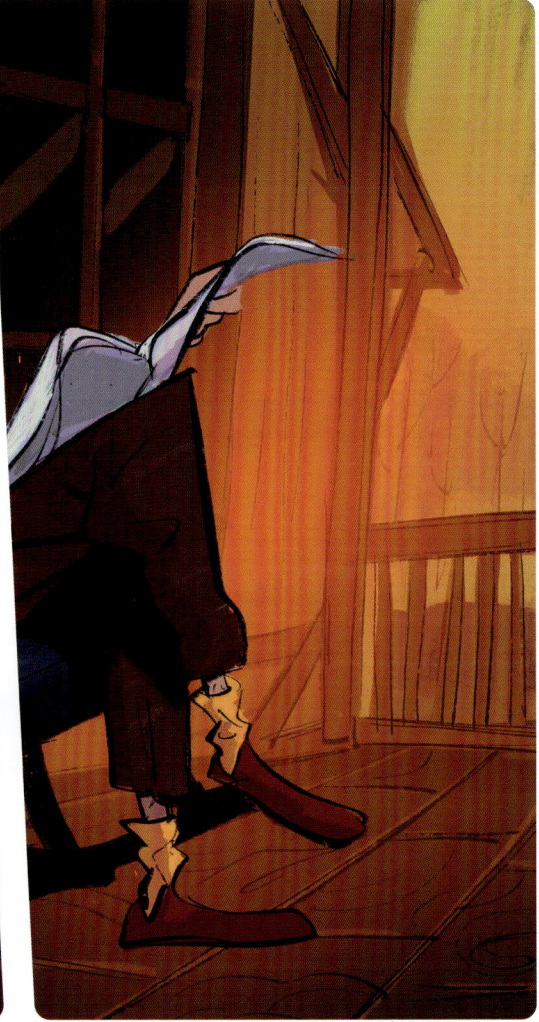

▲ It's important to have a plan before adding extra layers on top of your drawing – how you create depth on one layer may not necessarily work with another

ARTIST TIP BRUSH TEXTURES

Using different brush textures when painting in lighting will give your artwork a unique and expressive feel. Adding texture to shadows or rim lights can create depth and emotion, turning simple details into powerful storytelling elements. Even a bit of roughness can make the overall look more dynamic and engaging.

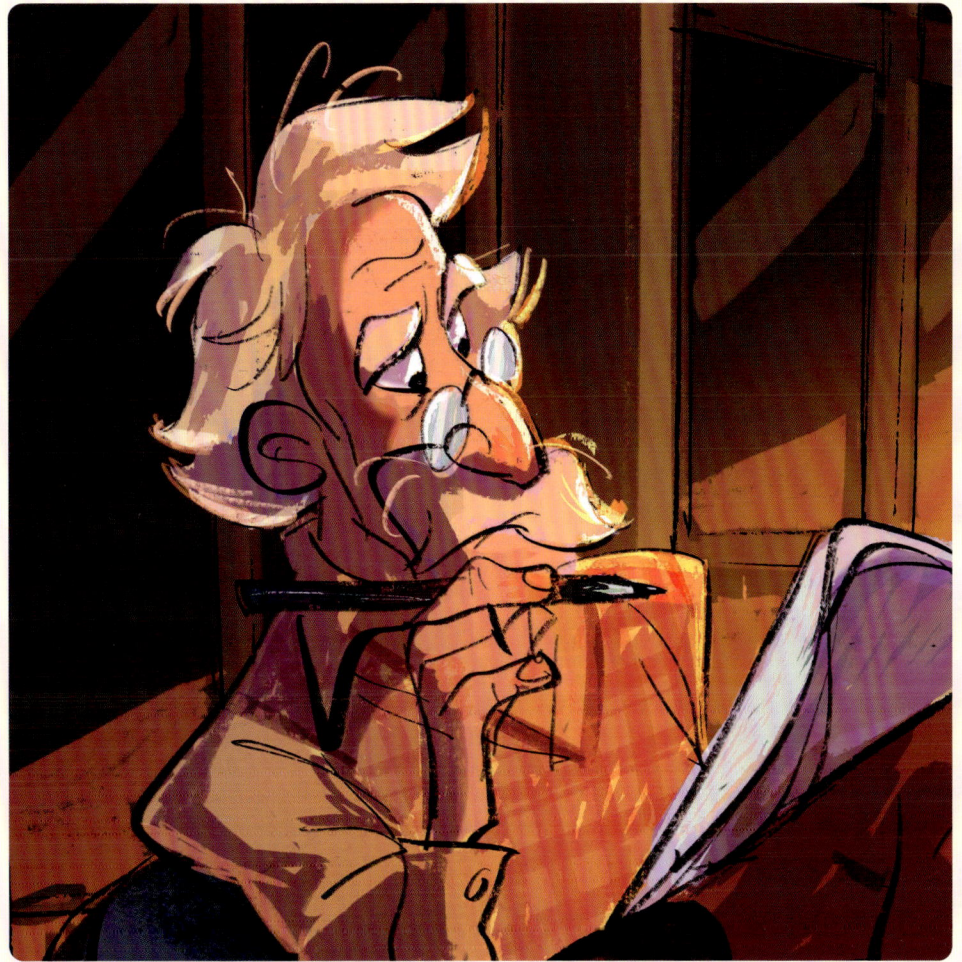

▲ Here a sharp white rim light is added to the character using a textured brush, creating a focal point and contrast with the smoother elements in the rest of the image

10 EXPERIMENT WITH DIFFERENT COLOUR SETTINGS

Try out various colour settings to see how they affect the mood and storytelling. In this example, a flatter lighting approach is used on the blue version, while the warm version features more dramatic, playful lighting. This contrast not only makes it more enjoyable to compare the two, but also enhances your learning experience. Each colour setting provides unique insights into how lighting influences the narrative, so don't hesitate to experiment and discover what works best for the story you're trying to tell.

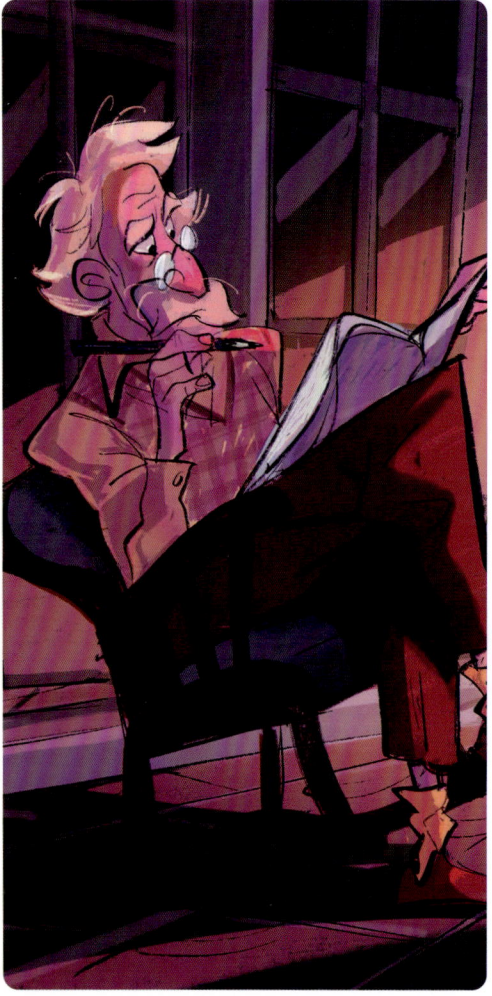 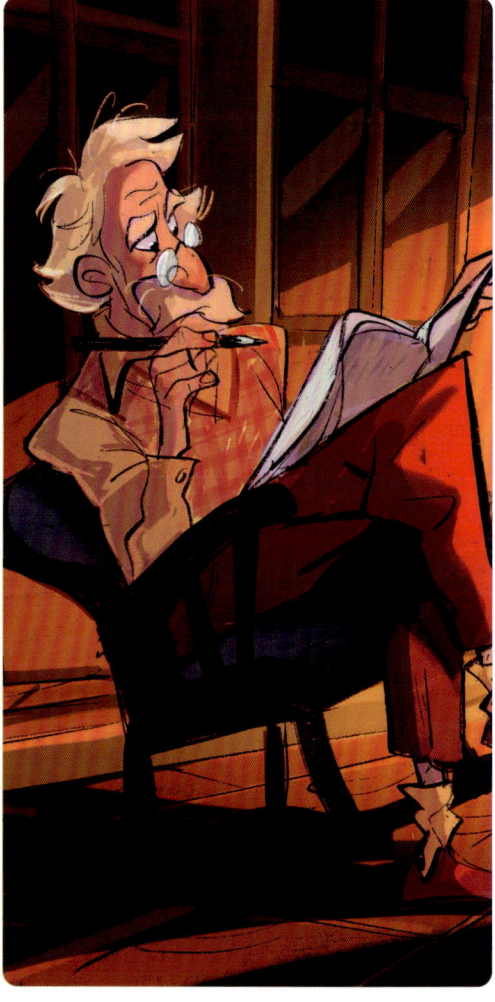

▲ While any changes at this stage are relatively minor, they are still important – introducing an extra layer of light or shade can make an image appear drastically different

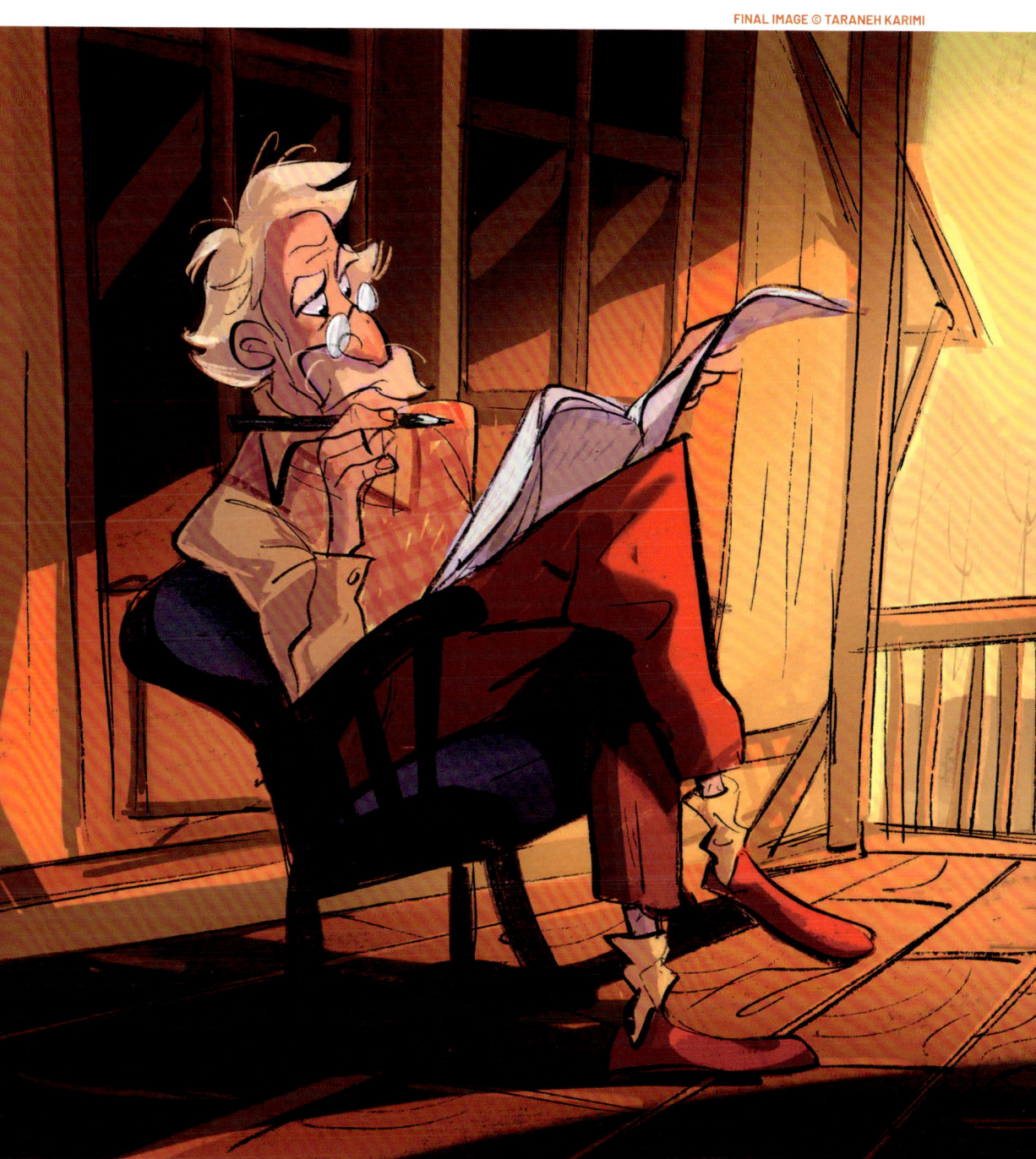

▲ With the use of blending modes, the final scene is rich with atmospheric colour and light

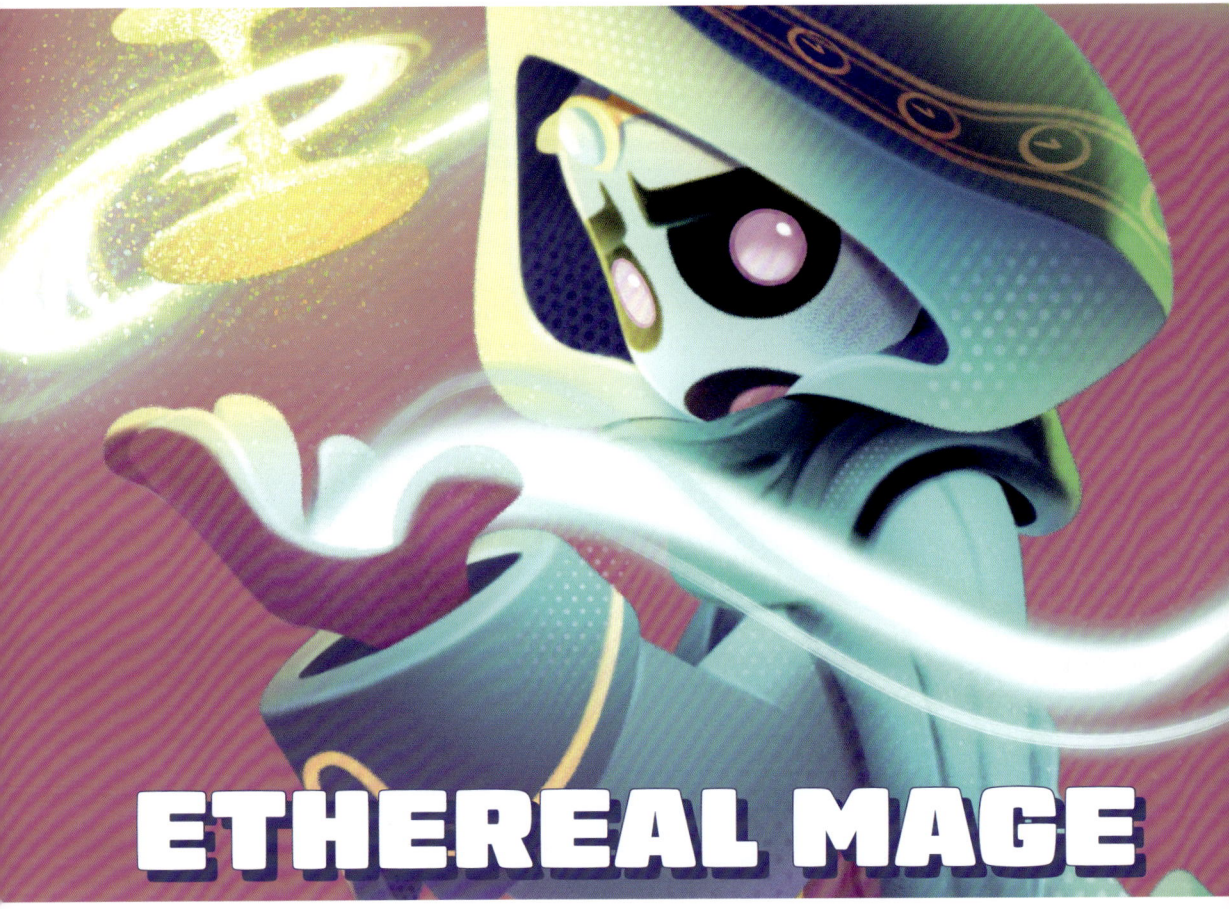

ETHEREAL MAGE

USING LIGHT WITHIN A CHARACTER DESIGN

Introducing visually interesting lighting techniques is a great way to take a character design to the next level. This tutorial will teach you how to design a character from scratch, incorporating light as an integral part of the design. The following pages will explore the use of storytelling, silhouettes, lighting, and texture to create a balanced and dynamic concept. From brainstorming ideas to finalizing the piece, you will learn how to integrate light into your design so it enhances the character without overwhelming the composition.

This artwork is created using Procreate, but you can follow along in your preferred choice of software.

By Isabella Agosti

01 BRAINSTORM THE CONCEPT

Begin by thinking about your character's story and their connection to light. Is the light a physical object, magical effect, or part of their anatomy? Consider their role and background. Are they a mage manipulating light, or an archer wielding a bow with glowing arrows? Jot down ideas and arrange them into a coherent structure. Next, choose your favourite concept and expand it with more details to refine and inspire the design further.

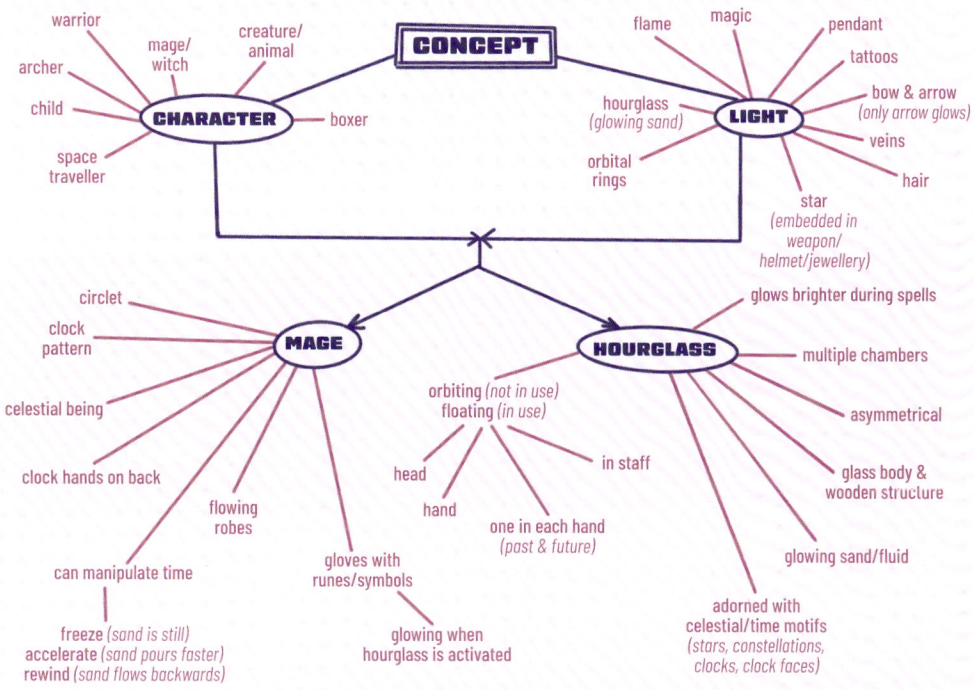

▲ A mind map exploring the theme of light as a character's core aesthetic

ARTIST TIP RESEARCH

Research plays a crucial role in character design. After creating your mind map, gather reference images that align with your idea. Create a vision board to inspire your design, from clothing styles to lighting effects to colour palettes. By exploring different sources, you can enrich your design and ensure it is grounded in reality, making your character more compelling and believable.

02 EXPERIMENT WITH SILHOUETTES

Create a series of rough silhouettes focusing on the character's overall shape and composition. A strong, clear silhouette will ensure your design is recognizable at a glance, even without colour or detail. If your light element is an object, use this step to explore silhouettes and shapes for that as well. Start thinking about how the light element could integrate into the character's silhouette, ensuring it complements the overall form.

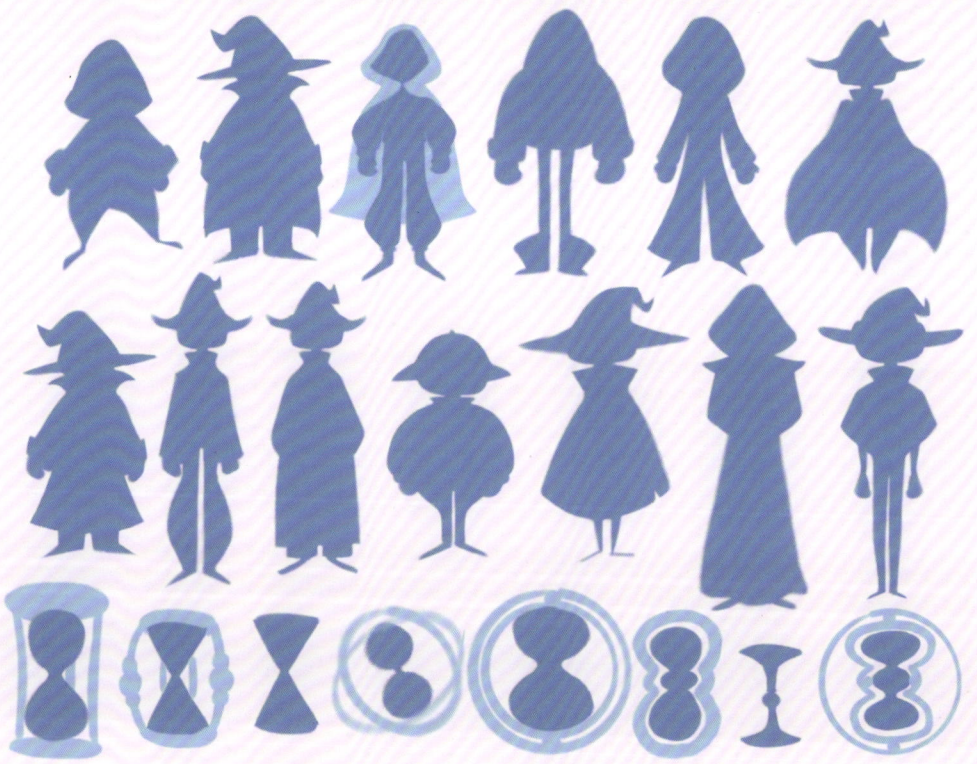

▲ Rough silhouettes exploring various shapes for both character and light element

03 THUMBNAIL SKETCHES

Using your silhouettes as a foundation, create a few thumbnail sketches to explore details, clothing, and accessories. Keep these sketches loose and rough to encourage experimentation and emphasize storytelling potential. Once you've developed a variety of ideas, select the most promising thumbnails and combine their strongest elements. Mix and match features to refine your design and create a more interesting and engaging character concept.

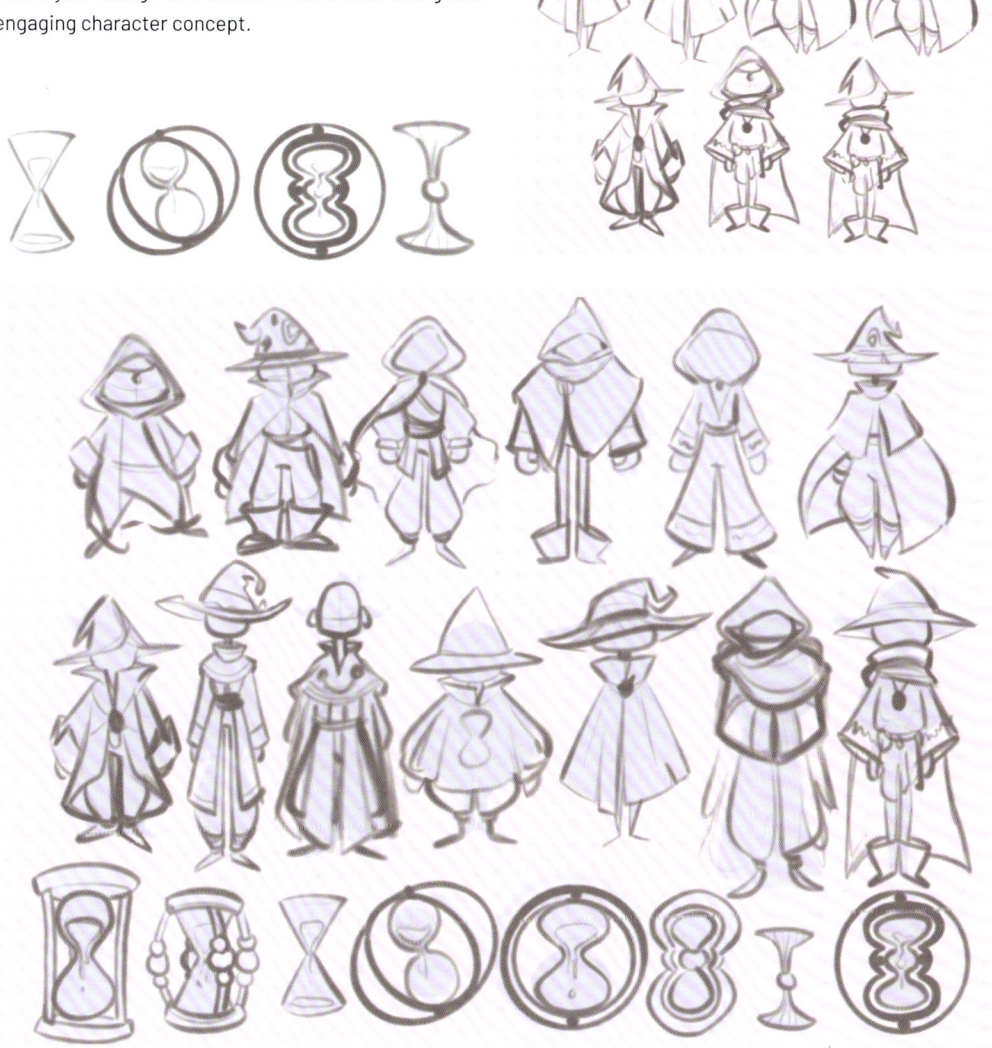

▲ Thumbnail concepts showcasing different ideas for the character and light element

04 REFINE THE VISION

Select a rough sketch to move forward with, then explore the design further. Add details, if necessary, and experiment with different facial features to give the character more personality and depth, considering how their expression and appearance tie into the story. Additionally, sketch out a clearer idea for the placement and integration of the light object, ensuring it feels natural and enhances the overall composition.

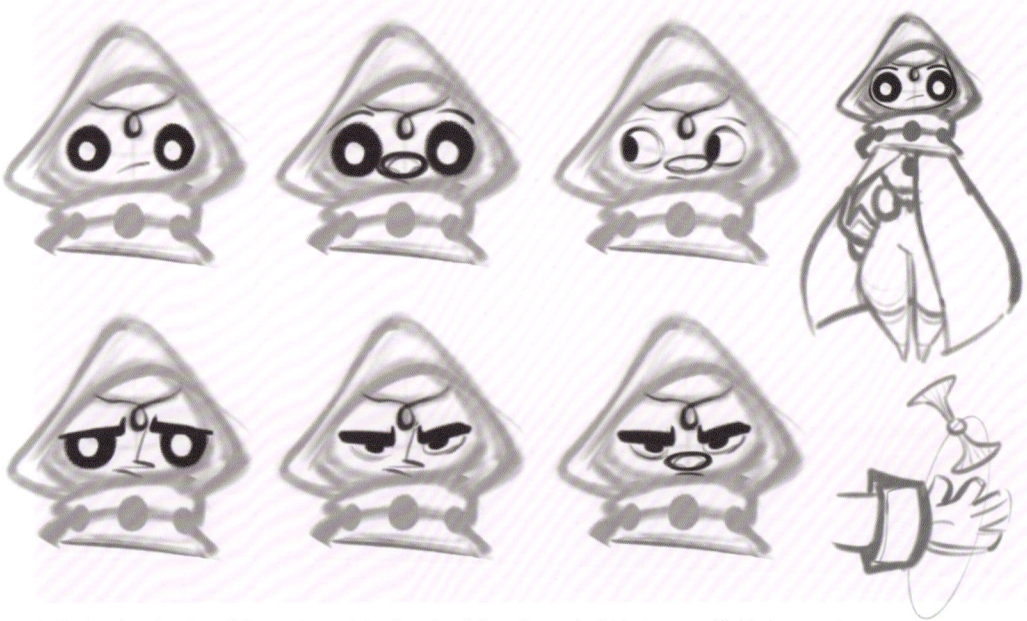

▲ Exploration sketches of the most promising thumbnail, focusing on facial features and light placement

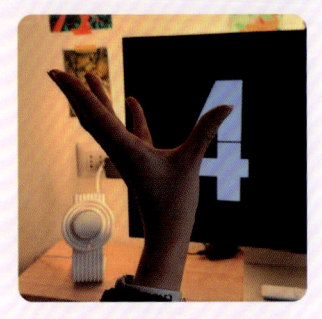

ARTIST TIP USE YOURSELF AS REFERENCE

When it comes to drawing tricky poses, expressions, or even hands, use a mirror or take photos to study how your own body moves and expresses emotion. This can help you to capture more realistic and dynamic poses, as well as understand how light interacts with different angles and surfaces.

0️⃣5️⃣ EXPLORING POSES

Explore potential poses for your character. Sketch simple stick figures to explore different actions and stances, then use the chosen design from the previous step as a reference to refine them. Focus on creating a sense of flow and movement to make the design more engaging and visually appealing. Don't forget to include the light element – magic hourglasses – and experiment with how it interacts with the pose to ensure it feels natural and enhances the design.

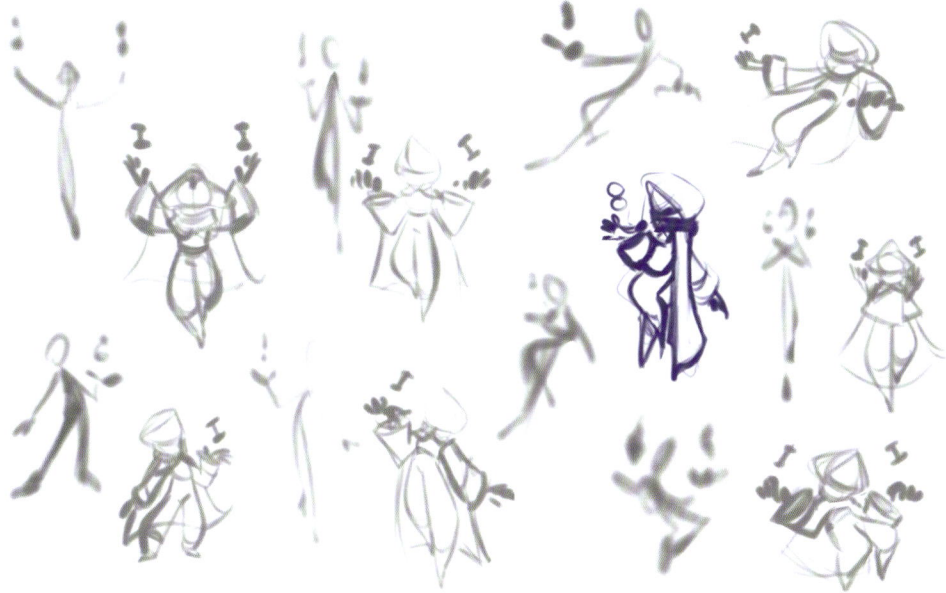

▲ Rough figure sketches showing dynamic poses, emphasizing flow and interaction with the light element

0️⃣6️⃣ FINALIZE THE POSE

Choose the pose that best captures dynamic movement and storytelling potential. Next, refine its line work and key elements while making sure the light-source object is well integrated with the design. Focus on achieving balance – let the light element enhance the character without overpowering the overall composition to avoid distracting the viewer from the focal point (in this case, the character's face).

▶ Final polished sketch of the chosen concept, depicting the character in a dynamic pose

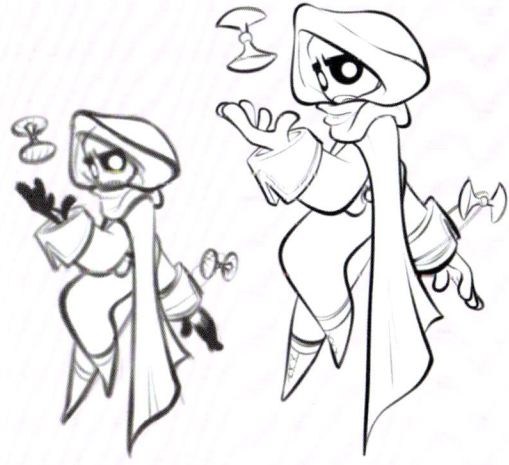

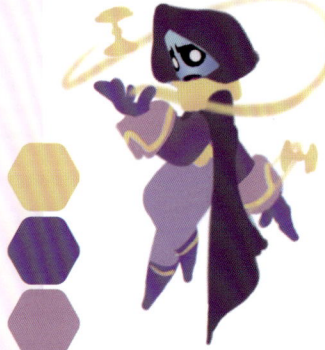

07 COLOUR PALETTE EXPLORATION

Create a few different colour palettes with the light source as a supporting element to enhance the focal point. Use complementary colours to create contrast between the character and the light. For example, pairing yellow with purple or orange with teal. This contrast will help draw attention to the focal point, while the light element subtly guides the viewer's eye towards it. Experiment with different combinations, then select the most visually appealing one with which to move forward.

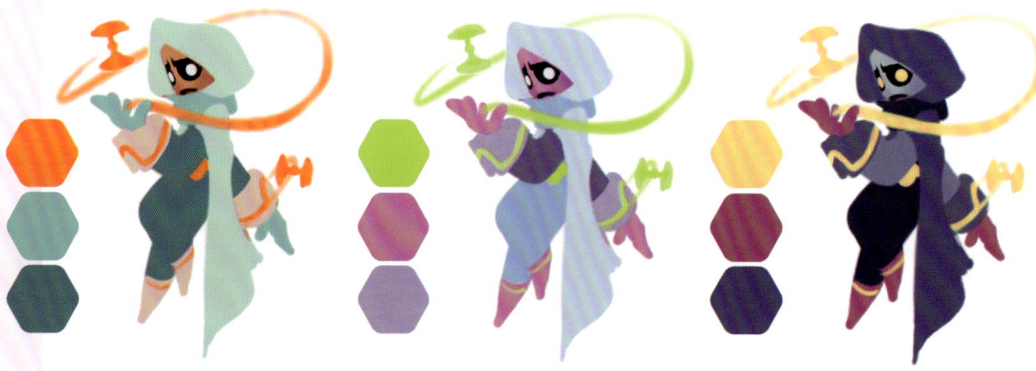

▲ Swatches of colour palettes focused on creating contrast between the character and light element

ARTIST TIP CONTRAST TO EMPHASIZE THE FOCAL POINT

Maximize contrast in the focal point to guide the viewer's eyes towards it and prevent them from getting lost in less important areas. Contrast can be achieved using various techniques, such as pairing dark and light values, complementary colours, low and high saturation, detailed and empty areas, and differing patterns.

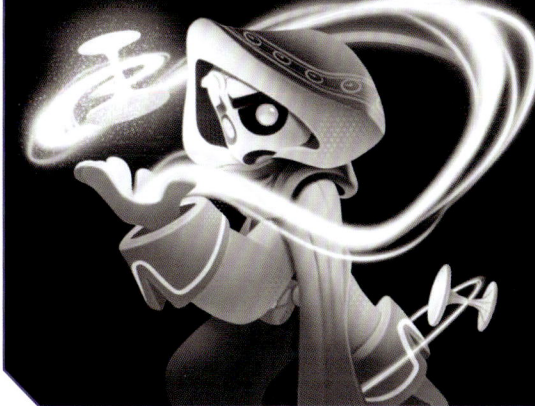

ARTIST TIP **TEST YOUR DESIGN IN GREYSCALE**

Remember to periodically test your design in greyscale to ensure the focal point remains the area of highest contrast, and the light source is properly emphasized without disrupting the overall balance. To do this, add a new layer above all others, fill it with black, and change its blending mode to Colour.

08 BLOCK IN THE COLOURS

Using the chosen palette as a guide, block in the local colours – those that define how the design would appear without any light – for both character and light elements. At this point, adjusting the line art colour to match the palette might be helpful to further unify the design. Colour each element on a different layer to maintain clarity and separation. This step establishes a solid foundation for the lighting and rendering process, making it easier to build depth and dimension in the following stages.

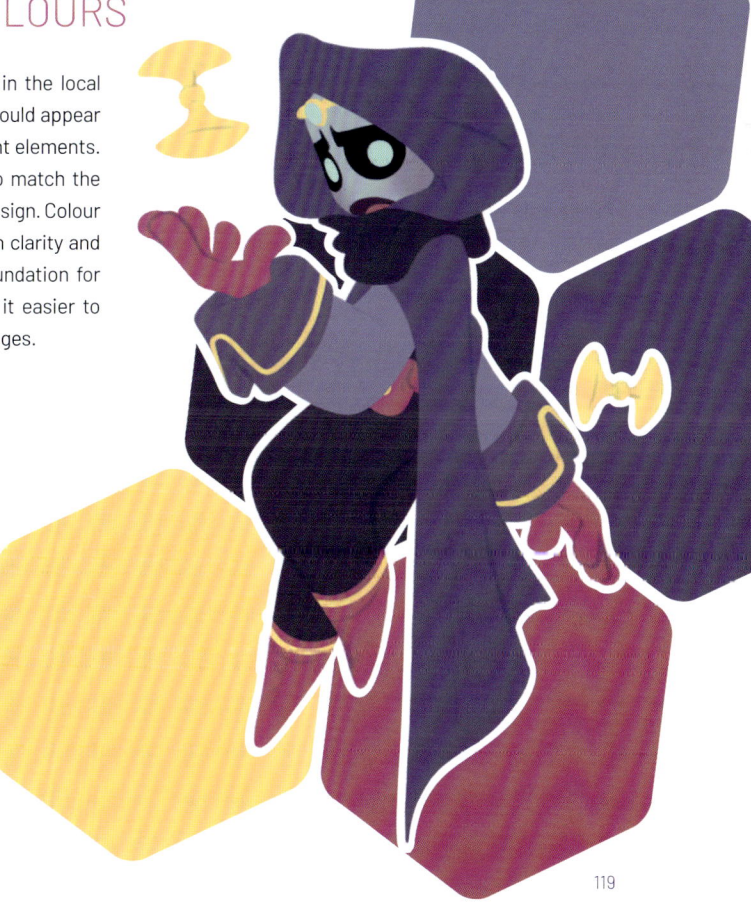

▶ Local colours mapped across the design, separating different elements and setting up a strong base

09 INTRODUCE LIGHTING

Now you can further define your light source's behaviour and effect. Add shadows on a Multiply layer, focusing on increasing contrast in the focal point while making sure the shadows fall realistically based on the light source. Next, decide on the intensity of the glow and how it affects the character. It should be bright enough to stand out, but not be overwhelming. Finally, consider the environment and how it might bounce light back onto the character to create more depth.

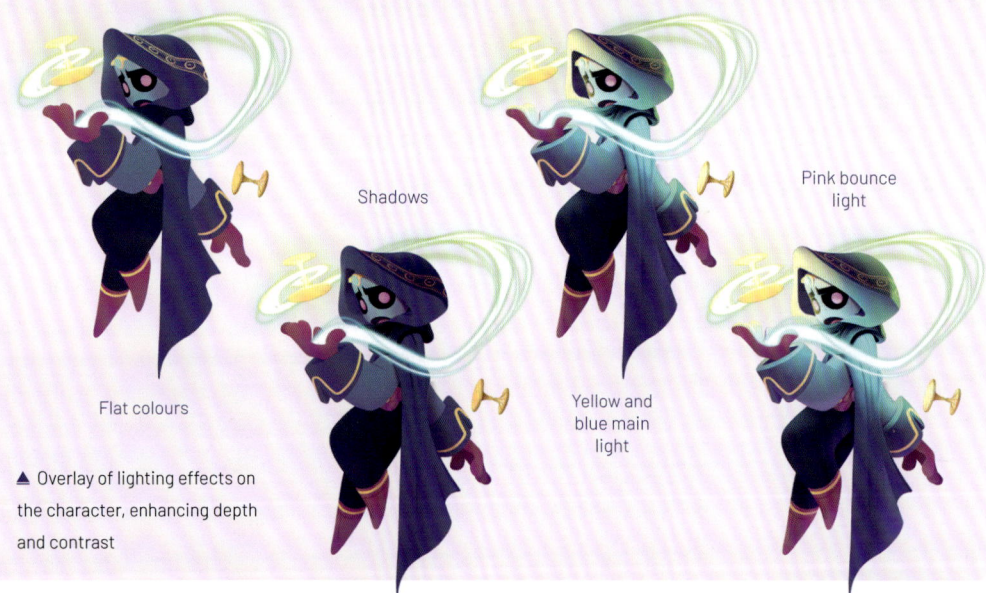

Shadows

Pink bounce light

Flat colours

Yellow and blue main light

▲ Overlay of lighting effects on the character, enhancing depth and contrast

10 FINAL TOUCHES & ADJUSTMENTS

Step back and evaluate the piece. Enhance the design by refining any weak areas, then add subtle elements – such as patterns and textures – to guide the viewer's eye towards the focal point. Adjust the intensity of the light if needed, then apply final colour adjustments – using tools like Colour Balance, Curves, Chromatic Aberration, and Noise – to enhance the visual appeal and ensure the design feels cohesive.

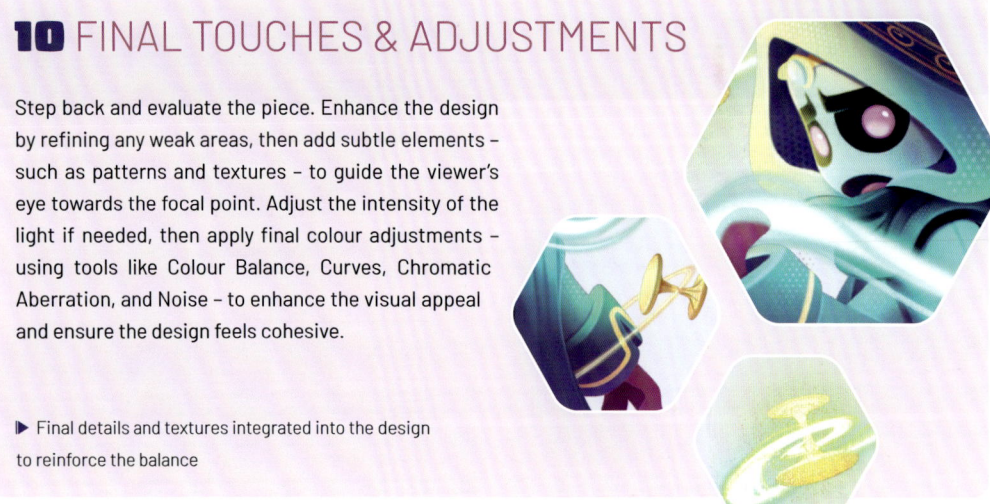

▶ Final details and textures integrated into the design to reinforce the balance

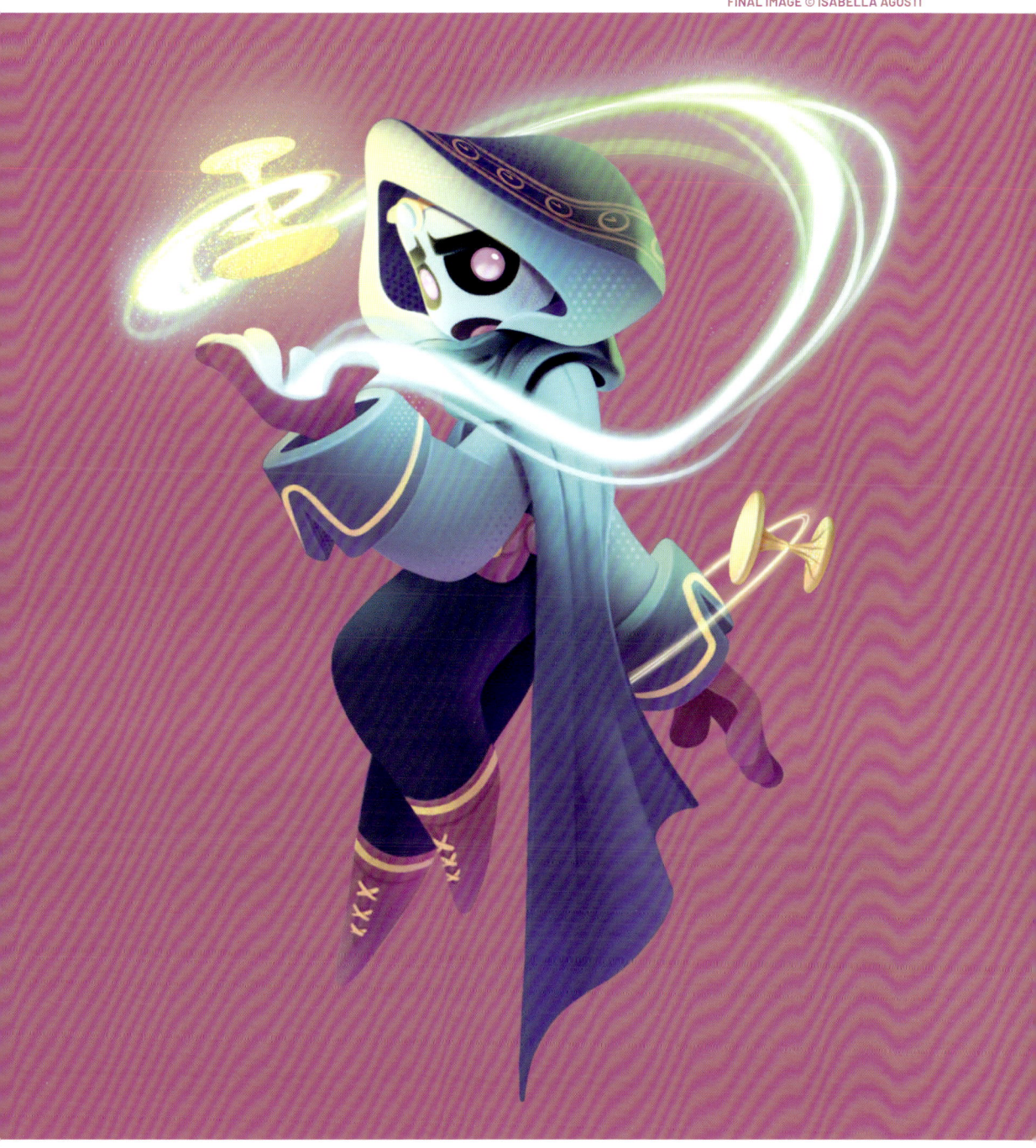

▲ A time-manipulating mage holding their glowing magical hourglasses

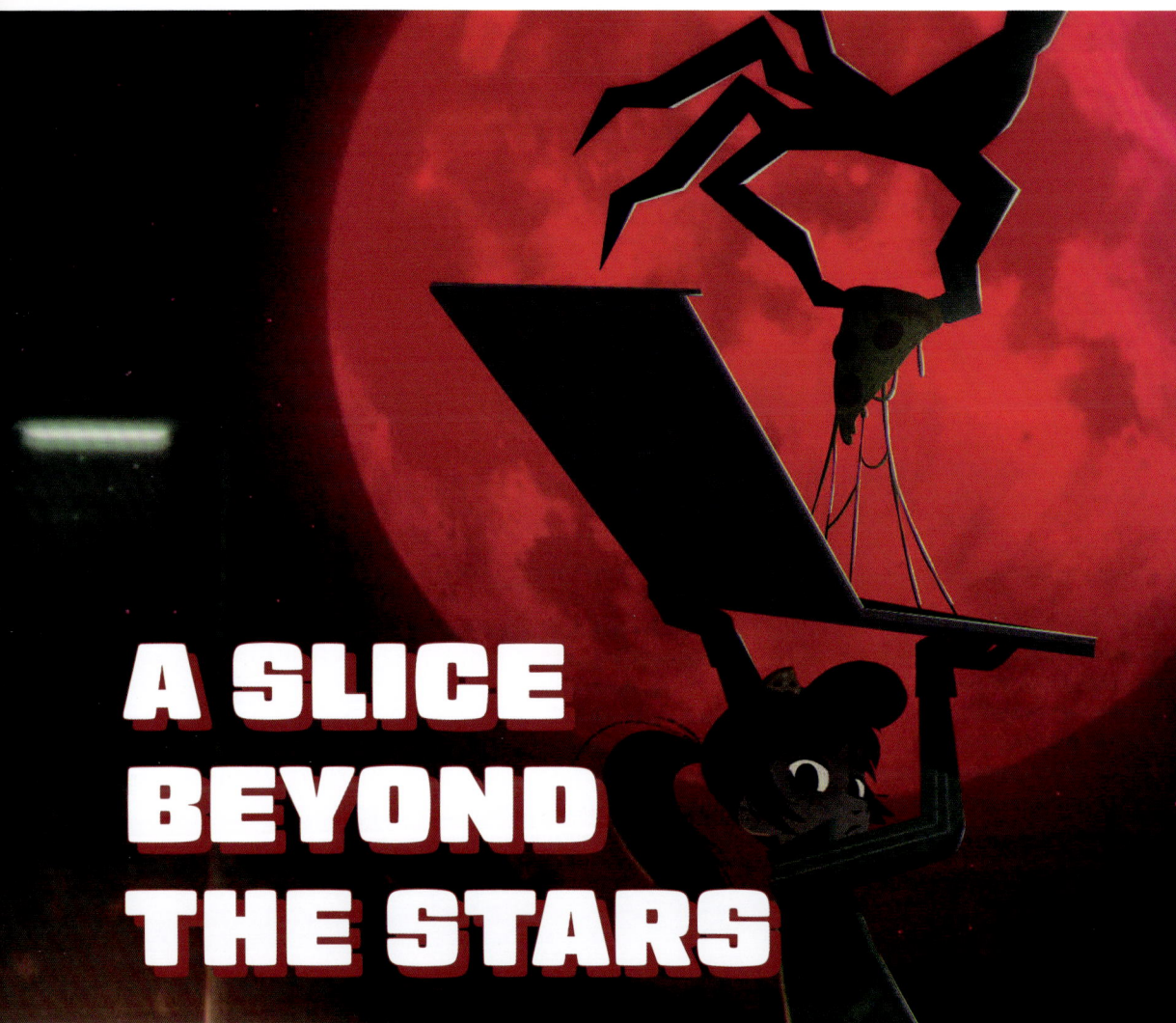

A SLICE BEYOND THE STARS

TELLING A CHARACTER STORY WITH LIGHTING

This tutorial will walk you through how to create a character in an environment with a dark, spooky vibe. Broken into simple steps, it will show you how to use shadow and light to tell the story and produce an eerie mood. With these techniques, you can make any character design atmospheric.

The tutorial is created in Photoshop using basic tools, along with a few optional extras. Keeping it simple and flexible allows your ideas to evolve as you work.

By Teo Skaffa

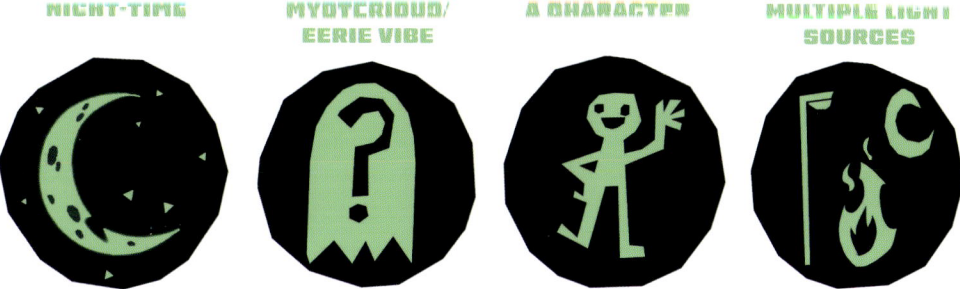

NIGHT-TIME   MYSTERIOUS/ EERIE VIBE   A CHARACTER   MULTIPLE LIGHT SOURCES

01 UNDERSTAND THE BRIEF

The goal is to create a mysterious character, using spooky light and shade to convey their story. Let the following guidelines be a springboard for your imagination; ingredients you can use to shape the drawing. Placing monsters in a fantasy setting is somewhat predictable. After all, a spooky castle crawling with ghouls and ghosts is expected. But a ghost waiting at a bus stop, or a couple of vampires out shopping, can give an illustration a unique and memorable twist.

Before you put digital pencil to digital paper, spend some time figuring out the key elements of the character and scene you wish to create. Illustration is all about storytelling, so deciding what to draw is already half the battle won.

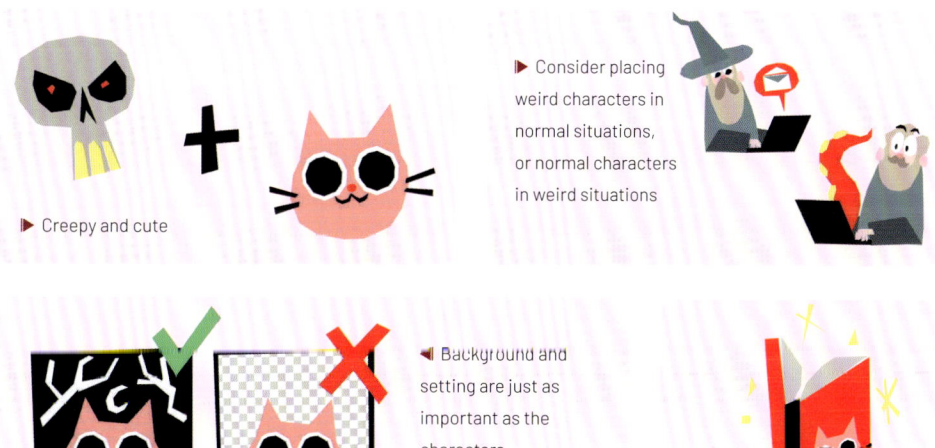

▶ Creepy and cute

▶ Consider placing weird characters in normal situations, or normal characters in weird situations

◀ Background and setting are just as important as the characters the characters need to inhabit their environment

▲ Tell a story

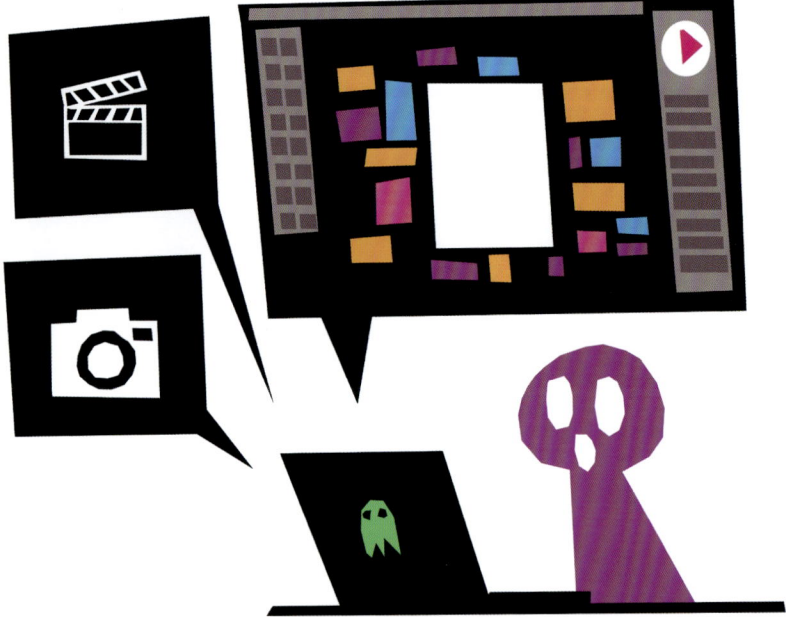

▲ Create a mood board of ideas

02 GET INSPIRED

Coming up with ideas can be the most time-intensive part of making an illustration. Create a mood board of the kinds of characters, lighting scenarios, and settings that would meet the brief. Open a blank canvas in Photoshop and line the margins with images that speak to you. You may find that you like the lighting or reflections in a certain photo, even though it has nothing to do with your subject matter.

Look up photos of car parks at night. A slightly strange character in a deserted car park immediately speaks to the imagination... Why are they there? What are they doing? Where did that monster come from?! There is potential for multiple light sources: street lights, a shopfront in the background, and lights from cars in the distance.

ARTIST TIP REFERENCE IMAGERY

Look up eerie lighting set-ups in movie scenes and photographs. They contain lots of valuable information, such as lighting, composition, mood, and how the lens used affects the overall look of the image.

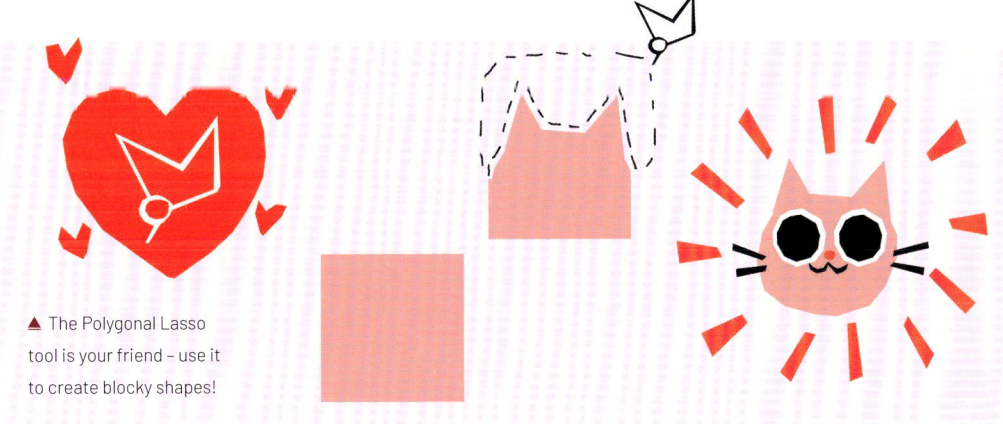

▲ The Polygonal Lasso tool is your friend – use it to create blocky shapes!

03 FIRST DRAFT

Once you've gathered a sufficient number of ideas, begin to compose a first draft of an eerie car park at night. Start with the placement of the main light sources: the street lights. How bright they are and how many there are, as well as the height or angle they're placed at, will determine the mood of the entire scene. Add a metal fence for light to bounce off, plus a car as another potential light source. These details immediately determine the modern-day setting and allow for further light sources to be introduced.

Think in shapes and don't get distracted by details. You're not at the actual drawing stage yet, but simply exploring ideas. Use the Polygonal Lasso tool to quickly block out the main shapes, drawing simple blocky lines for the lamp posts. Next, think about colour and atmosphere. The background can be just as much a character as the actual character. Don't worry about exact shapes or details just yet – try to focus on the mood instead.

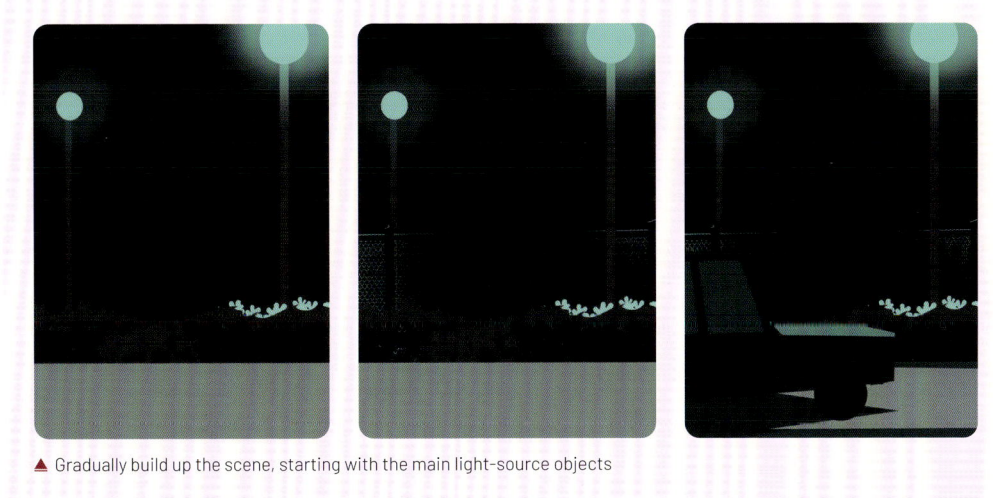

▲ Gradually build up the scene, starting with the main light-source objects

125

04 COMPOSITION

Introduce a rough idea of character placement. Consider the story you're trying to tell and the action you want the character to perform. Keep this very loose – vaguely humanoid-shaped figures are all that's needed.

Next, review the compositions and choose one to take forward. The sixth composition depicts the character standing on top of the car, looking at something off-screen, which adds an element of intrigue and suspense.

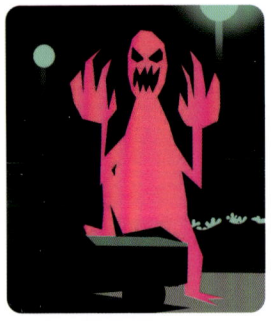
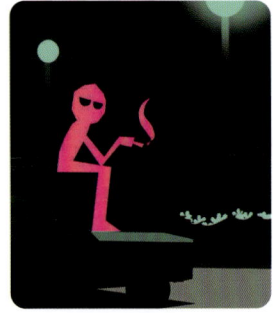
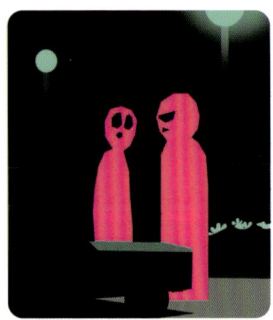
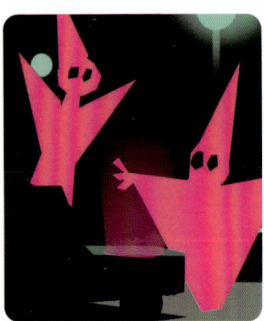
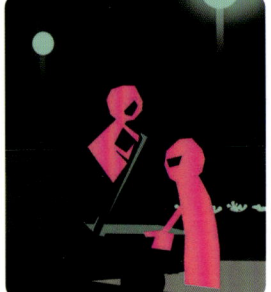
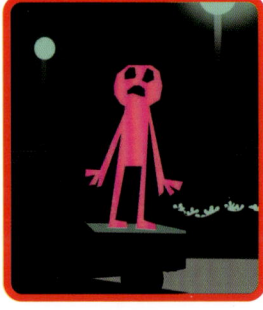

◀ Choose the most compelling composition with which to continue

05 DEVELOP THE STORY

The character will be a pizza-delivery driver, standing on top of the car to feed pizza to an off-screen monster in some kind of ritualistic offering. This gives the character a reason to stand on the car's bonnet and allows the viewer a sneak peek at what the character is looking up at. Loosely block in these elements, then paint a blood-red moon in the background to enhance the creepy mood. Introduce an extra light source coming from the car – this will create some eerie reflecting light on the lower part of the character.

▶ Add in details as you develop the story, always considering how lighting could add to the atmosphere

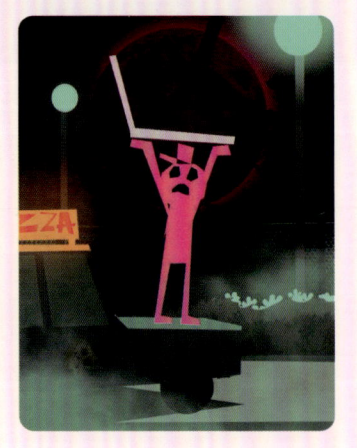

06 CHARACTER DESIGN

Loosely rough-in the pizza-delivery girl character. Create a general idea of her pose and size in relation to the background, then block in the base colours. Once you're happy with the character, place her into the background to review the design.

There are two colour tests below. Notice how the red outfit doesn't really work with the environment, as it gets lost in the red moon behind. The green cap and jacket strike a better contrast against the moon. The colours of her uniform – red, green, and white – are also those of the Italian flag, which ties in nicely with the pizza theme.

Paint in rough, blocky light to show the reflection from the car. It doesn't need to be pixel-perfect – shapes and details can be changed in later steps.

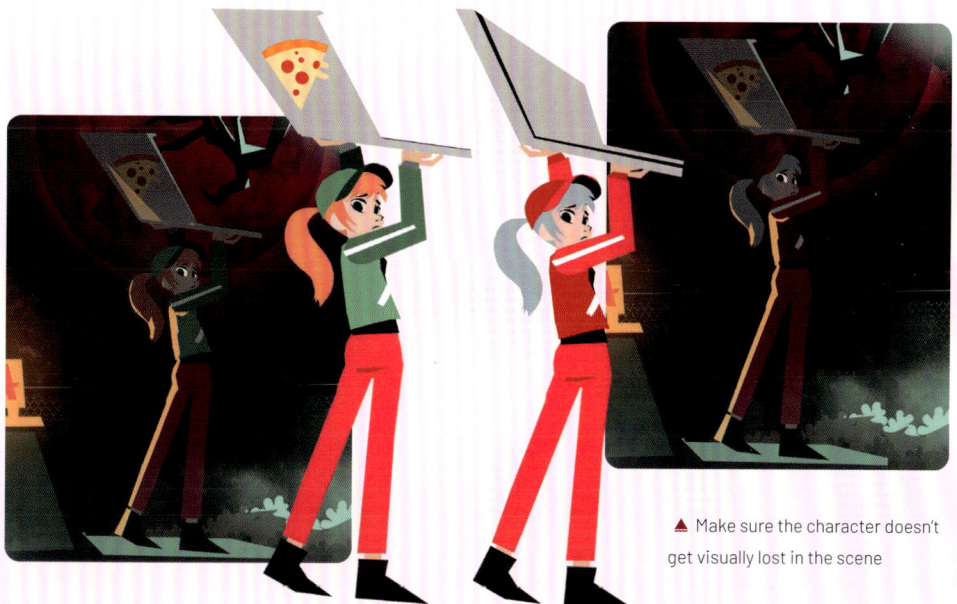

▲ Make sure the character doesn't get visually lost in the scene

ARTIST TIP SEPARATE FILES

One approach is to draw the characters and various elements that make up an illustration in separate files. By having each detail on its own layer, and each character in its own file, everything is adjustable. Starting with a clean file, you can simply drag each element into the illustration as it's ready.

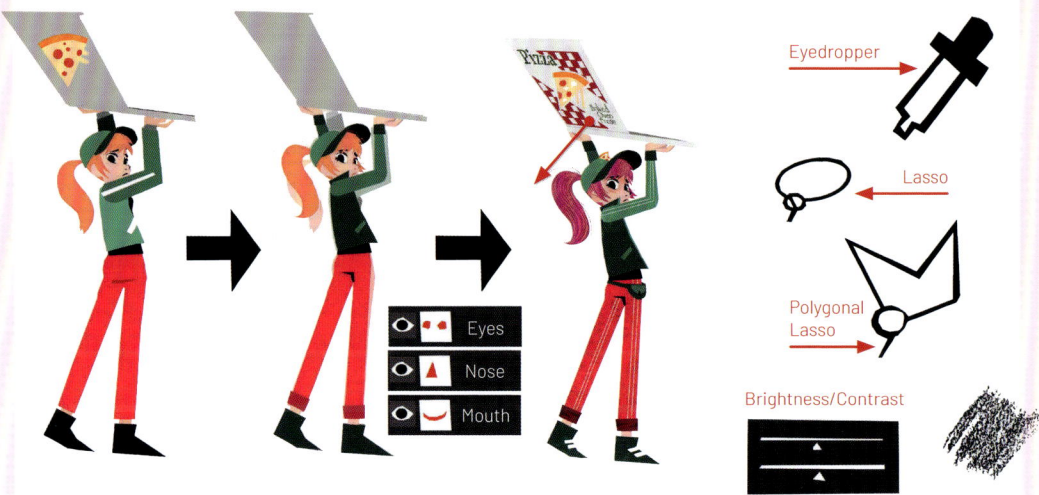

▲ Refine the shapes, add details, and adjust the colours

07 CLEAN UP & ADD TEXTURE

Merge the rough character layers together, then lower the new layer's opacity. Redraw the character on new layers above this one. The aim is to make her look less like a blocky sketch and more like an actual drawing by adding finer details. Keep each element on its own layer, as you will need to make colour adjustments later. For now, render your character as if there is no atmospheric lighting at all.

Next, add basic texturing to give the character some visual interest. Use the Eyedropper tool to select the base colour of the element you want to texture; the character's face, for example. Use the Brightness/Contrast sliders to increase the brightness of the face layer, then select Lock Transparent Pixels to ensure whatever you paint next will stay within the shape of that layer. Use a textured brush to paint the original colour back onto that shape, creating a two-toned, chalky effect. Make adjustments as you work, such as tweaking her hair colour and adding more outfit details. Once you're happy, group all of the character layers together in a folder.

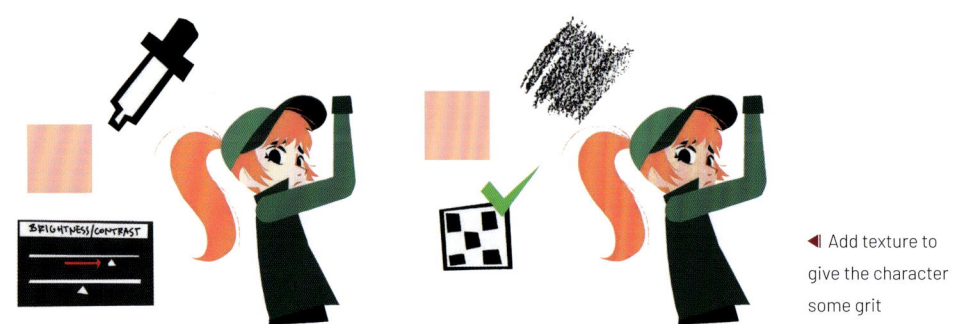

◀ Add texture to give the character some grit

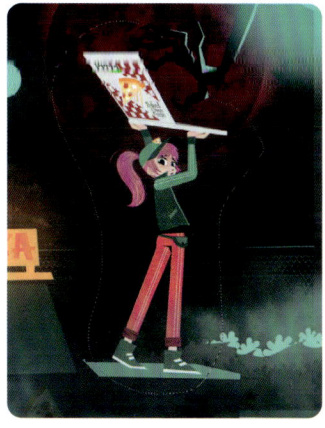  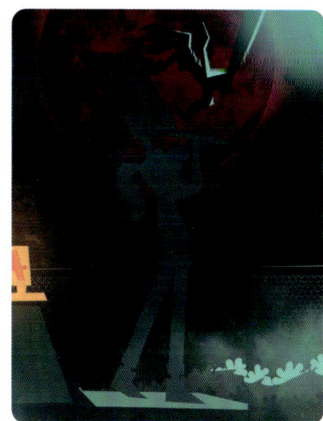

▲ Apply a dark layer as a clipping mask, otherwise the character will be too bright

08 QUICK READABILITY CHECK

Add the newly adjusted character to the background to see how they sit together. She is currently very bright, whereas her colours need to be dark and moody to fit the eerie vibe. On a new layer above the character folder, make a rough selection of the whole character and fill with a dark colour picked from the background. Make that layer a clipping mask for the folder, set it to Multiply, and adjust the layer's opacity until the character fits with the moody tones of the background.

If the character is too dark, however, the illustration will be unreadable. Notice how her hair disappears into the background on the bottom left. Turning the image to greyscale will help you to spot any character elements that have been lost. Select the layers that need work and change the colours until they are clearly readable. Next, experiment with the brightness and contrast of each layer, as well as the hue and saturation. Tweak colours as needed to fit the spooky atmosphere.

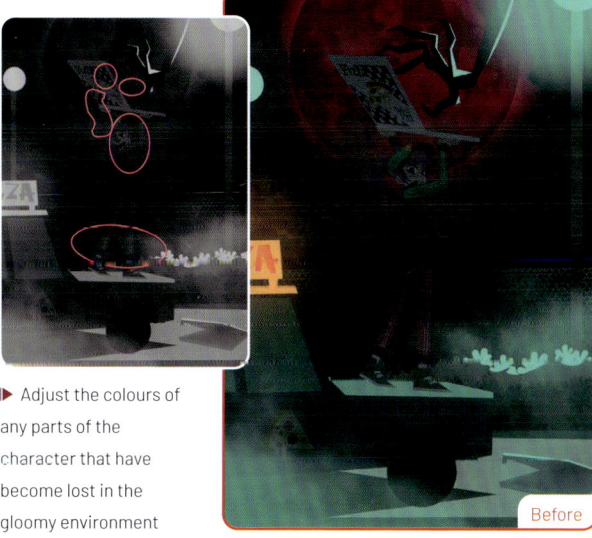

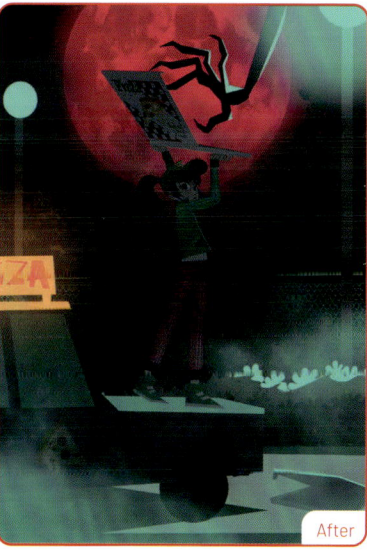

▶ Adjust the colours of any parts of the character that have become lost in the gloomy environment

Before

After

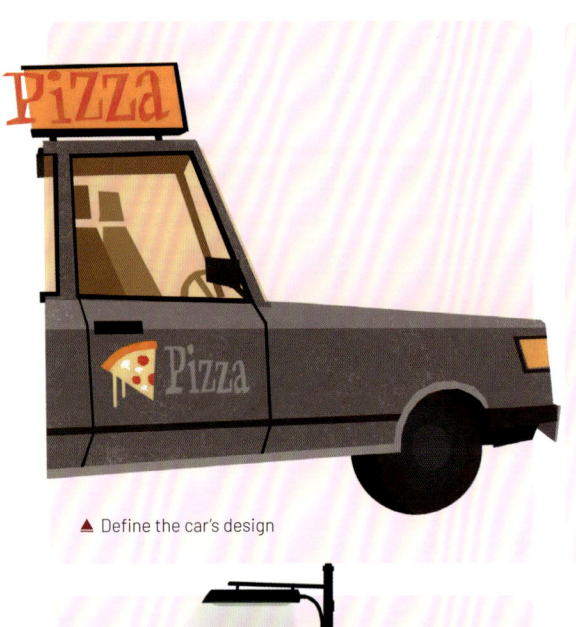

▲ Define the car's design

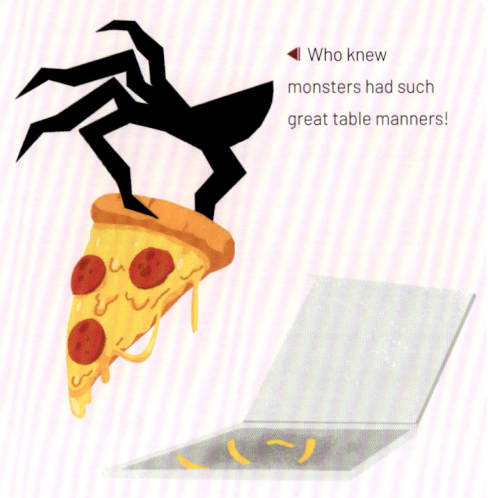

◀ Who knew monsters had such great table manners!

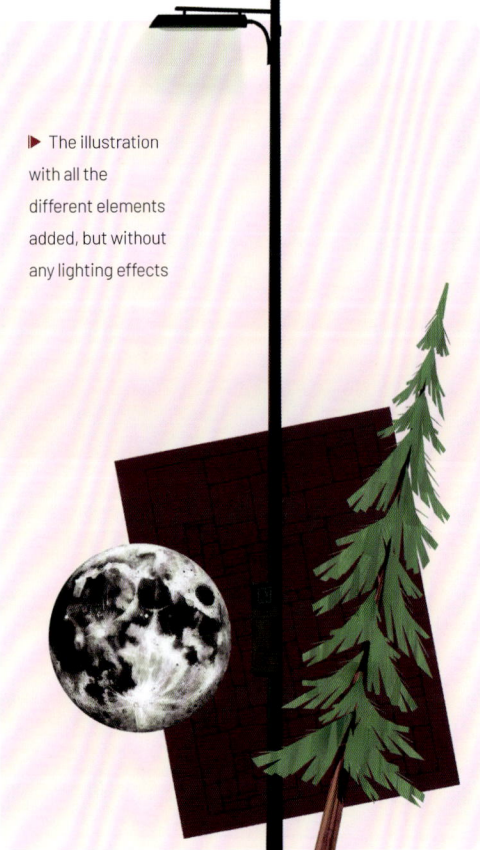

▶ The illustration with all the different elements added, but without any lighting effects

09 THE BACKGROUND

Develop the background following the same process as applied to the character. Replace the blocky sketch props with properly drawn versions and introduce some texture for visual interest. Organize every object in its own folder, then apply Multiply layers as clipping masks until each background elements fits the spooky mood. Tweak the colours of both the background and the character to ensure they fit well together.

Adjust the monster's hand so it is very elegantly taking a slice of pizza from the box, pinky finger in the air. Though this may seem like a small change, it creates a fun physical interaction between the girl and monster. It also gives the monster, who is completely off-screen, more personality.

10 FIRST LIGHTING PASS

Now it's time for a rough light pass, developing the various light sources. On a layer, or several, on top of the illustration, use a basic soft brush to lightly add a soft glow. Give each light-source colour its own layer.

Next, adjust the opacity and blend modes to your liking. Here the yellow light is set to Screen mode and the blue light to Colour Dodge. Next, add a slight reflecting glow on the pizza box.

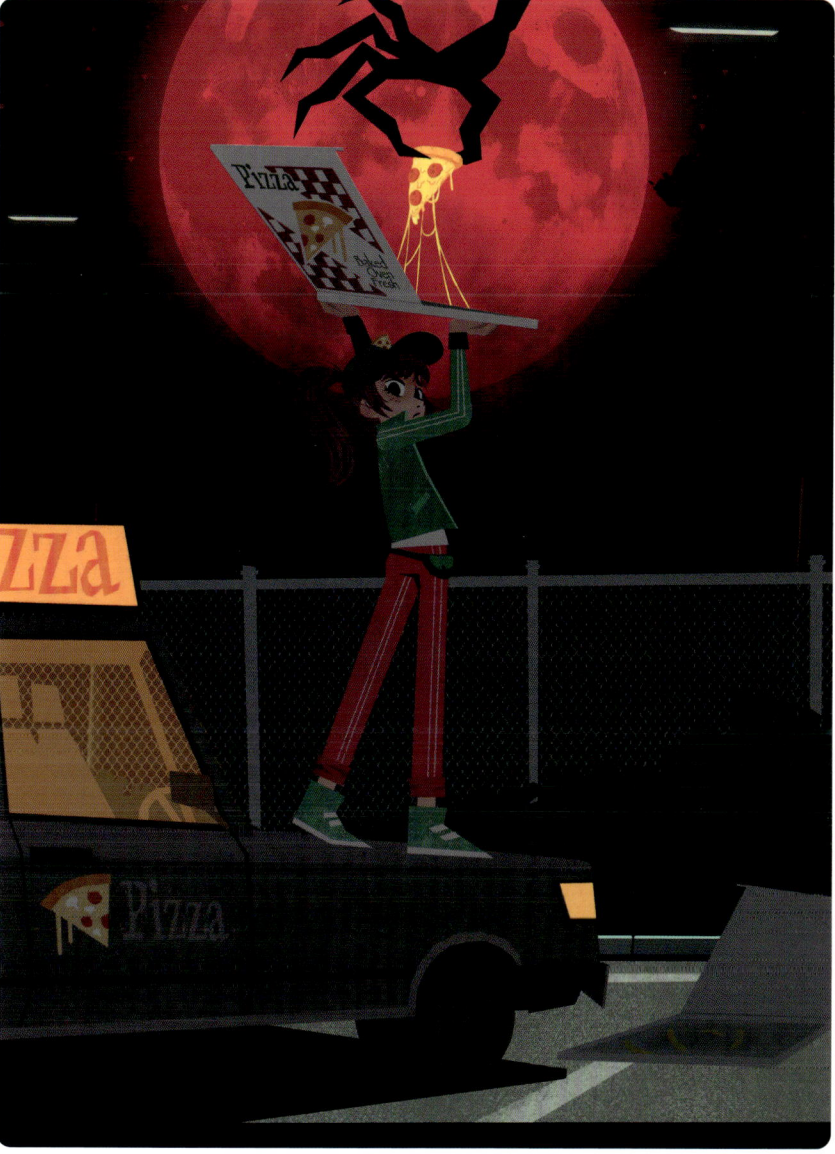

◀ Paint in yellow light from the car and blue light from the street lamps

11 LIGHTING FROM THE CAR

Before adding light to the character, try to visualize how the light sources affect the surrounding environment. Roughly block out the light if this helps you to imagine it, or guess where the light should fall. It doesn't need to be one hundred per cent realistic. The atmospheric mood the lighting creates and the clarity of the image are more important than realism here.

Using a clipping mask on the character folder, lightly brush in some reflecting light coming from the car windows and the pizza sign. This will make everything slightly warmer and help to ground the character in the environment. On another clipping mask, add some rim light onto the edges of the character. This will make her stand out against the background and make certain parts of her design, such as her hair, more readable.

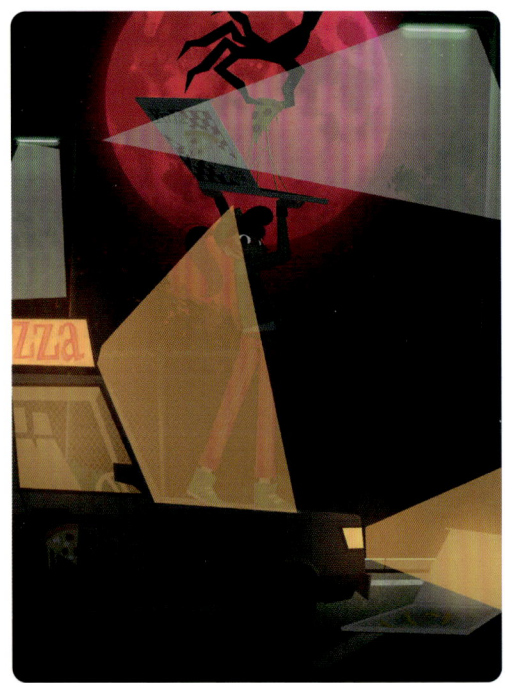

▶ Visualize the path of each light source

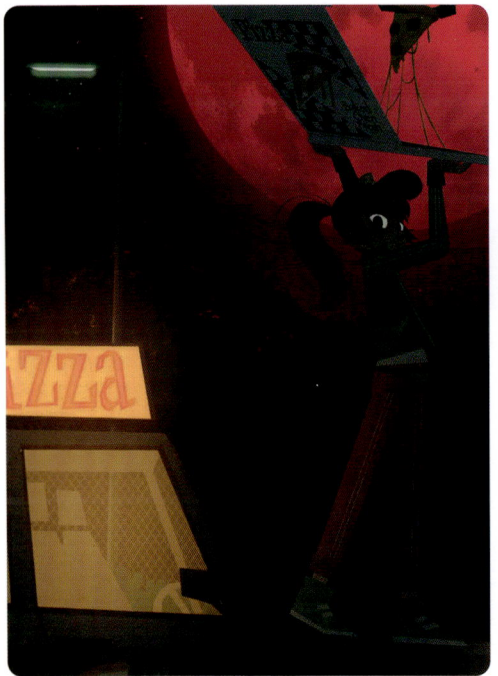

▲ Paint reflecting light onto the character

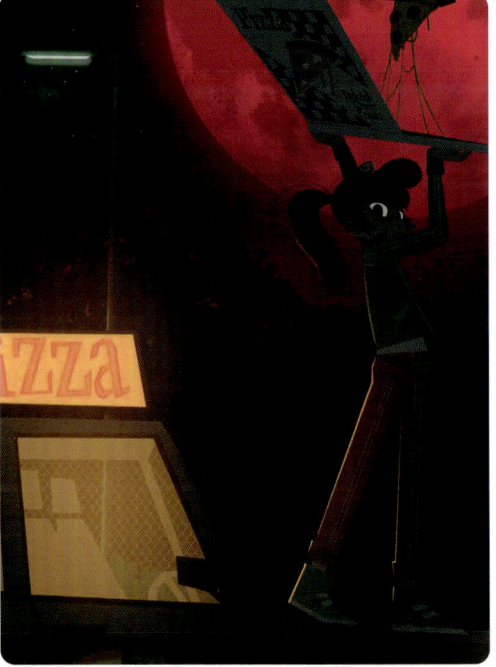

▲ Add rim light to the edges of the character

12 | LIGHTING & SHADOWS FROM THE STREET LAMPS

Think about where the shadows will fall in relation to the overhead street lamps. The character is holding a large pizza box above her head, which will block some of the light. On another clipping mask, paint in some shadow on the top part of the character. The more her face is obscured, the more mysterious she appears, which adds to the overall mood of the illustration. Next, repeat the process of adding soft light and rim light (from step 11) coming from the street lamp.

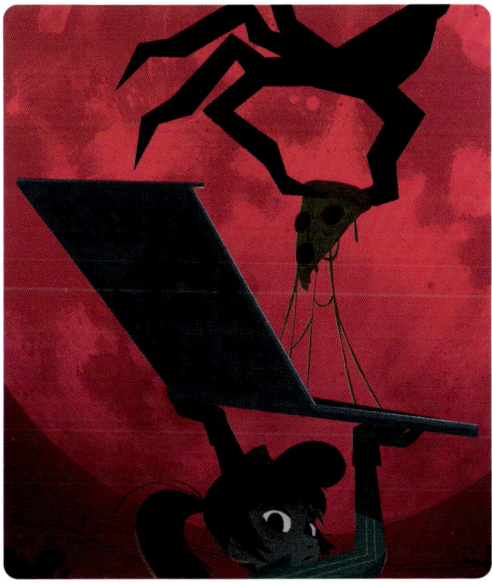
▲ Add the shadow created by the pizza box

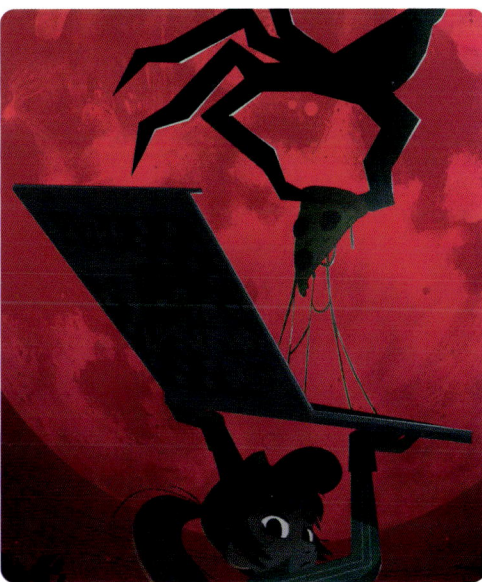
▲ Paint in soft light and rim light from the street lamp

ARTIST TIP STYLIZED LIGHTING

As this is a stylized character in a stylized illustration, the lighting doesn't need to be one hundred per cent accurate. If the scene were painted in a more realistic style, with more volume and fewer flat shapes, the lighting on the character would technically look more like the image on the right. However, this is too distracting and pulls the eye away from the top part of the image. The aim is to create the suggestion of lighting, inspired by – but not tied to – reality.

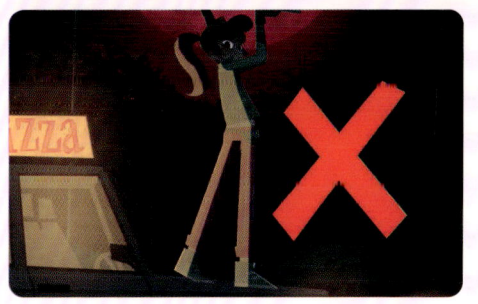

13 BACKGROUND LIGHTING & SHADOWS

Use the logic and workflow from steps 11–12 for the background, adding light and shadow where it makes sense. Remember, as this is a stylized illustration, you can break the rules. The suggestion of light is more important than realism. If there is a light source coming from the right, there should be a reflection of this light to the left, and so on.

ARTIST TIP **TAKE A BREAK**

Now you're nearing the finish line, turn off your computer and step away for a while. Return to the illustration the following day with fresh eyes.

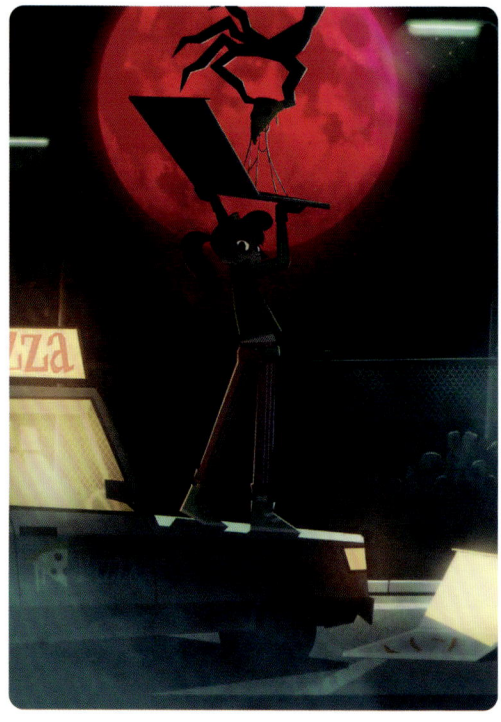

▲ Add shadows and light to the background

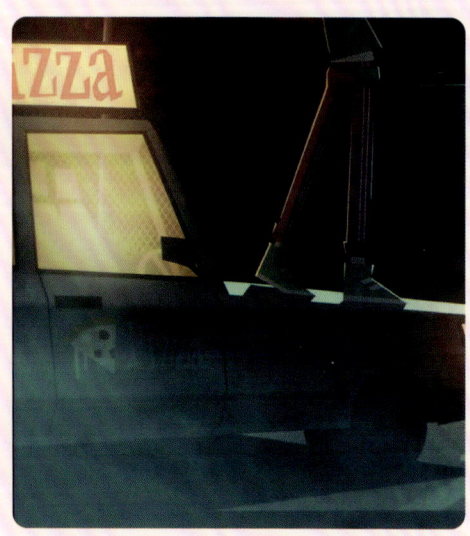

14 FINAL ADJUSTMENTS

Paint some misty fog on the lower part of the image to create an eerie mood. (You can create a fog brush yourself or find one online.) Environmental effects – whether gloomy rain, ethereal snow, or spooky fog – are a great way to give your illustration a little extra atmosphere. Finish by adding a slight film-grain texture, plus blurring the edges and background slightly, if you want to give the image more of a photographic feel.

◀ Finish by adding eerie fog and a film-grain texture

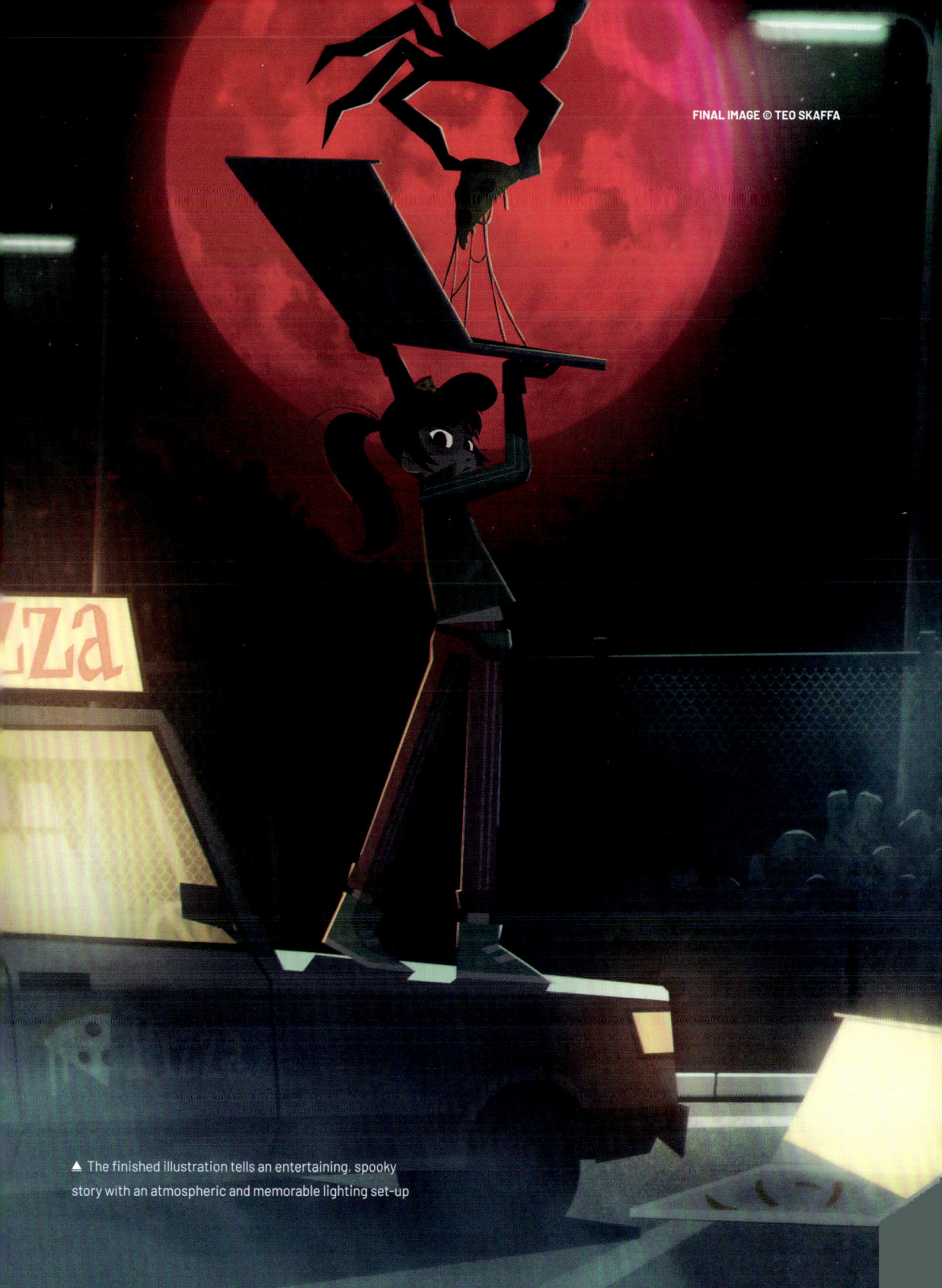

FINAL IMAGE © TEO SKAFFA

▲ The finished illustration tells an entertaining, spooky story with an atmospheric and memorable lighting set-up

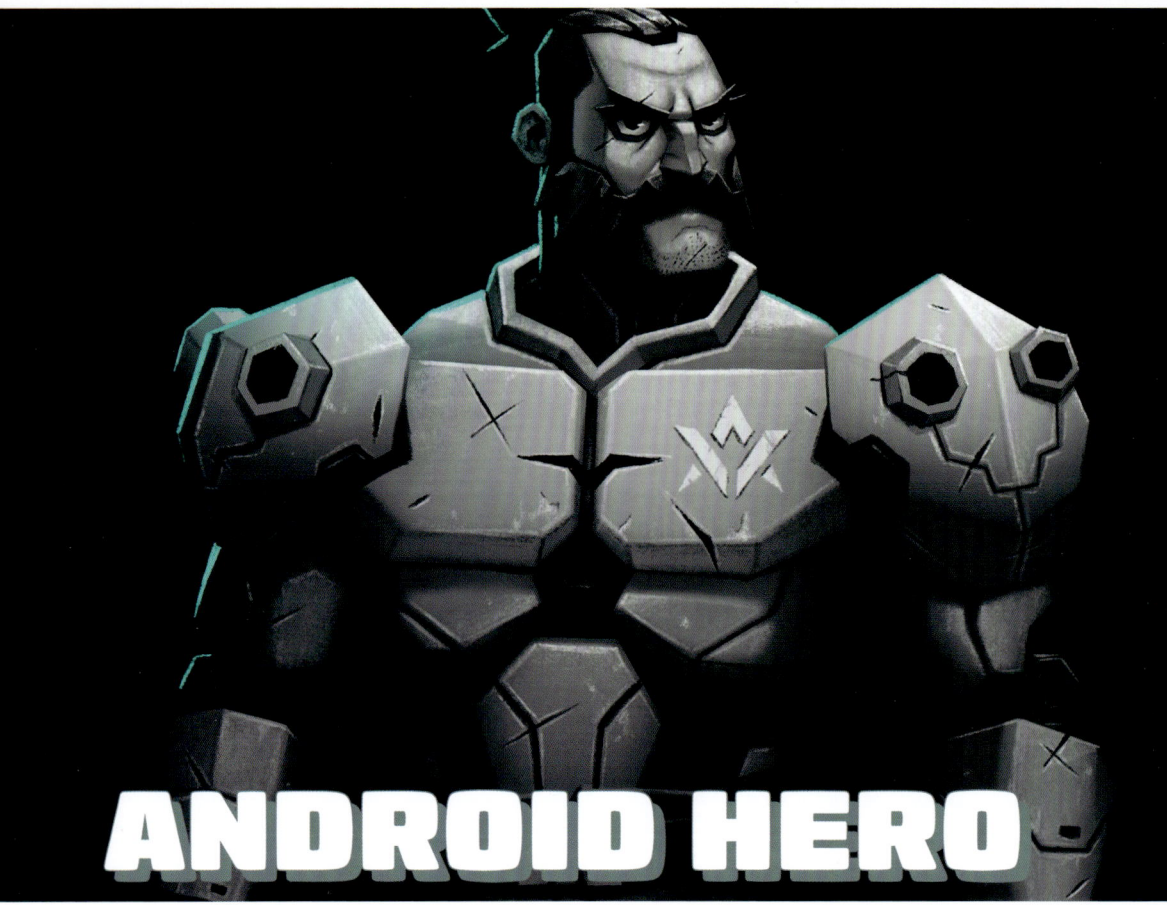

ANDROID HERO

USING LIGHT & SHADE TO CREATE STYLIZED FORM & VOLUME

Want to take your character designs to the next level? This tutorial will teach you how to apply shadows and highlights to give your shapes the illusion of volume. This android hero character will have a robotic body to simplify the shapes and allow you to see each individual component clearly. Working in black and white will stop you from getting distracted by colour, keeping the focus on lighting and shading. Additionally, the steps will show you how to create the character in a neutral pose. This will simplify the process and avoid any complex perspective issues.

This tutorial is created in Procreate, but you can use whichever software is available to you.

By Andrés Moncayo

01 INITIAL SKETCH

Start by thinking about the character you want to create. What kind of world do they exist in? What shape and size do you imagine their body to be? What's their personality like? Sketch out a few ideas until you find one you like.

Next, create a basic outline of the character: a simple silhouette without any facial features or clothing. The following steps will build up detail gradually, so starting simple will help you to remain in control.

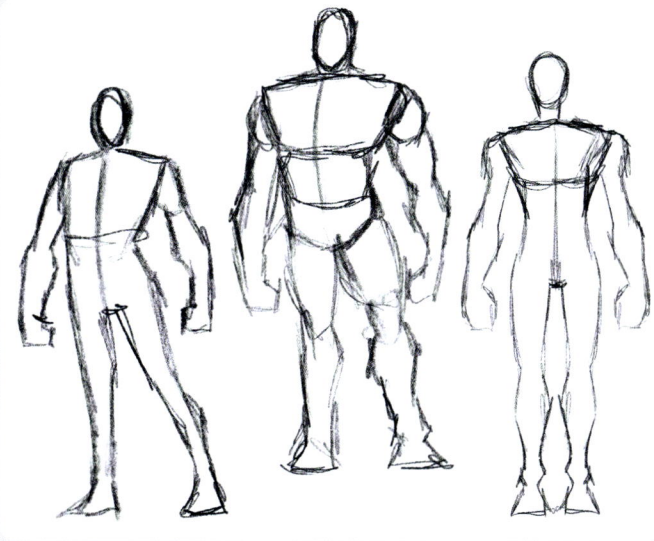

▼ Sketch a basic outline in a midtone grey – this is easier on the eyes and will make it simpler to add both lighter and darker tones later on

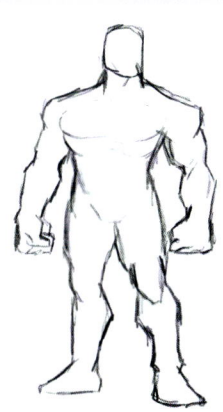

▲ Create a few exploratory sketches

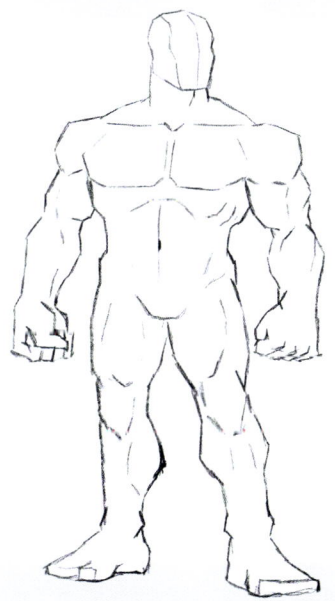

02 THE HUMAN SHAPE

Next, begin to define your character's body more clearly. Make it muscular and broad to help establish the character's overall physique and to provide a better idea of where and how to place the clothing. Use the Liquify tool to adjust the shape of the character, making parts bigger or smaller, or simply moving them around. Even though the character will have robotic parts, building a fully human body first will help you to decide which human structures to keep and which to modify.

◀ Define the character's body, adjusting size and shape

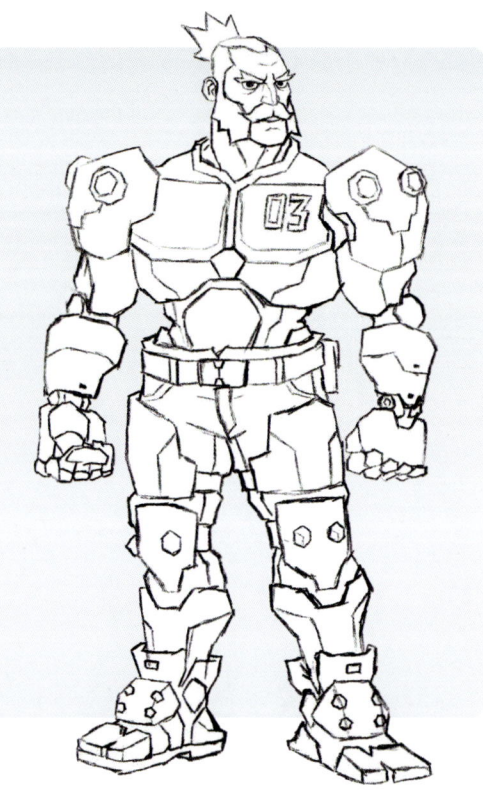

03 CHARACTER SKETCH

Once you're happy with the sketch, draw over it to add facial features, clothing, and any other details. Every detail can reveal something about your character's personality, world, and backstory. This heroic android has a rugged appearance with a broad, muscular body and facial hair. The robotic parts of his body suggest he lives in a futuristic world.

▶ Try to draw clean lines, as they will allow you to create the colour blocks in the next step more easily

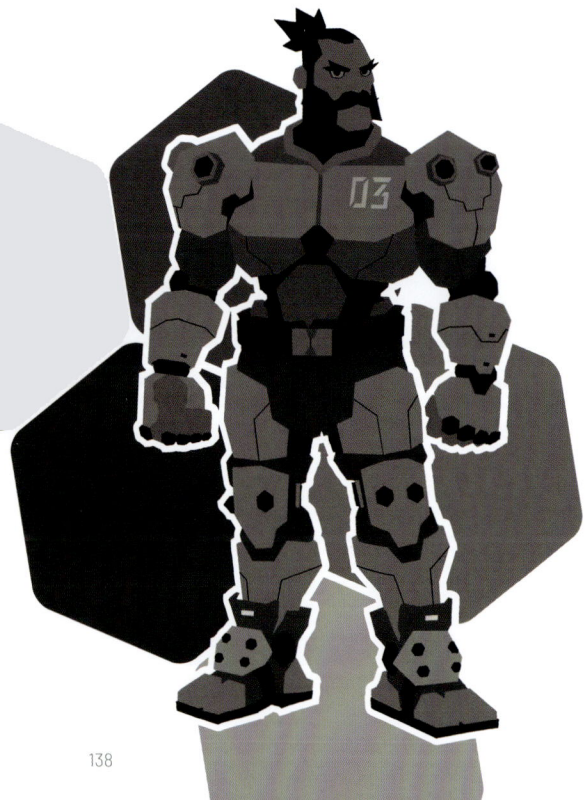

04 COLOUR BLOCKS

Reduce the opacity of your previous sketch layer. Next, create the solid base colours for your character. Avoid using very light or very dark tones, as this will allow you to add shadows (darker tones) and highlights (lighter tones) later on. For example, using pure white on the character's face would make it difficult to define highlights later in the process and would only let you apply darker colours.

◀ Create a new layer for each colour block; this will make it much easier to apply shadows and highlights later on without affecting other parts of your character

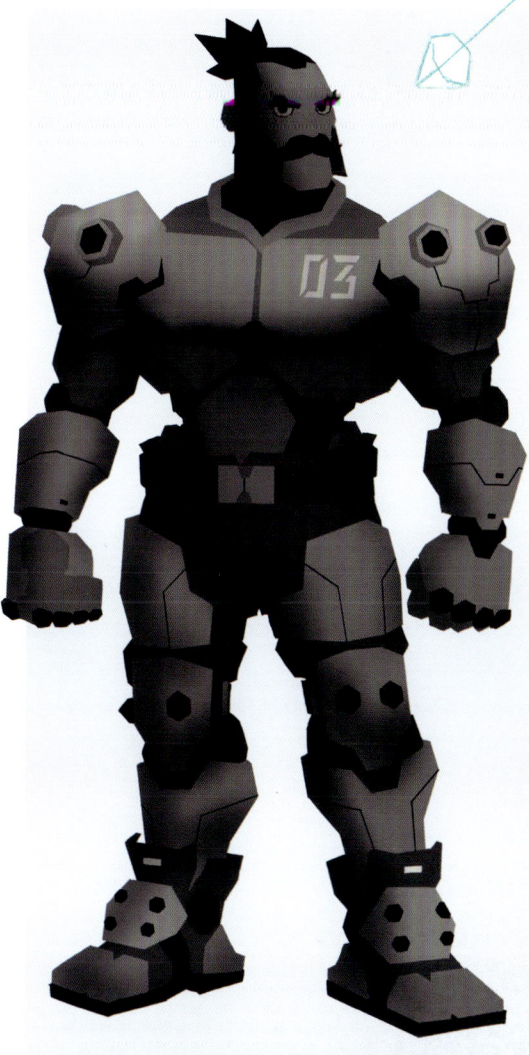

05 LIGHT SOURCE

Decide where your light source will be. Here it's in the top right, slightly in front of the character. You can then use this light to draw attention to specific parts. The light is close to the character's face, making it the most illuminated area that will naturally draw the viewer's eye. Also, keep in mind that brighter lighting can make a character seem more approachable, while darker lighting can create a more mysterious atmosphere.

Create a shadow study. On a new layer set to Multiply mode, lightly paint shadows over your drawing – this will help you to plan your shading before you start adding the darker tones.

◀ Choose the direction of the light source – this will dictate the most illuminated parts of the character

ARTIST TIP REFERENCES

Don't be afraid to use references and live models when figuring out lighting set-ups for characters. Even the most celebrated artists draw inspiration from the world around them.

06 BASIC SHADOWS

Hide the shadow layer created in the previous step. Then, for each of your base colour layers, activate Alpha Lock. This will restrict your painting to within the boundaries of that layer. Paint a simple, darker shadow onto each colour block, referencing the shadow study created in the previous step. This should only be a quick pass to establish the initial shadow areas.

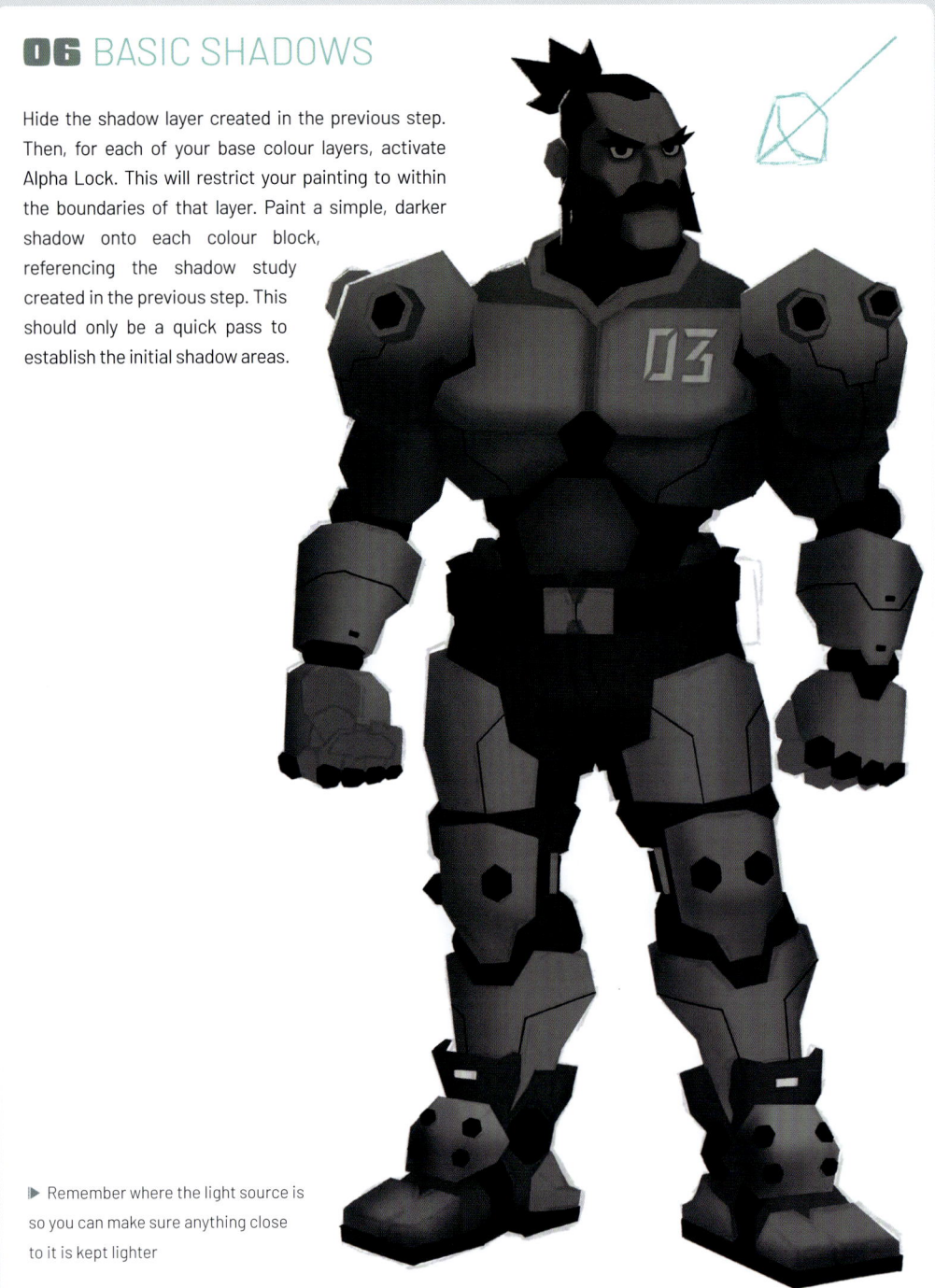

▶ Remember where the light source is so you can make sure anything close to it is kept lighter

07 ADVANCED SHADOWS

Revisit each colour block and refine the shadows. Start by focusing solely on the darkest tones, leaving the highlights for later. You could apply both shadows and highlights to each block, but here they are separated to emphasize the importance of midtones and the dramatic impact that light and dark values can have.

◀ The 6B Pencil brush in Procreate has a realistic pencil texture that is perfect for creating both shadows and highlights, as well as adding texture

08 ADDING LIGHTS

Now it's time to add the highlights: the lightest tones in your illustration. This can really bring a character to life, elevating it from a sketch to a finished piece. Begin by using a light colour on areas facing the light source, then add even more light to the edges of certain shapes and planes. This will help to emphasize them and define the contours.

▶ Add highlights to the character, adding a brighter light on the edges of planes closest to the light source

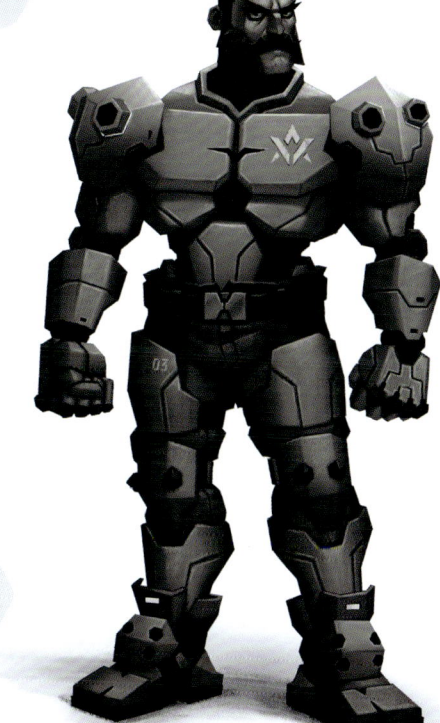

09 DETAILS & SECOND LIGHT

Paint in small details and imperfections to make the character feel more realistic, such as scratches and wear and tear on the metal parts. Next, add a second light source in a different colour to separate it from the main light source. This rim light technique brightens up the darker side of the character's head, helping to separate him from the background.

▶ Introduce rim lighting to lift the character from the background

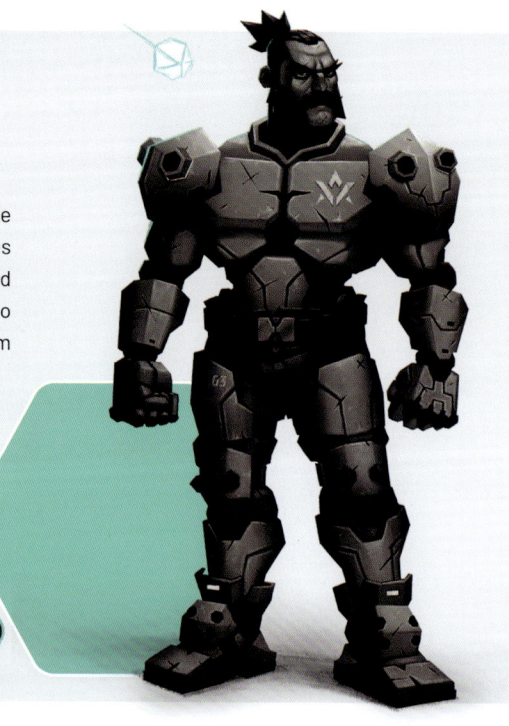

10 BRIGHTNESS & COLOUR CORRECTIONS

Use this step to make any final adjustments. Here the character's body is leaning forwards too much, so the Distort tool is used to reduce the size of his head. To emphasize the main light source, you can darken the lower half of the body by selecting the area and then reducing its brightness with a dark-coloured brush. This produces a better result than using a dark brush with the Multiply blend mode. Next, add a white Overlay layer to the top part of the design to further brighten it. Adjust the brightness and contrast, then use the Selective Colour adjustment to add a touch of magenta to the darkest tones. This will give the shadows more depth and prevent them from looking flat.

▶ Darken the lower part of the image and lighten the upper section

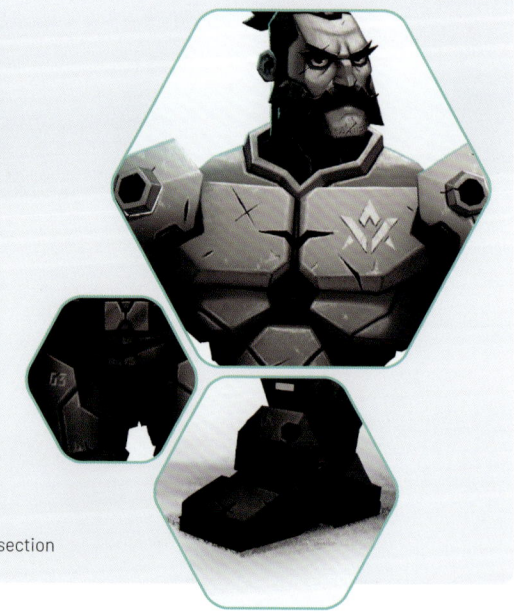

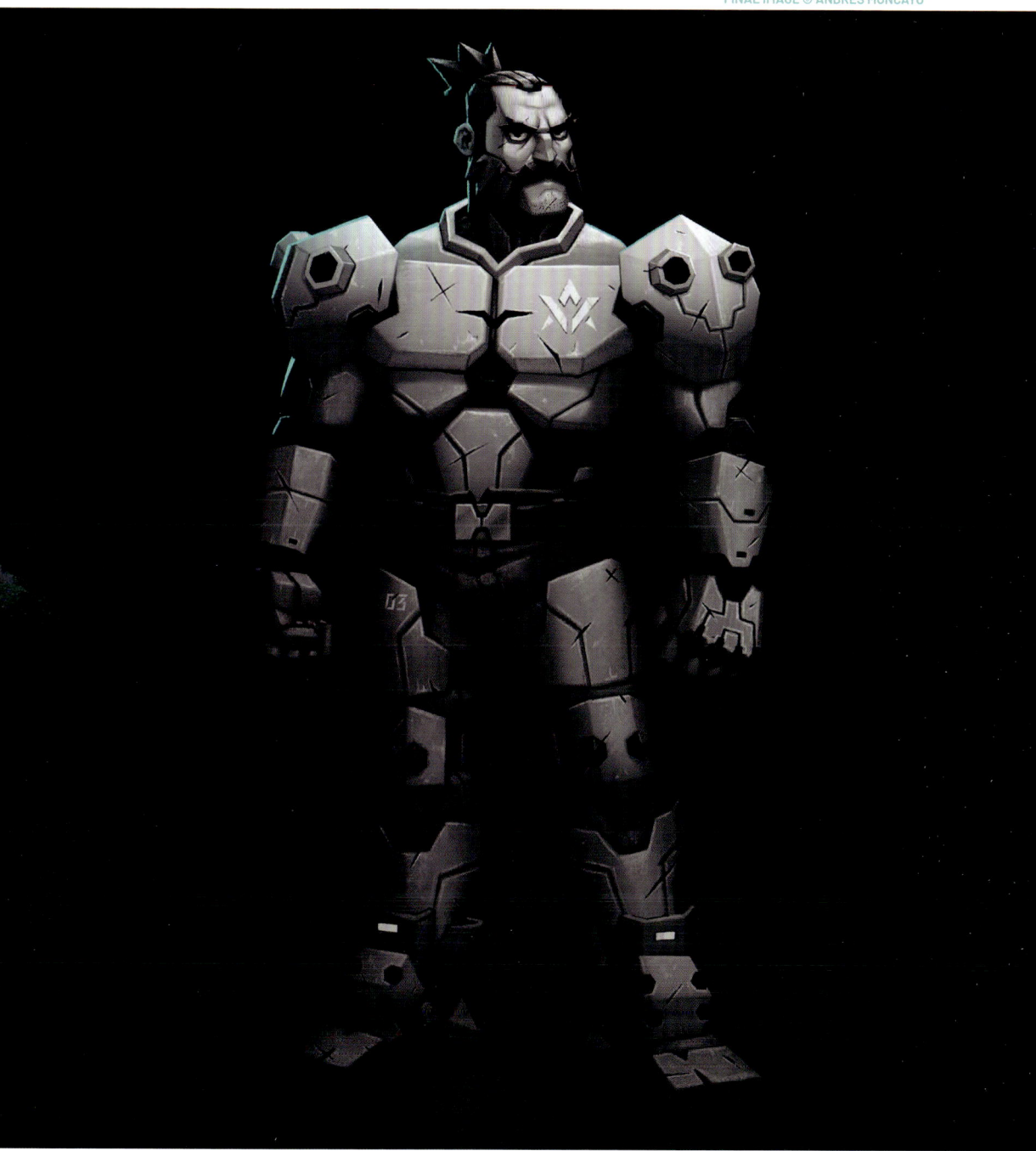

▲ The final character is stylized and three-dimensional, with shadows and highlights to create a sense of depth and volume

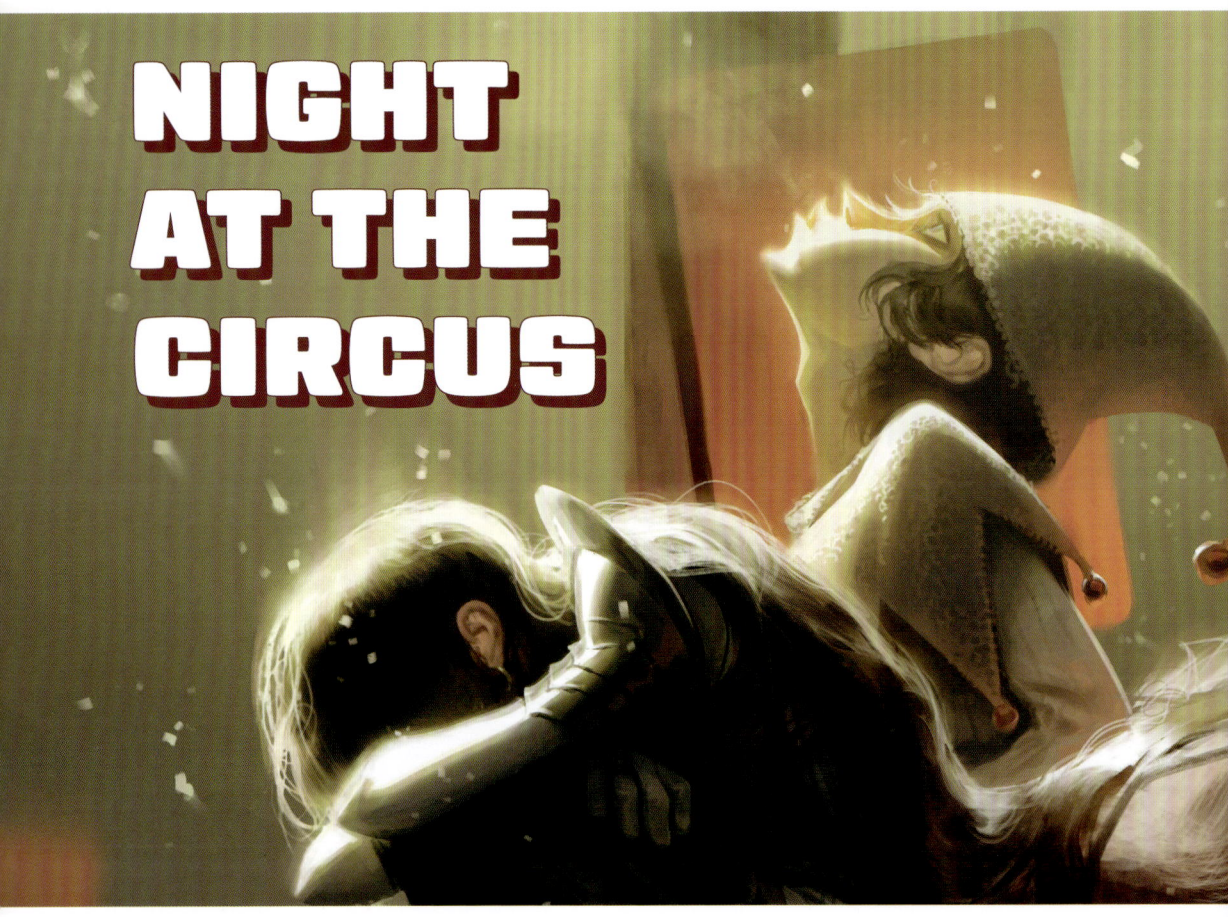

NIGHT AT THE CIRCUS

REALISTIC CHARACTER CONCEPT ILLUSTRATION

This tutorial will walk you through how to use advanced light and shade to create a dramatic, realistically lit character-concept illustration. Don't worry if you only have a vague idea for a character, narrative, or mood. You can explore these things, plus composition and lighting, as you go. Starting with set expectations can often place unnecessary pressure on the process and self-imposed limitations on the final image. Consider whether you wish to use soft atmospheric lighting or a single intense light source, or even a combination of types for a more complex set-up, but don't feel pressured to make a final decision until after you've created the initial thumbnails.

This tutorial is created in Adobe Photoshop, but you can follow along with the software of your choosing.

By Ognjen Sporin

01 INITIAL THUMBNAILS

Begin by generating ideas and exploring possibilities, without worrying about creating 'good' drawings. The only goal at this stage is to use simple lines to sketch out rough ideas you can build on. You may find that you naturally associate each composition with a lighting set up. For example, the sketch of a character looking up could work well if he were looking directly up into an intense, soaking light, his face illuminated with an almost ethereal glow. Asking yourself 'What would happen if...?' is a helpful way to come up with ideas for compositions.

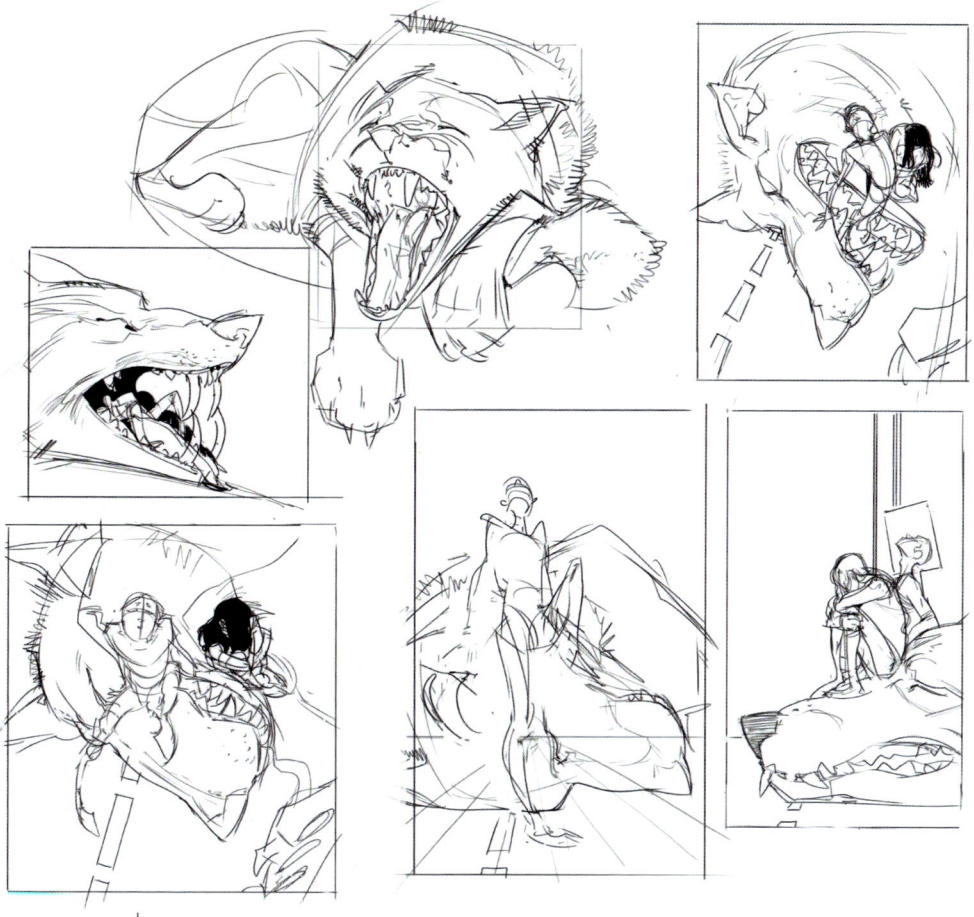

▲ Sketch out loose compositions, letting them spark ideas for potential lighting scenarios

02 ROUGH FLAT COLOUR BLOCK-IN

Decide which thumbnail best communicates your narrative intention, then paint a simple colour block-in on a new layer underneath the original scribbly drawing. You may wish to explore a few different colour options, on separate layers, or you may already have colours in mind based on the atmosphere and mood you want to create.

▶ When creating a colour sketch, start by establishing silhouettes and indicating flat colours

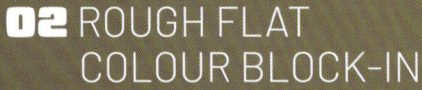

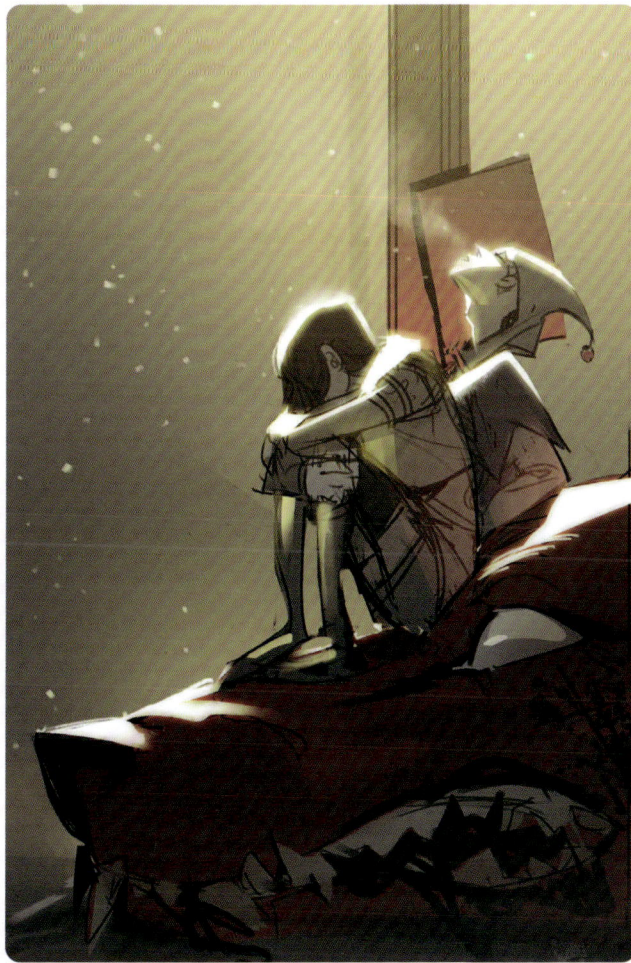

◀ Create a rough block-in as a map to guide you throughout the painting process

03 ROUGH LIGHTING

Once you have a rough base of flat colours, experiment with adding light and shadow. Paint the light and shadow on separate layers – this will allow you to alter them easily without having to paint over or worry about ruining the layers underneath. Play around with various options, such as the Value, Hue, and Saturation sliders. Though you don't want to waste time on detail just yet, try to include all of the elements, lights, colours, and effects that will be present in the final illustration. Here the off-screen light source will play a big part in creating a strong mood. To achieve this, intensify the glow in the top-right as the light disperses through mist particles. To further communicate the strength of the light source, blow out the light shapes on the characters themselves, so they are overexposed to the point of glowing.

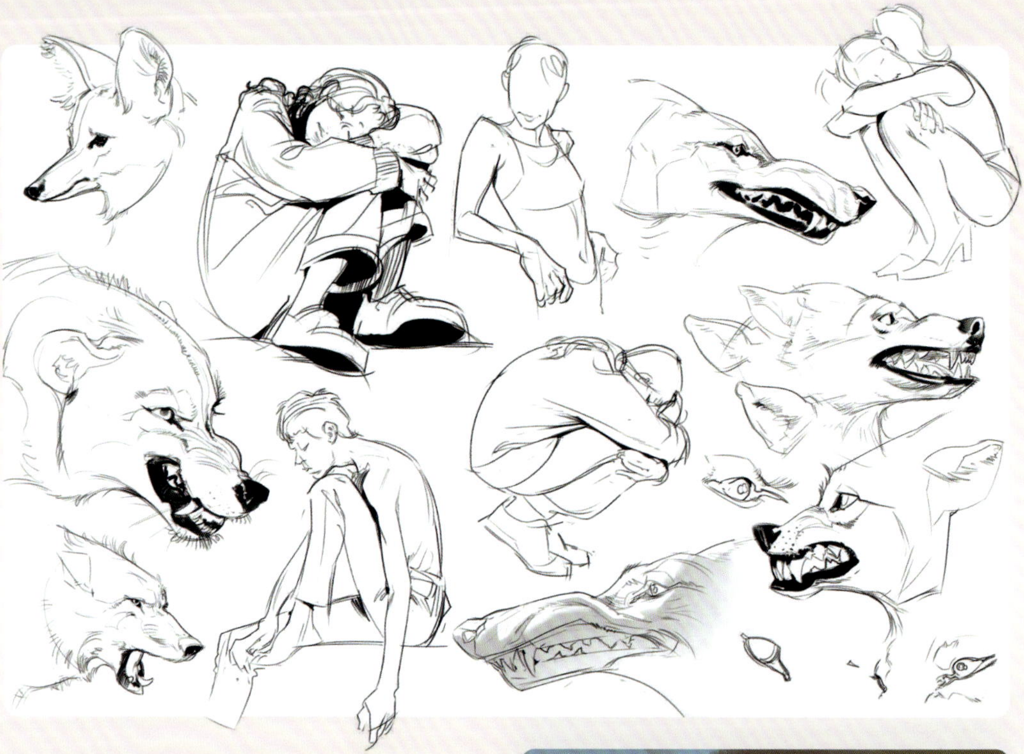

▲ Practise drawing small studies of
different elements of the illustration

04 PRELIMINARY DRAWING STUDIES

Before starting the drawing phase, spend some time studying references for your subject matter, especially if it's something you find difficult or don't have a lot of experience drawing. Sketch small studies of wolf heads, as well as potential crouching poses for the character. If you already know what kind of light or atmospheric effect you plan to paint, create a few preparatory studies for that as well. Here you may wish to create a few quick armour reflectivity studies.

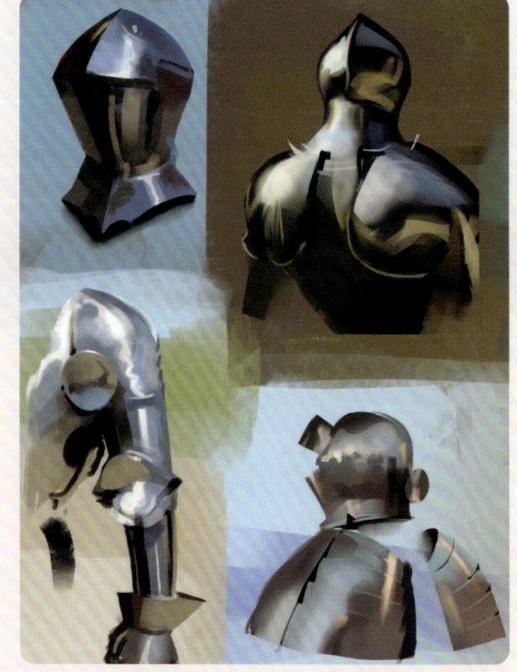

▲ It can be helpful to paint studies of challenging materials

05 ROUGH DRAWING

The drawing stage forms the foundation of the image, so make sure to figure out proportions, shapes, forms, and perspective before you begin layering colour and light on top. When drawing in the first line-work pass, use the rough sketch as a vague compositional base, but avoid mindlessly reiterating the lines already drawn. Take the time to reconsider and reposition most elements.

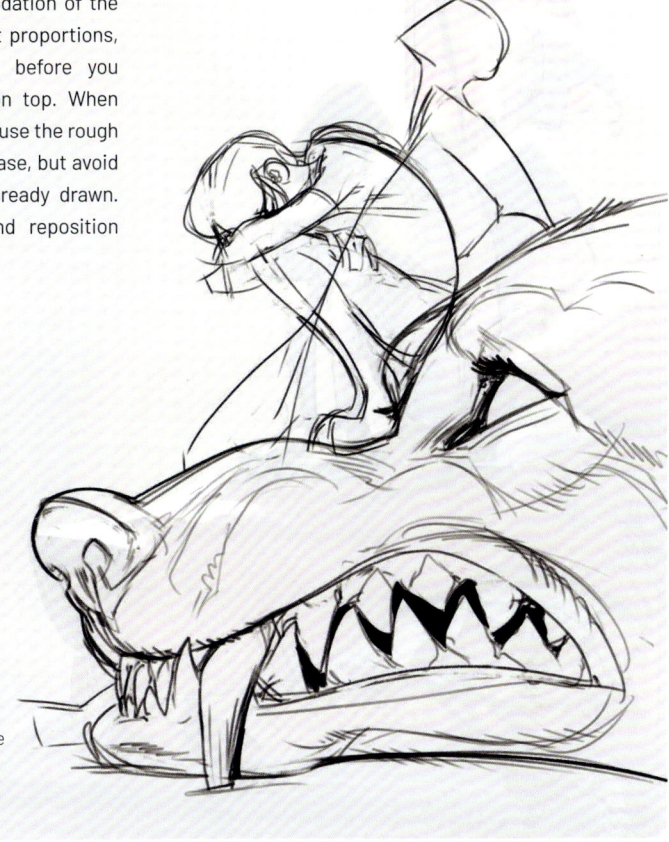

▶ Draw the characters as simple gestural mannequins that you can refine with additional drawing passes

ARTIST TIP FIGURE OUT THE DRAWING

Drawing characters requires a lot of construction and 'drawing through' (sketching out transparent 3D forms) to ensure they are built solidly and interact believably with the space they inhabit. As uncomfortable as struggling with placement and perspective can be, it will make the painting and rendering stage much easier, as you won't have to sort out drawing problems. Rushing Into painting with a weak, vague drawing, hoping that it somehow figures itself out, rarely produces good results.

06 REFINED DRAWING

The drawing stage can be broken up into as many passes as you need. For example, you may wish to refine the figures in three passes: the simple gesture, followed by the refined figure, and finally, the costuming. Build the drawing up step by step, ensuring a solid base. An unambiguous drawing will make the process of painting and rendering much more straightforward. Other elements that are not so layered, such as the wolf, you may decide to draw directly.

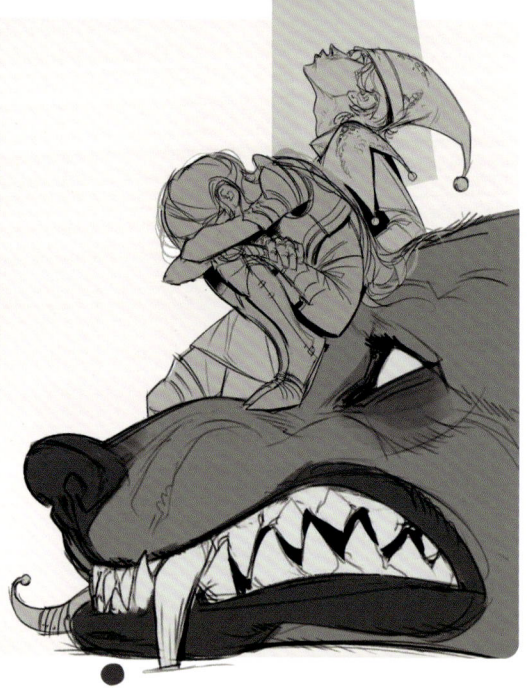

▶ Refine the characters step by step, from a simple gesture to refined, clothed figures

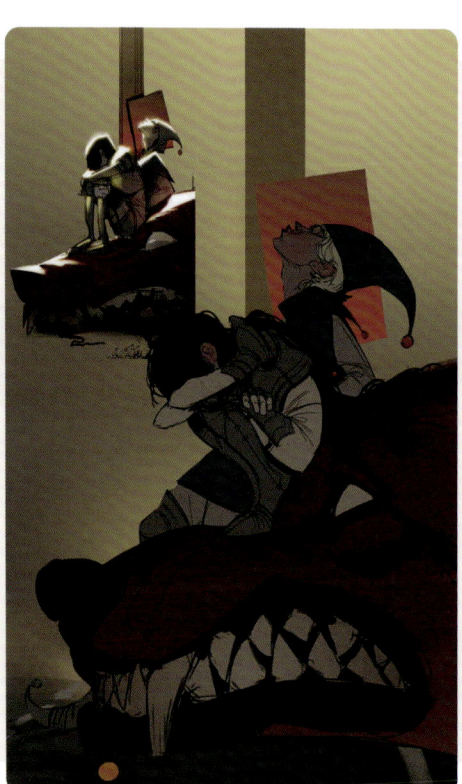

07 FLAT COLOURS

Start the painting process by laying in a simple flat colour base for each of the objects in the scene, referring back to your original colour rough. Here, the shadows form the base, on top of which light shapes will be added later. Try to be fairly clean with each shape, but don't worry too much – you will eventually paint over everything anyway.

As everything is technically in shadow at this point, take care to group your values. (Strong light will be added in later steps.) If the values of your flats are too spread out, they might eventually interfere with your intended clear separation of light and shadow.

◀ Notice how the flat colours already establish basic silhouette shape and separation

08 AMBIENT OCCLUSION

To further refine the shadows and give them more depth and form, begin to introduce deeper, darker areas where objects close to one another prevent atmospheric light from reaching. Some parts of the drawing, such as the solid shadows inside the wolf's mouth or on the characters' bodies, already serve as stand-ins for this ambient occlusion. Simultaneously soften or paint out the lines as well.

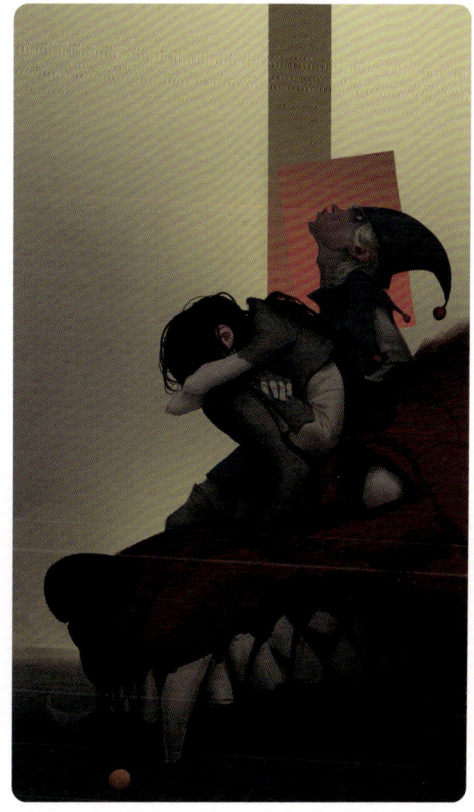

▶ Paint deeper shadows to give each object form and shape, ultimately making them appear more believable

ARTIST TIP SEPARATING LIGHT SOURCES

If a lighting set-up seems complex, break it down into different light sources, and then further into different modelling factors within each light source. Once you understand the separate pieces, you can layer them one by one. Here, the more intense, directional overhead light simply pastes on top of the weaker, softer ambient light. Similarly, within the ambiently lit shadows, begin with a single simple layer of the base colour, then add ambient occlusion, bounce light, and reflections, approaching each of those modelling factors separately, rather than painting everything at once.

09 LIGHT SHAPES

When adding a light source on top of the shadow base, start with a kind of cel-shaded (or in this case, cel-lit) approach. Only paint in the simple, flat shapes of the light areas without being concerned with edges, transitions, rendering, or even colour. Using an off-white colour, make sure the shapes are distinct, clear, and well-designed. Opt for an almost direct overhead light – compositionally, this allows for fairly small light shapes, which in turn leaves the huge, grouped shadow shapes mostly untouched. These largest shapes are what will make the image clear and readable, even when seen from afar. In terms of the narrative, this light could be coming from a street lamp above the characters.

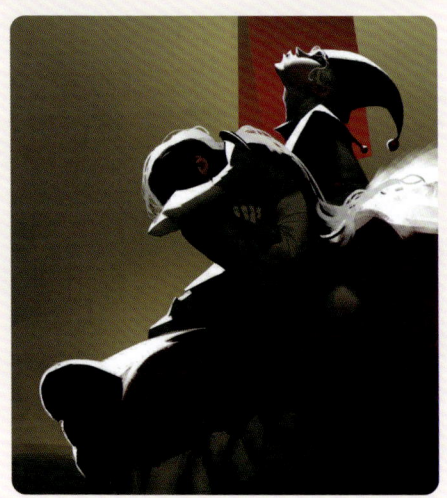

▲ Set up the light with a simple shape separation

10 LIGHT REFINEMENT

After establishing the shape of the light, begin to create a more believable illusion of light by introducing various local colours and soft transitions across forms. Tint the light on the wolf to a slightly reddish tone to distinguish it from the local colours of the characters. Soften the edges of the light shape, giving it an appropriately smooth transition, depending on how curved and gradual the surface of the underlying object is. As with the previous steps, try to focus on one small element of the light at a time to avoid becoming overwhelmed with detail.

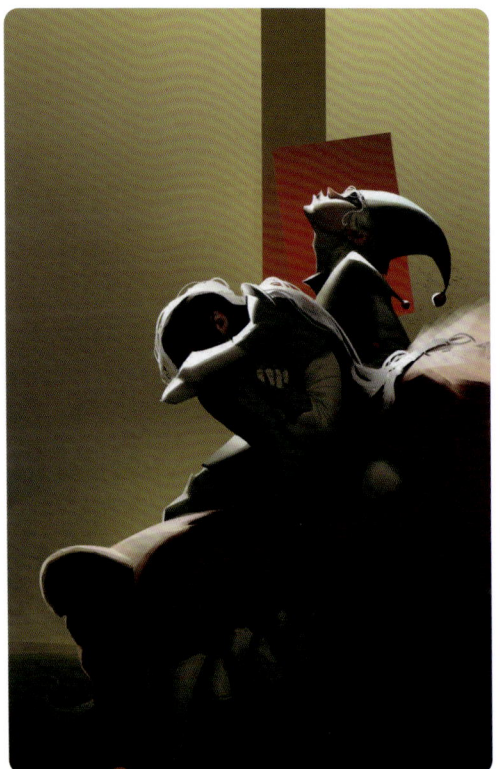

◀ Paint soft transitions from light to shadow to produce an illusion of form

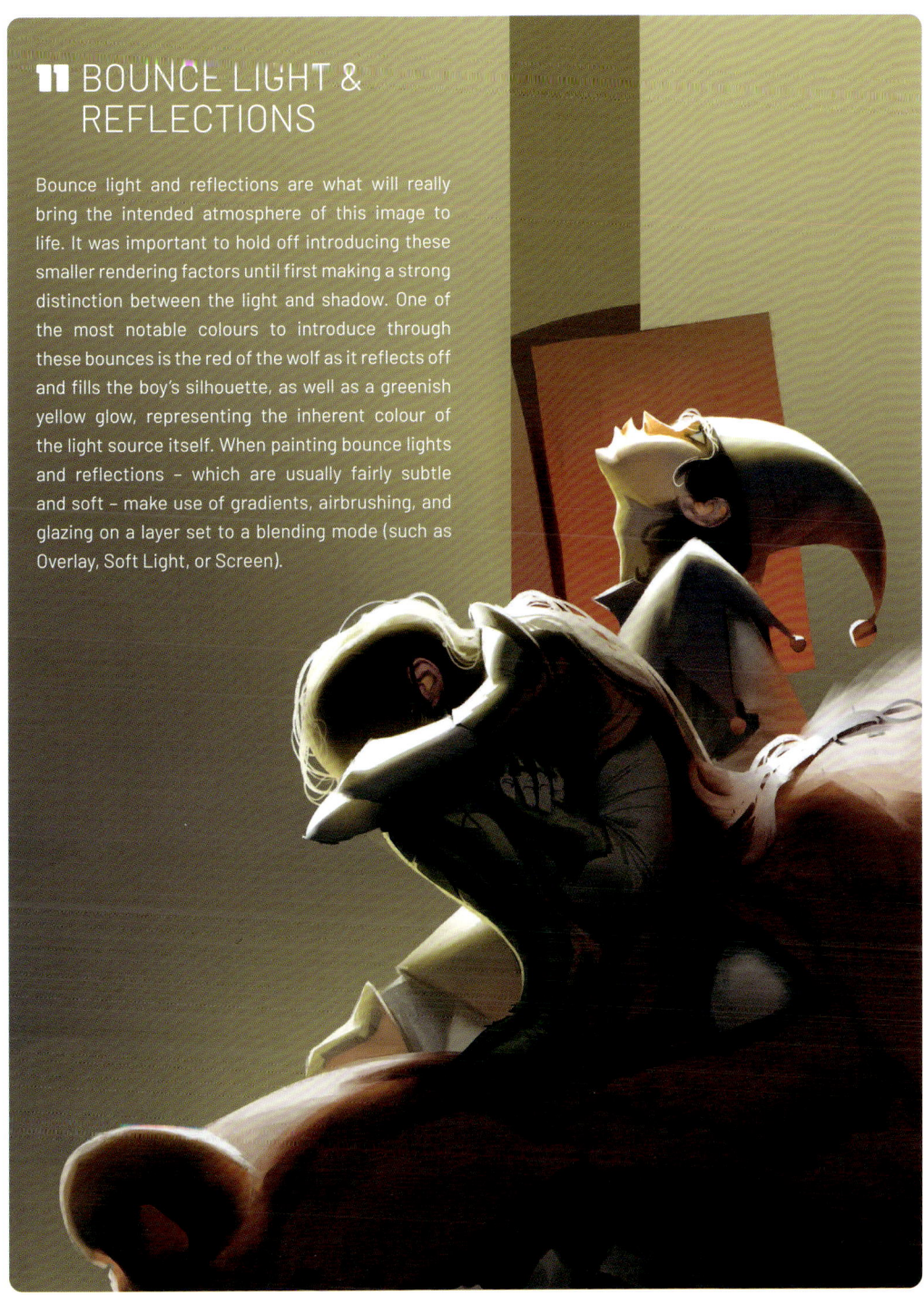

11 BOUNCE LIGHT & REFLECTIONS

Bounce light and reflections are what will really bring the intended atmosphere of this image to life. It was important to hold off introducing these smaller rendering factors until first making a strong distinction between the light and shadow. One of the most notable colours to introduce through these bounces is the red of the wolf as it reflects off and fills the boy's silhouette, as well as a greenish yellow glow, representing the inherent colour of the light source itself. When painting bounce lights and reflections – which are usually fairly subtle and soft – make use of gradients, airbrushing, and glazing on a layer set to a blending mode (such as Overlay, Soft Light, or Screen).

12 RENDERING

While the rendering stage takes the most time, it's the step where the fewest obvious visual changes are seen. There's nothing wrong with making a few last-minute revisions, but the more patience and care you put into the previous steps, the less there will be to fix or adjust at this stage. The primary concern here is to maintain what has worked from previous steps, rather than feeling you have to add anything new. Save work-in-progress images and keep them on a hidden layer over your working file, occasionally flipping them on and off for comparison.

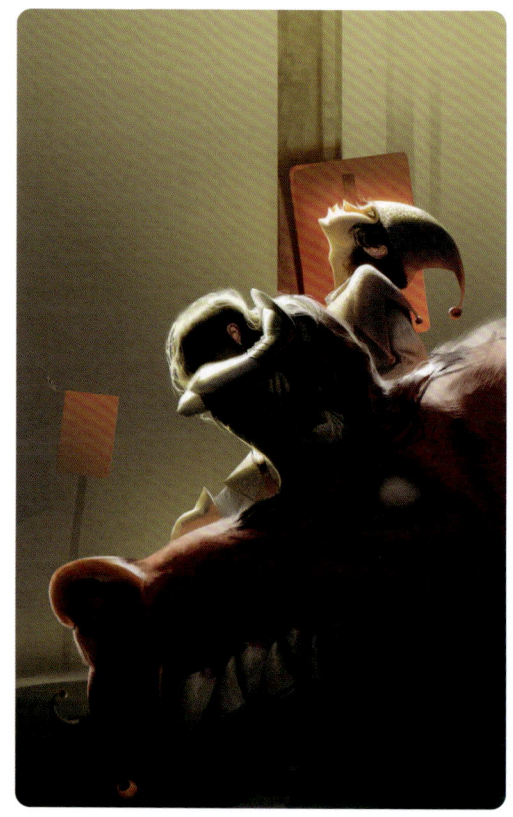

▶ Paint in and clean up details, textures, and small transitions

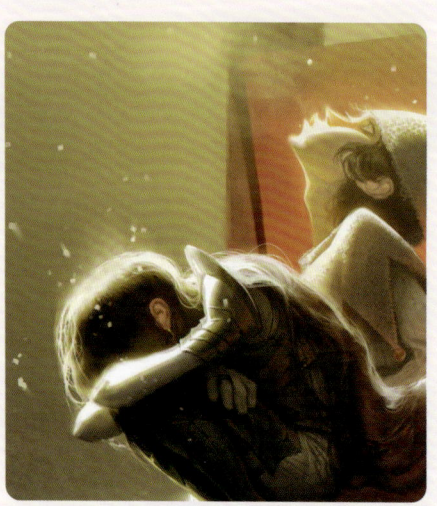

13 FINAL EFFECTS

Paint in small particles and light effects – such as smoke, speckles, or glow – creating final enhancements using layer modes and adjustments. Referring back to the distinct glowing effect from the original colour sketch, where the overhead street lamp diffuses light through the mist, airbrush in fog on a Screen layer. Adjust the Colour Balance settings to make the scene slightly greener, and brighten the value levels overall to further the misty atmosphere.

▶ Paint in soft atmospheric glow, particles, and fog to enhance the otherworldly mood

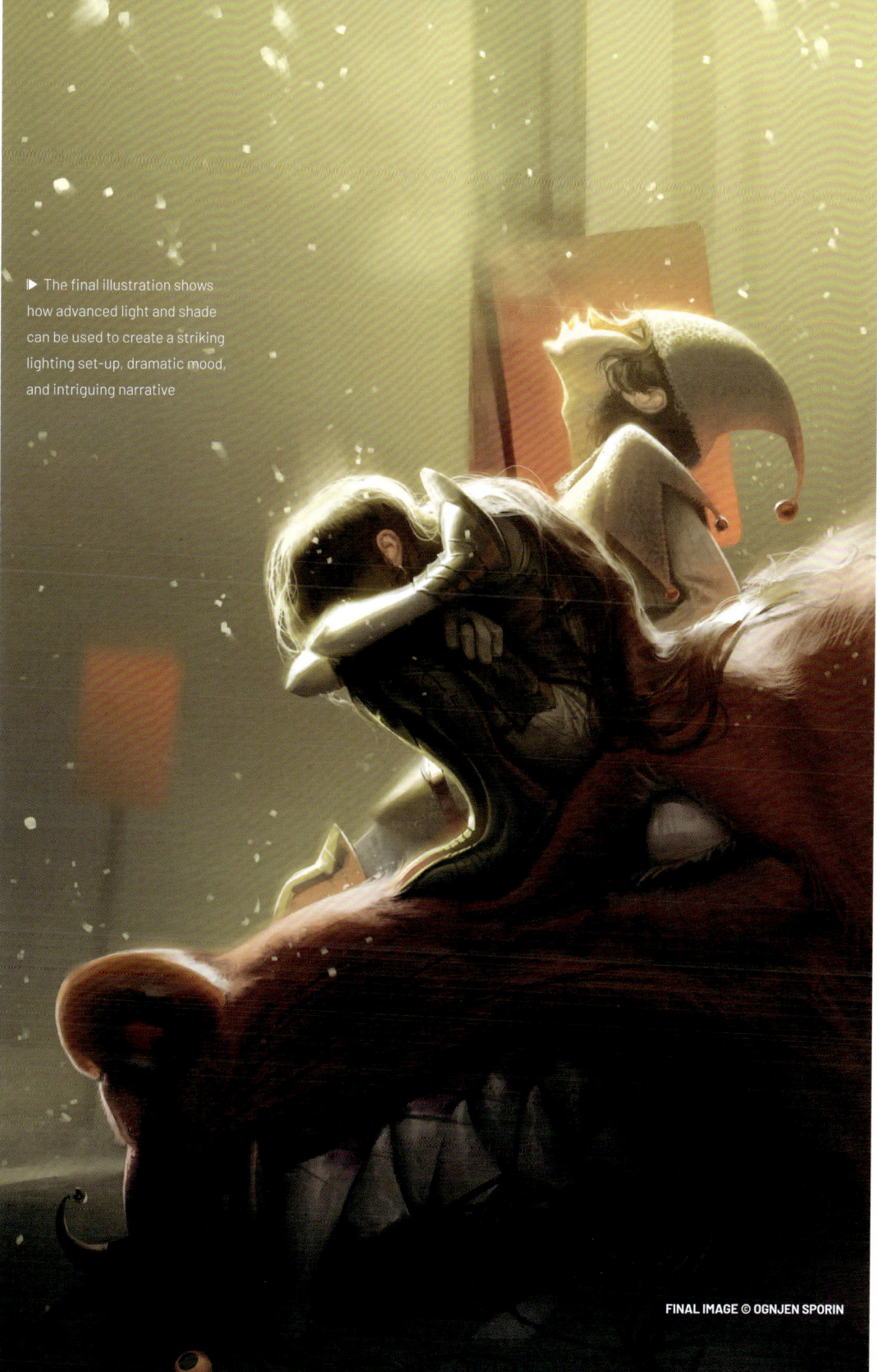

▶ The final illustration shows how advanced light and shade can be used to create a striking lighting set-up, dramatic mood, and intriguing narrative

FINAL IMAGE © OGNJEN SPORIN

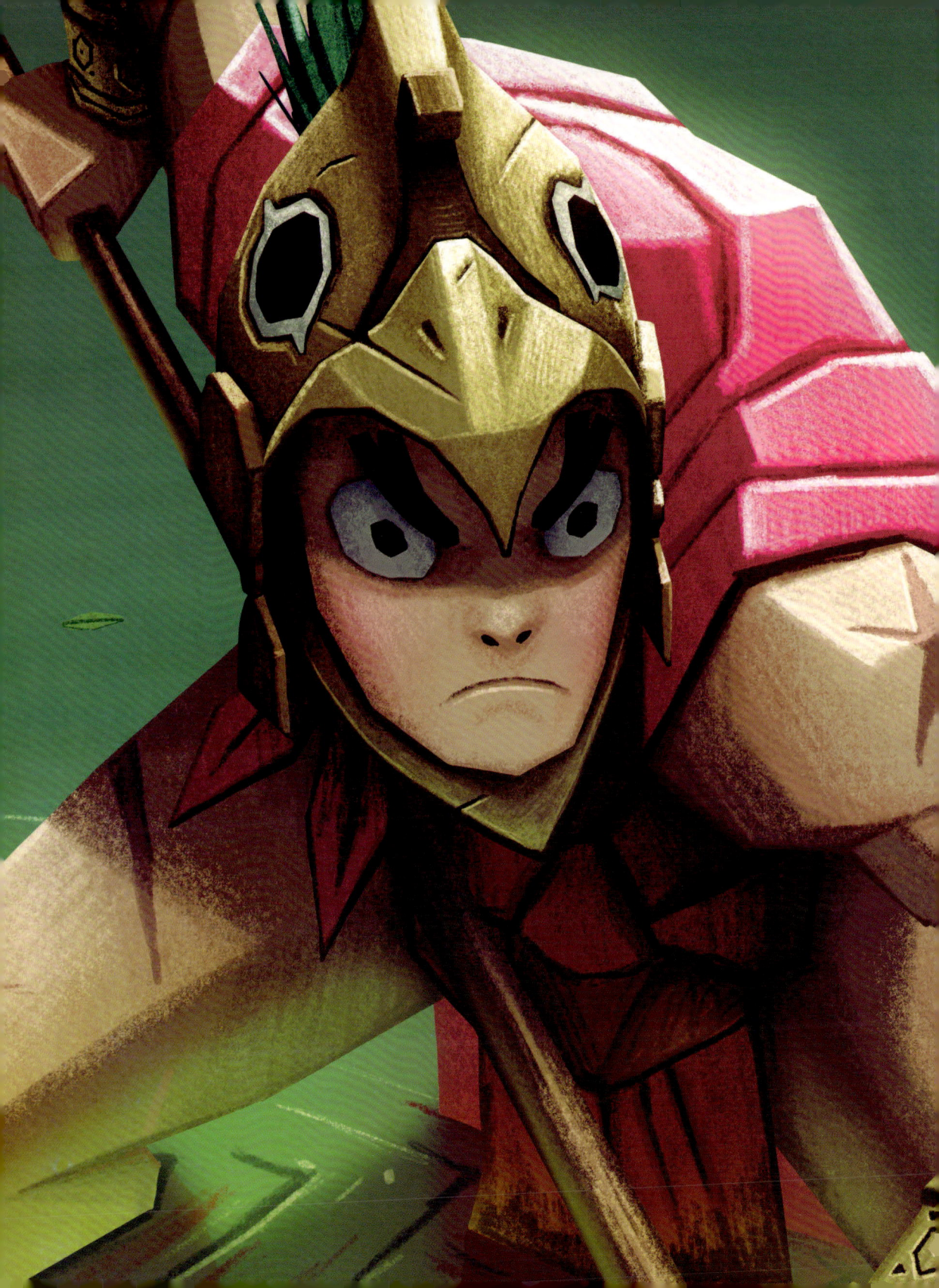

GALLERY

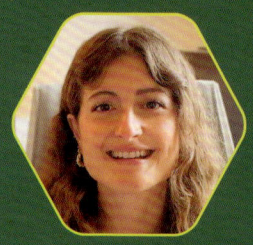

Isabella Agosti
Illustrator & character designer
isabellaagosti.com

Isabella is a freelance illustrator and character designer from Italy. She loves designing characters and illustrating compelling stories about them to make their personalities shine through.

IMAGE © ISABELLA AGOSTI

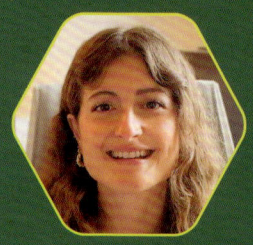

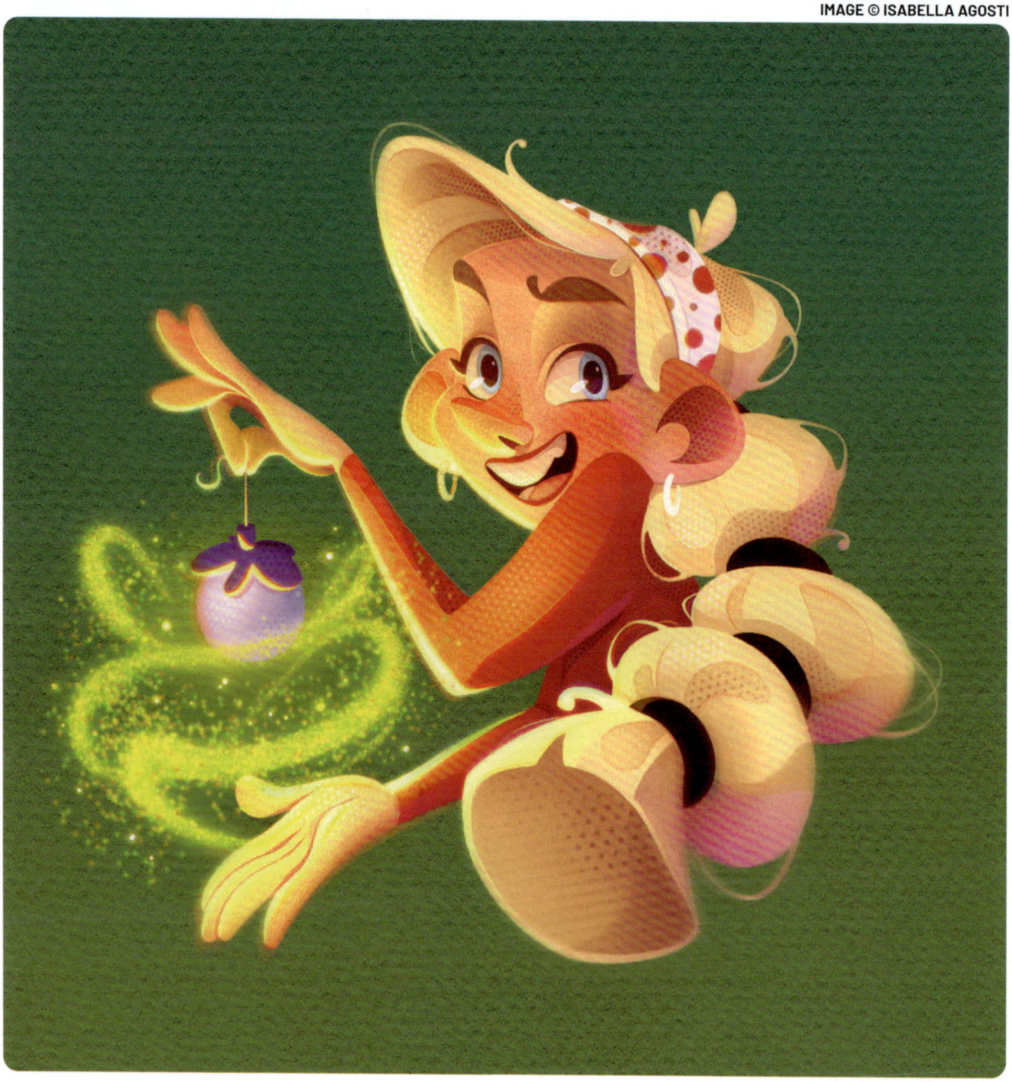

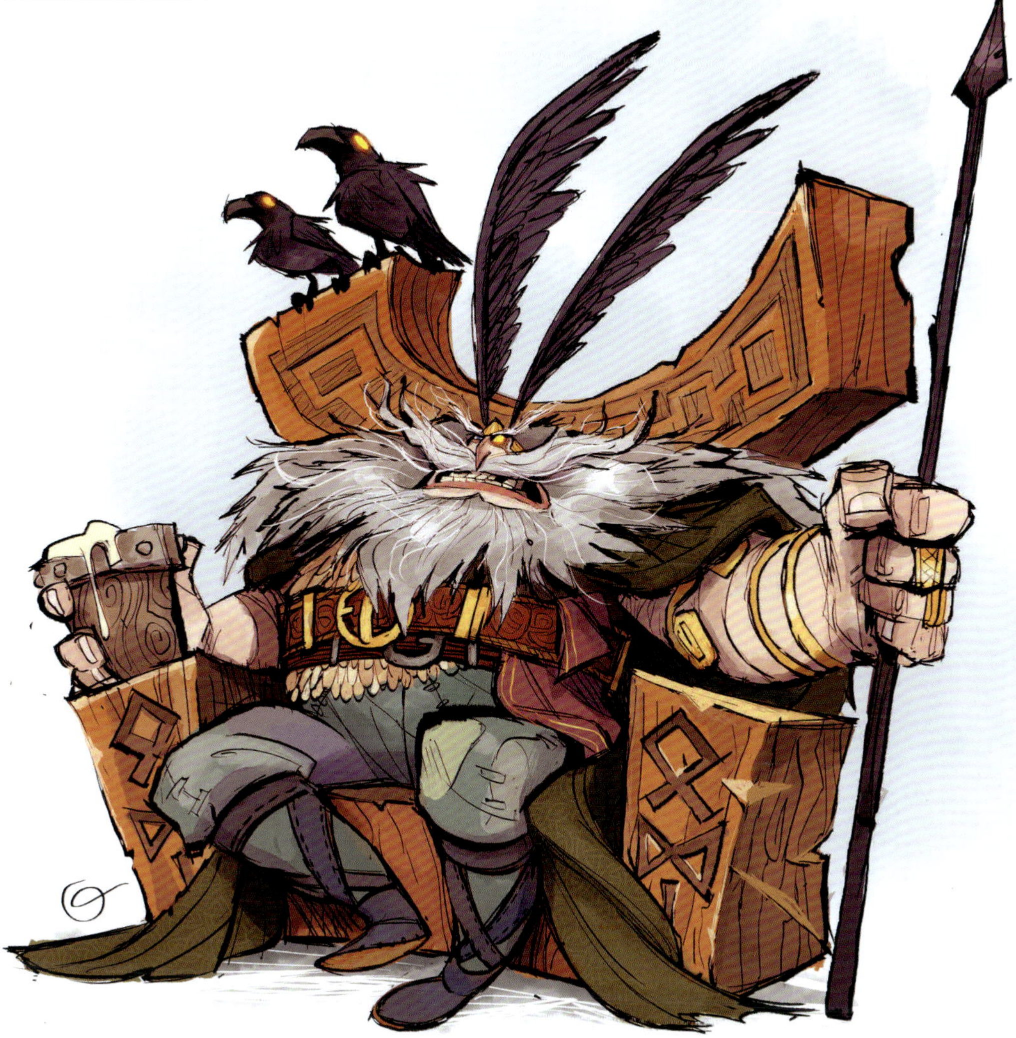

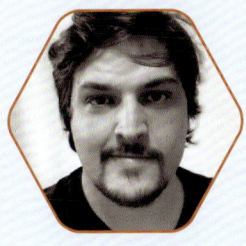

Guilherme Franco

Character designer & concept artist

guilhermefranco.com.br/projects

Guilherme is a Brazilian artist with experience in TV and feature animation. For the past seven years his work has focused on the games industry. He likes to create stylized and exaggerated characters that can visually tell a story.

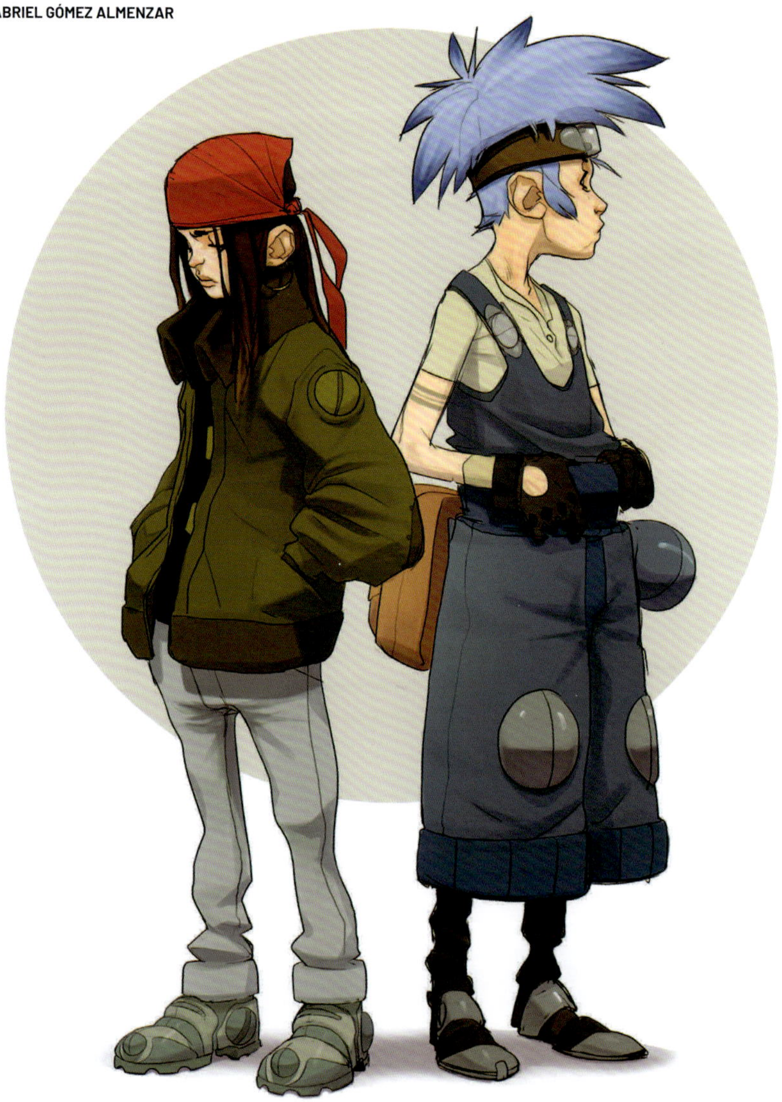

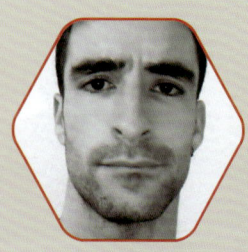

Gabriel Gómez Almenzar

Freelance illustrator

artstation.com/zar

Based in Granada, Spain, Gabriel works as an illustrator for board games, as well as a concept artist creating character design and illustrations for various projects.

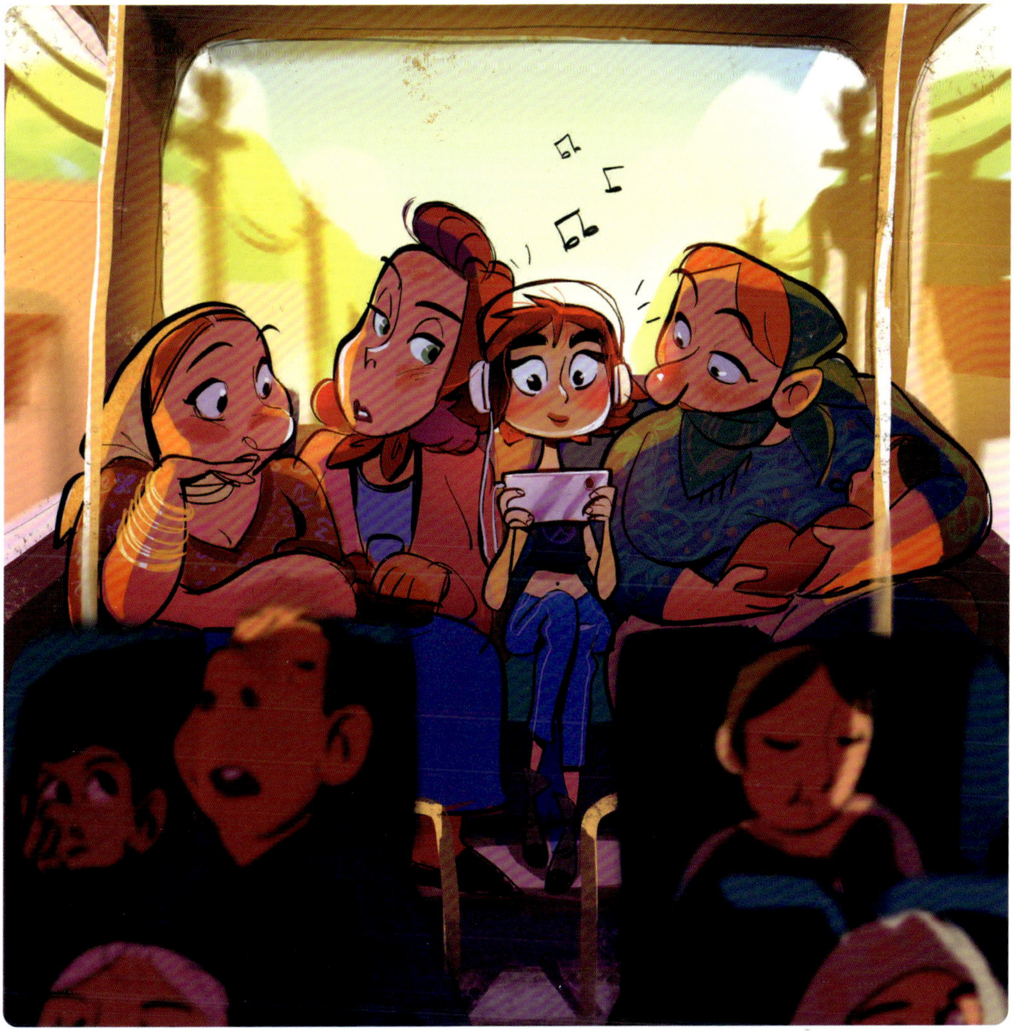

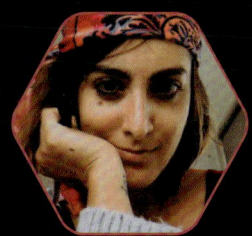

Taraneh Karimi
Concept artist & character designer
instagram.com/taraneh.artworks

Taraneh has over a decade of experience working with companies including Disney Animation, Netflix, and various other game and animation studios. She loves studying the interplay of colours and emotions, and the challenge of creating vibrant character designs that resonate with audiences.

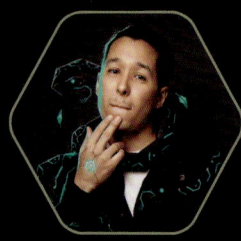

Andrés Moncayo

Illustrator

andresmoncayo.com

Andrés is an art director and illustrator from Colombia. He lives in New York City, USA, where he has worked with brands including Apple, Capcom, Paramount Pictures, and Adobe, among others.

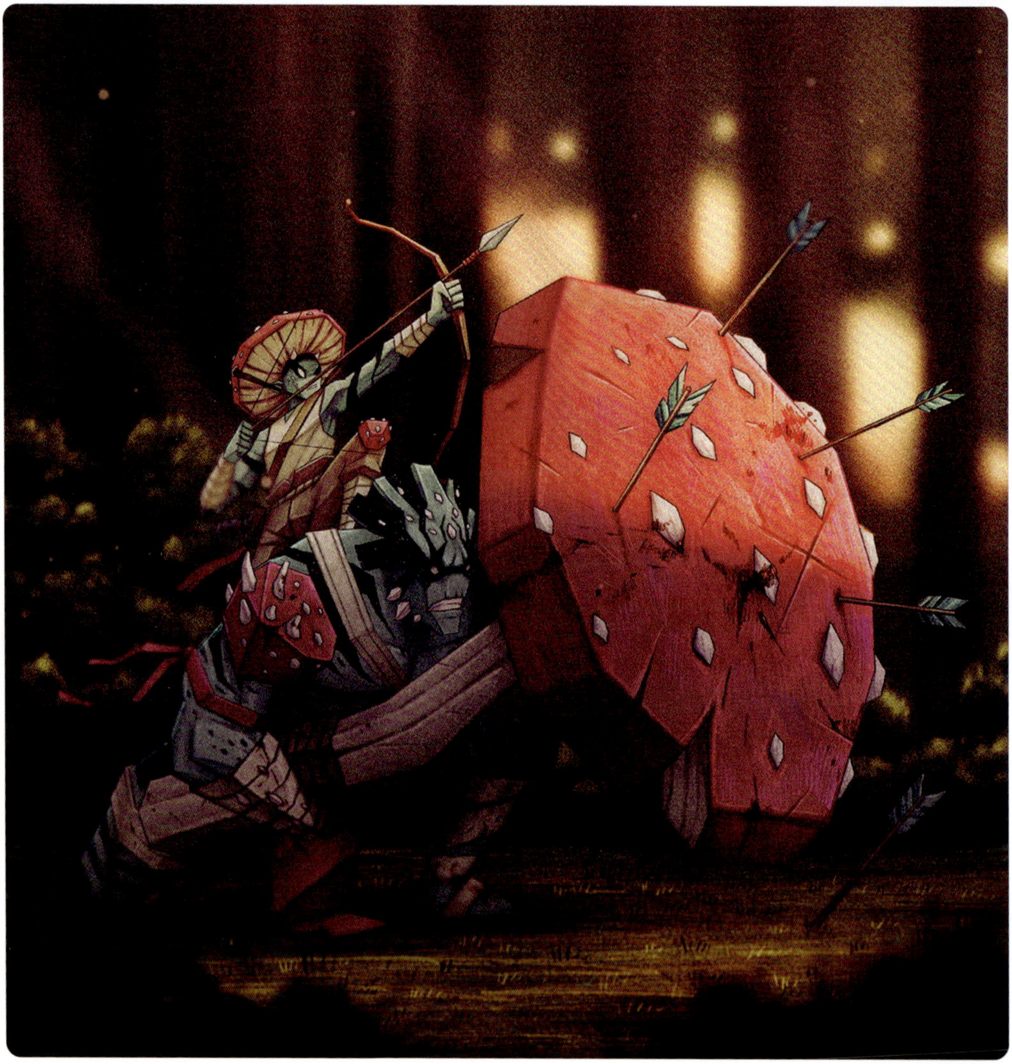

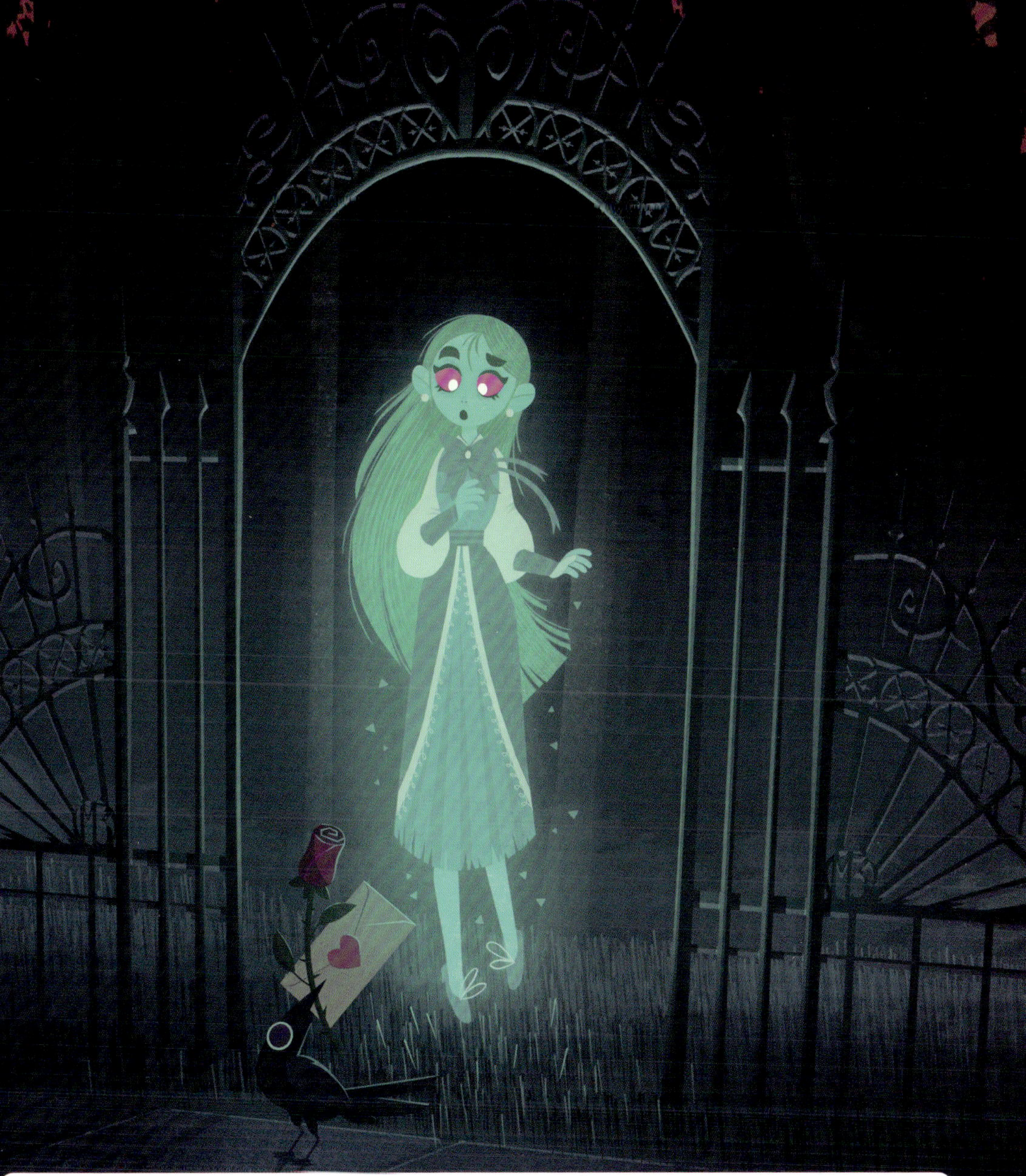

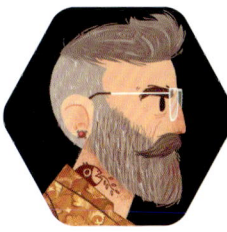

Teo Skaffa
Illustrator
teoskatta.com

Originally from the Netherlands, Teo now lives in the Italian countryside. He illustrates creepy children's books as well as working on visual development for animation and video games.

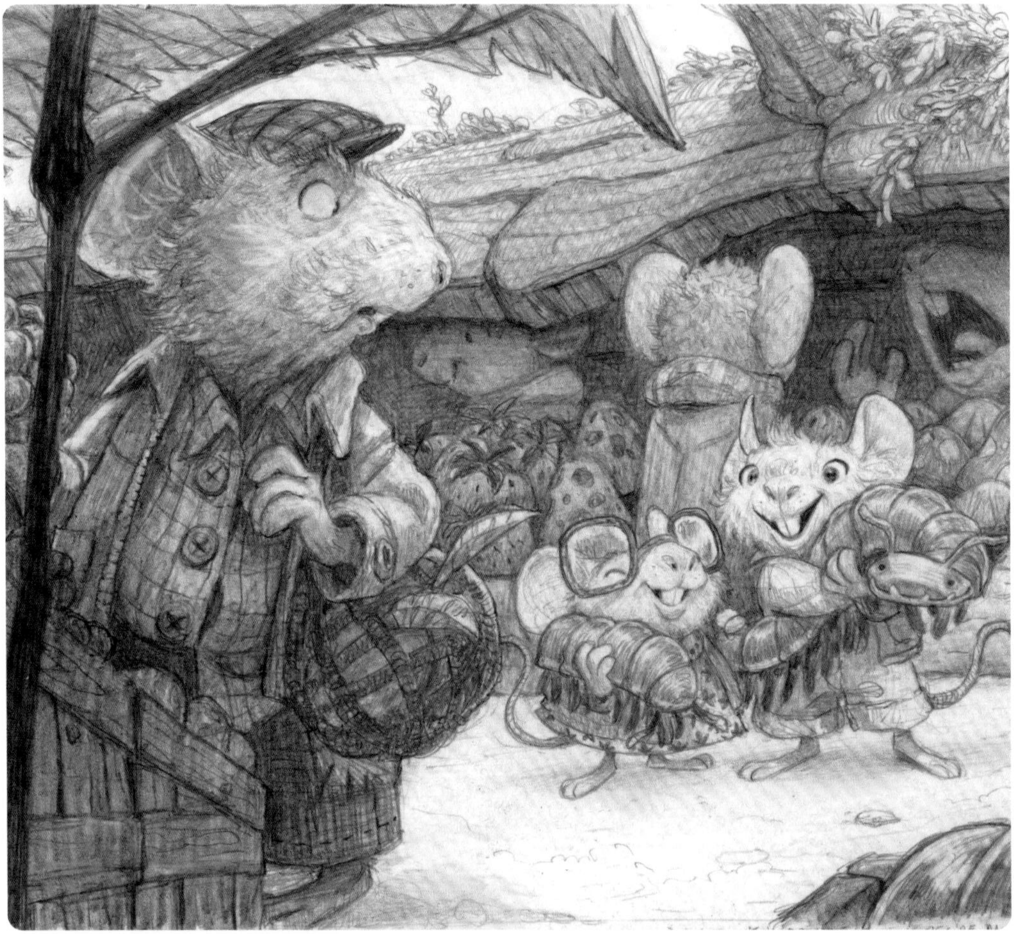

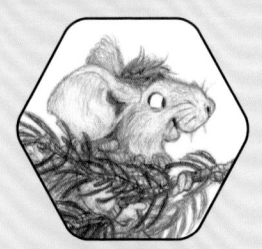

Rachelle Joy Slingerland
Visual development artist & illustrator
rachellejoys.com

Rachelle works as a freelance illustrator in Rotterdam, the Netherlands, where she creates artwork for advertising, animation, and children's books.

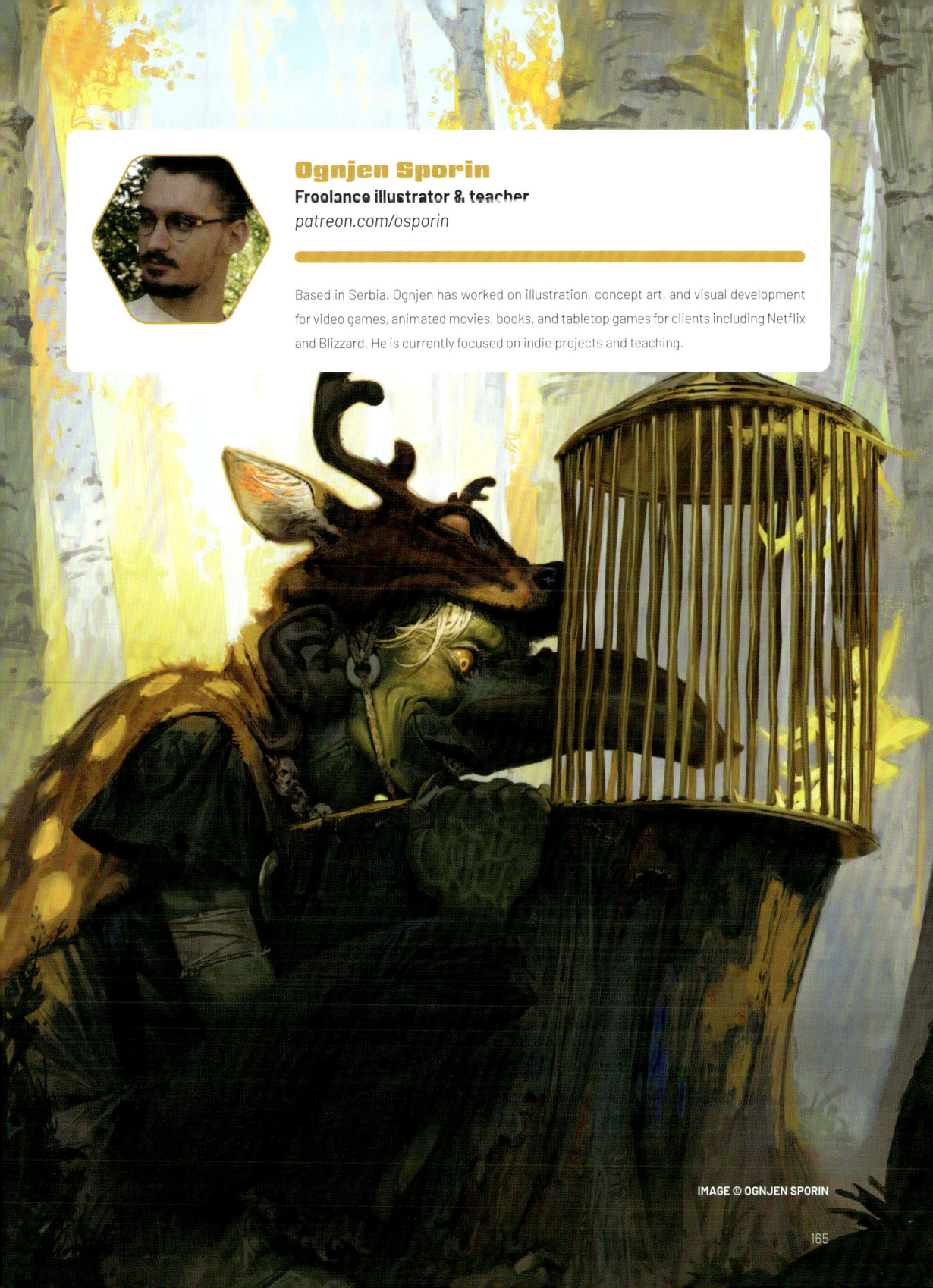

Ognjen Sporin

Freelance illustrator & teacher

patreon.com/osporin

Based in Serbia, Ognjen has worked on illustration, concept art, and visual development for video games, animated movies, books, and tabletop games for clients including Netflix and Blizzard. He is currently focused on indie projects and teaching.

IMAGE © OGNJEN SPORIN

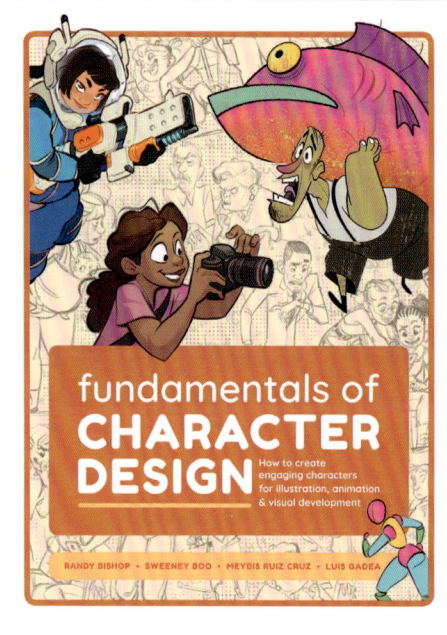

fundamentals of
CHARACTER
DESIGN

**How to create
engaging characters
for illustration, animation
& visual development**

Why do the characters in our favorite books, animations, and games stay with us long after the final scene? The heroic protagonist, evil villain, comedic sidekick – even the supporting cast – have been crafted by clever character designers with incredible skills at their fingertips. This comprehensive character-design toolkit, written by industry professionals, includes everything you need to design successful and compelling characters.

store.3dtotal.com

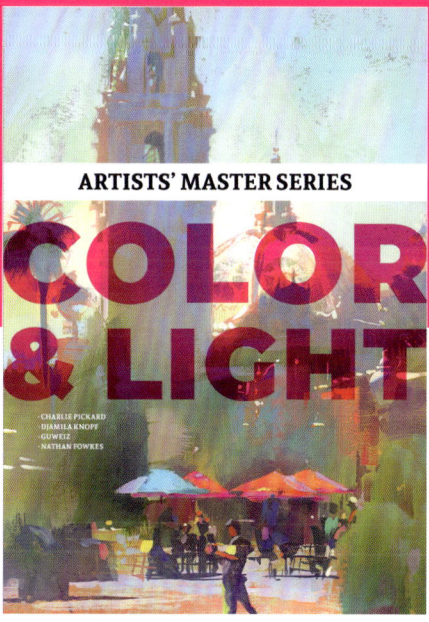

ARTISTS' MASTER SERIES

COLOR & LIGHT

A select few industry experts reveal techniques they use to infuse their images with the advanced levels of color and light that make their work instantly recognizable and universally admired. Their in-depth illustrated theory, detailed step-by-step tutorials, and enlightening case studies provide a distinctive and invaluable blend of advanced knowledge that can't be found anywhere else. For both digital and traditional artists and designers aiming to raise their game to an expert level, the Artists' Masters Series is the key to success.

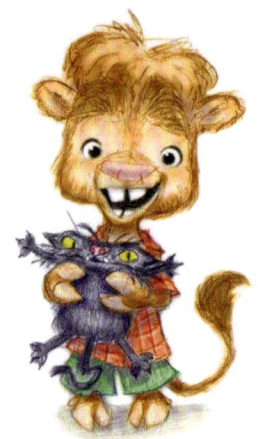

3dtotalPublishing

3dtotal Publishing is a trailblazing, creative publisher specializing in inspirational and educational resources for artists.

Our titles feature top industry professionals from around the globe who share their experience in skilfully written step-by-step tutorials and fascinating, detailed guides. Illustrated throughout with stunning artwork, these bestselling publications offer creative insight, expert advice, and essential motivation. Fans of digital art will enjoy our comprehensive volumes covering Adobe Photoshop, Procreate, and Blender, as well as our superb titles based around character design, including *Fundamentals of Character Design* and *Creating Characters for the Entertainment Industry*. The dedicated, high-quality blend of instruction and inspiration also extends to traditional art. Titles covering a range of techniques, genres, and abilities allow your creativity to flourish while building essential skills.

Well-established within the industry, we now offer over 100 titles and counting, many of which have been translated into multiple languages around the world. With something for every artist, we are proud to say that our books offer the 3dtotal package:

LEARN · CREATE · SHARE

Visit us at store.3dtotal.com

3dtotal Publishing is part of 3dtotal.com, a leading website for CG artists founded by Tom Greenway in 1999.

IMAGE © RACHELLE JOY SLINGERLAND